The Habitual Entrepreneur

Increasingly, entrepreneurship research recognizes a wide variety in entrepreneurial behaviour. One such difference is marked between experienced or habitual entrepreneurs and novices. This book, authored by established experts in the field, introduces and explores the habitual entrepreneur phenomenon. Building upon an international body of research, the authors analyse business behaviour to demonstrate how experience relates to the performance of new ventures. In employing a range of methodological techniques, the authors provide insight into how prior business ownership experience produces different outcomes when it comes to the key success factors associated with entrepreneurial ventures. With detailed coverage of finance, networking, opportunity discovery and learning, the book is a uniquely comprehensive resource. This concise book is a complete research guide which provides an introduction for advanced students and researchers of entrepreneurship worldwide.

Paul Westhead is a Professor of Entrepreneurship at Durham University Business School, UK, and he is the visiting professor of entrepreneurship at Bodø Graduate School of Business, Nord University in Norway. In collaboration with Mike Wright, the book *Entrepreneurship: A Very Short Introduction* (Oxford University Press) was published in 2013. His research focuses on wealth creation and entrepreneur behaviour.

Mike Wright is a Professor of Entrepreneurship at Imperial College Business School, UK, Director of the Centre for Management Buyout Research and visiting professor at the University of Ghent. He was previously Chair of the Academy of Management Entrepreneurship Division and is co-editor of the *Strategic Entrepreneurship Journal* and *Academy of Management Perspectives*.

Routledge Studies in Entrepreneurship

Edited by Susan Marlow and Janine Swail (University of Nottingham, UK)

For a full list of titles in this series, please visit www.routledge.com

This series extends the meaning and scope of entrepreneurship by capturing new research and enquiry on economic, social, cultural and personal value creation. Entrepreneurship as value creation represents the endeavours of innovative people and organizations in creative environments that open up opportunities for developing new products, new services, new firms and new forms of policy-making in different environments seeking sustainable economic growth and social development. In setting this objective, the series includes books which cover a diverse range of conceptual, empirical and scholarly topics that both inform the field and push the boundaries of entrepreneurship.

4 **Entrepreneurship in the Informal Economy**
   Edited by Mai Thi Thanh Thai and Ekaterina Turkina

5 **Enterprising Initiatives in the Experience Economy**
   Transforming social worlds
   *Edited by Britta Timm Knudsen, Dorthe Refslund Christensen
   and Per Blenker*

6 **Entrepreneurial Learning**
   The development of new perspectives in research, education and
   practice
   David Rae and Catherine L. Wang

7 **Entrepreneurship and Knowledge Exchange**
   Edited by Jay Mitra and John Edmondson

8 **Entrepreneurship in Small Island States and Territories**
   Edited by Godfrey Baldacchino

9 **Entrepreneurship and Cluster Dynamics**
   Edited by Cristina Boari, Tom Elfring, and F. Xavier Molina-Morales

10 **The Habitual Entrepreneur**
   Paul Westhead and Mike Wright

The Habitual Entrepreneur

Paul Westhead and Mike Wright

NEW YORK AND LONDON

First published 2017
by Routledge
711 Third Avenue, New York, NY 10017

and by Routledge
2 Park Square, Milton Park, Abingdon, Oxon OX14 4RN

First issued in paperback 2018

Routledge is an imprint of the Taylor & Francis Group, an informa business

© 2017 Taylor & Francis

The right of Paul Westhead and Mike Wright to be identified as authors of this work has been asserted by them in accordance with sections 77 and 78 of the Copyright, Designs and Patents Act 1988.

All rights reserved. No part of this book may be reprinted or reproduced or utilised in any form or by any electronic, mechanical, or other means, now known or hereafter invented, including photocopying and recording, or in any information storage or retrieval system, without permission in writing from the publishers.

Trademark notice: Product or corporate names may be trademarks or registered trademarks, and are used only for identification and explanation without intent to infringe.

Library of Congress Cataloging-in-Publication Data
Names: Westhead, Paul, 1962– author. | Wright, Mike, 1952– author.
Title: The habitual entrepreneur / by Paul Westhead and
    Mike Wright.
Description: New York : Routledge, 2016. | Series: Routledge studies
    in entrepreneurship ; 10 | Includes bibliographical references
    and index.
Identifiers: LCCN 2016027670 | ISBN 9781138231054 (cloth :
    alk. paper) | ISBN 9781315316123 (ebook)
Subjects: LCSH: Entrepreneurship. | Businesspeople.
Classification: LCC HB615 .W4723 2016 | DDC 658.4/21—dc23
LC record available at https://lccn.loc.gov/2016027670

ISBN 13: 978-1-138-34018-3 (pbk)
ISBN 13: 978-1-138-23105-4 (hbk)

Typeset in Sabon
by Apex CoVantage, LLC

Detailed Contents

List of Tables and Figures	*xi*
Preface	*xiii*

1 Introduction   **1**

  1.1 Learning Objectives 1
  1.2 Entrepreneur Diversity 2
  1.3 Definitional Issues 3
  1.4 Scale of the Habitual Entrepreneur Phenomenon 5
  1.5 Knowledge Gaps and Research Themes 6
  1.6 Organizing Framework and Book Structure 8
  1.7 Summary 10
  1.8 Reflection Questions 11

2 Entrepreneur Resources: Theoretical Insights   **12**

  2.1 Learning Objectives and Overview 12
  2.2 Human Capital Theory 12
    2.2.1 General Human Capital 12
    2.2.2 Specific Human Capital 14
  2.3 Cognition and Heuristics 14
  2.4 Resource-Based View of the Firm 17
  2.5 Dynamic Capabilities 19
  2.6 Signalling Theory 19
  2.7 Learning 20
  2.8 Summary 20
  2.9 Reflection Questions 21

3 Entrepreneur Resource Profiles   **22**

  3.1 Learning Objectives and Overview 22
  3.2 Entrepreneur Resource Profile: General Dimensions 23
    3.2.1 Gaps in the Knowledge Base and Research Questions 23
    3.2.2 Descriptive Analysis 24

vi *Detailed Contents*

3.2.3 Methodology 24
   3.2.3.1 Data 24
   3.2.3.2 Techniques 24
3.2.4 Findings 24
   3.2.4.1 Entrepreneur and Business Ownership Profiles 24
   3.2.4.2 Portfolio Entrepreneurs Compared with Novice and Serial Entrepreneurs: Human Capital 25
   3.2.4.3 Serial Entrepreneurs Compared with Novice and Portfolio Entrepreneurs: Human Capital 26
   3.2.4.4 Portfolio Entrepreneurs Compared with Novice and Serial Entrepreneurs: Personal Capabilities Toward Opportunity Identification and Sources of Opportunities 26
   3.2.4.5 Serial Entrepreneurs Compared with Novice and Portfolio Entrepreneurs: Personal Capabilities Toward Opportunity Identification and Sources of Opportunities 26
   3.2.4.6 Portfolio Entrepreneurs Compared with Novice and Serial Entrepreneurs: Financing Businesses 27
   3.2.4.7 Serial Entrepreneurs Compared with Novice and Portfolio Entrepreneurs: Financing Businesses 27
   3.2.4.8 Portfolio Entrepreneurs Compared with Novice and Serial Entrepreneurs: Organizational Capabilities 28
   3.2.4.9 Serial Entrepreneurs Compared with Novice and Portfolio Entrepreneurs: Organizational Capabilities 28
3.2.5 Conclusions and Implications 28
3.3 Entrepreneur Resource Profile: Assets, Liabilities and Cognition 29
   3.3.1 Gaps in the Knowledge Base and Research Questions 29
   3.3.2 Hypothesis Tested 29
   3.3.3 Methodology 31
      3.3.3.1 Data 31
      3.3.3.2 Techniques 32
   3.3.4 Findings 32
   3.3.5 Conclusions and Implications 34
3.4 Entrepreneur Resource Profile: Comparative Optimism 35
   3.4.1 Gaps in the Knowledge Base and Research Questions 35
   3.4.2 Hypotheses Tested 37

Detailed Contents vii

    3.4.3 Methodology 39
        3.4.3.1 Data 39
        3.4.3.2 Dependent Variables 40
        3.4.3.3 Independent Variables 41
        3.4.3.4 Techniques 42
    3.4.4 Findings 43
    3.4.5 Conclusions and Implications 44
 3.5 Summary 45
 3.6 Reflection Questions 46

4   Entrepreneur Resource Accumulation: Finance   47

 4.1 Learning Objectives and Overview 47
 4.2 Finance: Debt 48
    4.2.1 Gaps in the Knowledge Base and Research Questions 48
    4.2.2 Hypotheses Tested 49
    4.2.3 Methodology 52
        4.2.3.1 Data 52
        4.2.3.2 Dependent Variable 53
        4.2.3.3 Independent Variables 53
        4.2.3.4 Technique 54
    4.2.4 Findings 54
    4.2.5 Conclusions and Implications 55
 4.3 Finance: Venture Capital 56
    4.3.1 Gaps in the Knowledge Base and Research Questions 56
    4.3.2 Hypothesis Tested 58
    4.3.3 Methodology 58
        4.3.3.1 Data 58
        4.3.3.2 Dependent Variable 60
        4.3.3.3 Independent Variables 60
        4.3.3.4 Technique 60
    4.3.4 Findings 60
    4.3.5 Conclusions and Implications 60
 4.4 Finance: Venture Capital Reinvestment in Serial Entrepreneurs 61
    4.4.1 Gaps in the Knowledge Base and Research Questions 61
    4.4.2 Hypotheses Tested 62
    4.4.3 Methodology 63
        4.4.3.1 Data 63
        4.4.3.2 Techniques 64
    4.4.4 Findings 65
    4.4.5 Conclusions and Implications 67

viii *Detailed Contents*

4.5 Summary 67
4.6 Reflection Questions 68

5 Entrepreneur Resource Accumulation: Networking and
Resource Orchestration   69

5.1 Learning Objectives and Overview 69
5.2 Networking 70
  5.2.1 Gaps in the Knowledge Base and Research Questions 70
  5.2.2 Methodology and Data 72
  5.2.3 Findings 73
    5.2.3.1 Patterns of Social Capital Development 73
    5.2.3.2 Nascent Entrepreneurs: Network Structure,
    Content and Governance 74
    5.2.3.3 Novice Entrepreneurs: Network Structure, Content
    and Governance 74
    5.2.3.4 Habitual Entrepreneurs: Network Structure,
    Content and Governance 75
    5.2.3.5 Development of Propositions 76
      5.2.3.5.1 Network Structure 76
      5.2.3.5.2 Network Content 76
      5.2.3.5.3 Network Governance 78
      5.2.3.5.4 Venture Development 79
  5.2.4 Conclusions and Implications 79
5.3 Resource Orchestration 80
  5.3.1 Gaps in the Knowledge Base and Research Questions 80
  5.3.2 Theoretical Background 80
  5.3.3 Methodology and Data 81
  5.3.4 Findings 82
    5.3.4.1 Sharing Resources and Capabilities 82
    5.3.4.2 Transforming Resources and Capabilities 83
    5.3.4.3 Harmonizing Resource and Capability
    Configurations 83
  5.3.5 Conclusions and Implications 85
5.4 Summary 85
5.5 Reflection Questions 86

6 Opportunity Discovery and Creation   87

6.1 Learning Objectives and Overview 87
6.2 Opportunity Discovery and Creation Theories 88
  6.2.1 Key Elements of Opportunity Discovery and Creation
  Theories 88

6.2.2 Innovation and Opportunity Creation 89

6.2.3 Opportunity-Based Conceptualization of Entrepreneurship 90

6.3 Opportunity Discovery: Nature of Experience 90

6.3.1 Gaps in the Knowledge Base and Research Questions 90

6.3.2 Hypotheses Tested 91

6.3.3 Findings 92

6.3.4 Conclusions and Implications 92

6.4 Opportunity Discovery: Extent and Nature of Experience 93

6.4.1 Gaps in the Knowledge Base and Research Questions 93

6.4.2 Hypothesis Tested 94

6.4.3 Methodology 98

6.4.3.1 Data 98

6.4.3.2 Dependent Variables 98

6.4.3.3 Independent Variables 100

6.4.3.4 Technique 100

6.4.4 Findings 101

6.4.5 Conclusions and Implications 101

6.5 Opportunity Creation 102

6.5.1 Gaps in the Knowledge Base and Research Question 102

6.5.2 Hypotheses Tested 105

6.5.3 Methodology 107

6.5.3.1 Data 107

6.5.3.2 Dependent Variables 108

6.5.3.3 Independent Variables 109

6.5.3.4 Techniques 110

6.5.4 Findings 110

6.5.5 Conclusions and Implications 111

6.6 Summary 112

6.7 Reflection Questions 114

7 Learning   **115**

7.1 Learning Objectives and Overview 115

7.2 Learning 115

7.2.1 Gaps in the Knowledge Base and Research Questions 115

7.2.2 Human Capital Perspective Explaining the Emergence of Types of Habitual Entrepreneurs 116

7.2.3 Methodology 116

7.2.4 Findings 118

7.2.5 Conclusions and Implications 122

7.3 Reflection Questions 123

x *Detailed Contents*

8 Entrepreneur and Firm Performance   **124**

8.1 Learning Objectives and Overview 124

8.2 Entrepreneur and Firm Performance: Growth 125

    8.2.1 Gaps in the Knowledge Base and Research Questions 125

    8.2.2 Hypotheses Tested 126

    8.2.3 Methodology 126

    8.2.4 Findings 126

    8.2.5 Conclusions and Implications 127

8.3 Entrepreneur and Firm Performance: Exporting 127

    8.3.1 Gaps in the Knowledge Base and Research Questions 127

    8.3.2 Hypotheses Tested 128

    8.3.3 Methodology 129

        8.3.3.1 Data 129

        8.3.3.2 Dependent Variables 129

        8.3.3.3 Independent Variables 130

        8.3.3.4 Techniques 130

    8.3.4 Findings 131

    8.3.5 Conclusions and Implications 131

8.4 Summary 132

8.5 Reflection Questions 132

9 Conclusions and Implications   **134**

9.1 Future Research Directions 134

9.2 Summary and Reflection Questions 136

References   137

Index   149

Tables and Figures

Tables

1.1	Categorization of Habitual Entrepreneurship	5
4.1	Length of the Debt Finance Gap by Lead Entrepreneur Type of Prior Business Ownership Experience	55
4.2	Multivariate Analysis of Variance for Investment Appraisal Criteria	66
5.1	Summary Findings of Social Capital Development Between Different Types of Entrepreneurs	77
6.1	Opportunity Discovery Versus Opportunity Creation	88
7.1	Demographic Characteristics of the Habitual Entrepreneurs and Their Ventures	119

Figures

1.1	The Mediating Relationships Between Prior Business Ownership Experience and Entrepreneur Behaviour and Performance	7
1.2	Themes Explored in Entrepreneurship Studies	9

Preface

Some two decades ago, the phenomenon of habitual entrepreneurship was generally seen as an intellectual curiosity of peripheral importance. The focus of entrepreneurship research and policy was on the start-up of private ventures, with the implicit assumption that this was a one-time event by individual entrepreneurs. However, surveys showed that habitual entrepreneurship was a widespread phenomenon in many countries, and it was evident to us at the time that it offered important opportunities for a new research agenda. Since then, increasing research has been directed toward the evolution of understanding relating to the habitual entrepreneur phenomenon. Here, we focus on habitual entrepreneurs who have the potential to mobilize their prior business ownership experience (PBOE) in subsequent ventures. Habitual and sub-groups of serial and portfolio entrepreneurs with PBOE are compared against novice entrepreneurs who do not have any PBOE to draw upon. Our aim is to reflect this complexity and ambiguity, but also to weave a pathway through the debate and offer some clarity to the reader. We highlight key themes across several articles that we have published over the past twenty years on habitual entrepreneurs. Drawing on these articles, we demonstrate the breadth and insight of evolving work relating to the habitual entrepreneur phenomenon, and the extent of the continuing research agenda. The themes we discuss will be of interest to academics, students and practitioners.

In developing the research programme behind this volume, we extend thanks to our team of co-authors and the survey respondents. We are also grateful to Susan Marlow for her encouragement in bringing this volume to fruition.

Paul Westhead
Mike Wright
January 2016

1 Introduction

1.1 Learning Objectives

Cantillon (1755) is often associated with the term 'entrepreneur'. He suggested that entrepreneurs react to profit opportunities, bear uncertainty and continuously serve to bring about a (tentative) balance between supplies and demands in specific markets. Entrepreneurs undertake activities, and the entrepreneur is the pivotal figure who operates within a set of economic markets. Unlike Cantillon, Knight (1921, 1942) does not believe everyone can become an entrepreneur. Knight suggests entrepreneurs are 'calculated risk takers' who assemble resources and co-ordinate scarce resources to exploit business opportunities.

Entrepreneurship occurs over time (Low and MacMillan, 1988) and is not a static event. The standard and uncritically assumed normative representation of the entrepreneurial actor relates to the owner of one single business, which sustains her or his lifetime career in business ownership (or self-employment). This view exists in isolation and does not correlate with the entrepreneurial careers of a growing number of entrepreneurs in developing and developing economies. The latter view ignores the habitual entrepreneur phenomenon.

Studying habitual entrepreneurs encourages a focus on the assets (and liabilities) of an individual's human capital to be viewed through a dynamic rather than a static lens (MacMillan, 1986). A dynamic view appreciates that rather than only being involved in one venture, entrepreneurs can vary in the nature and extent of their prior business ownership experience (PBOE).

Focusing on the entrepreneur rather than the firm as the unit of analysis, this chapter encourages reflection relating to the careers that can be followed by entrepreneurs with regard to different business ownership forms. We encourage reflection relating to the fact that entrepreneurial behaviour is not solely exhibited relating to the foundation of do novo private new firms. Entrepreneurs can exhibit entrepreneurial behaviour in family firm, management buyout and other contexts. Entrepreneurship can also relate to exit decisions. Some entrepreneurs over their entrepreneurial careers close and/or sell one or more of the businesses they own. We encourage reflection relating to the motives, resources, behaviour and performance of serial

2 Introduction

entrepreneurs. Studies focusing on the life cycle of the firm may ignore that some entrepreneurs may own two or more businesses at the same time for a variety of economic and non-economic reasons. We encourage reflection relating to the motives, resources, behaviour and performance of portfolio entrepreneurs. In this chapter, we define and describe the profile of habitual entrepreneurs, and highlight sub-groups of habitual entrepreneurs termed serial and portfolio entrepreneurs. A growing body of studies relate to the habitual entrepreneur phenomenon, but there are few dedicated texts that focus upon them (Ucbasaran et al., 2006, 2008). Students are encouraged to appreciate that academic articles focus on the habitual entrepreneur phenomenon or sub-groups of serial and portfolio entrepreneurs differ in their focus, purpose and contribution. Under the umbrella of the habitual entrepreneur phenomenon, we highlight that initial studies relating to this new and emerging sub-field in entrepreneurship generally described the profiles of habitual, serial and portfolio entrepreneurs. However, we encourage readers to appreciate that more recent studies are more clearly linked to policy, practitioner and/or theory, with more recent studies being theory-building or theory-testing studies and building on mainstream perspectives in entrepreneurship and management. Gaps in the knowledge base relating to the habitual entrepreneur phenomenon and with reference to themes relating to the entrepreneurial process key issues are highlighted. These issues are discussed in more detail in the following chapters. We focus on entrepreneur diversity with reference to the habitual entrepreneur phenomenon. Issues relating to habitual entrepreneur definition, resources, behaviour and performance are highlighted.

1.2 Entrepreneur Diversity

Entrepreneurship is about what entrepreneurs do, but debate surrounds the roles of entrepreneurs (Landström, 2005; Hébert and Link, 2006; Westhead and Wright, 2013). High-profile, successful entrepreneurs have fostered popular interest into the backgrounds and behaviour of entrepreneurs. Throughout the world, entrepreneurs and their firms are viewed as the panacea to solve national and local development issues (Department of Trade and Industry (DTI), 2004; Organisation for Economic Co-Operation and Development (OECD), 1998; Storey, 1994). The popular perception relates to entrepreneurs as heroic yet maverick individuals, single-handedly and relentlessly pursuing opportunity and enjoying exotic lifestyles as a result (Drakopoulou Dodd and Anderson, 2007). The latter perception fails to appreciate entrepreneur diversity, the fact that some entrepreneurs have careers in business ownership, entrepreneurs make mistakes and their ventures may fail and some entrepreneurs own two or more businesses at the same time.

Studies focusing on the entrepreneur as the unit of analysis may explore 'who the entrepreneur is' (i.e., the entrepreneur as a particular type of person or the entrepreneur as the product of a particular environment), or 'what the entrepreneur does' (i.e., the entrepreneur as the performer of a particular role in society, entrepreneurship as a specific input in the economy, entrepreneurial events and entrepreneurial processes). Generally, scholars have traditionally focused on the profiles of entrepreneurs and what the entrepreneur does. Here, we appreciate that entrepreneurship and entrepreneurs are complicated and ambiguous phenomena. Notably, we highlight that some people have careers in business ownership and entrepreneur exists relating to an individual's PBOE. We focus on entrepreneur diversity with reference to the habitual entrepreneur phenomenon. Issues relating to habitual entrepreneur definition, contribution, resources, behaviour and performance are highlighted.

Despite growing media, practitioner and academic interest relating to the entrepreneurship phenomenon, it is very difficult to present an overarching theory of entrepreneurship. This is because there is no consensus surrounding the definition of entrepreneurs or the entrepreneurial process (Westhead et al., 2011). Beyond definitional problems, an additional source of difficulty in understanding entrepreneurship stems from the heterogeneity of entrepreneurs. One notable source of heterogeneity is variations in the extent and nature of entrepreneurs' experience (Reuber and Fischer, 1999), in particular, PBOE. Entrepreneurship is not a single-action event, and some people have careers in entrepreneurship (Westhead and Wright, 1998).

Variations in PBOE have led to the distinction between experienced (i.e., habitual) entrepreneurs and first-time (i.e., novice) entrepreneurs. An individual's human capital needs to be viewed through a dynamic rather than a static lens. Rather than only being involved in one venture, entrepreneurs can vary in the extent and nature of their PBOE. Scott and Rosa (1996: 81) asserted that:

> The study of multiple ownership should be more than a specialist curiosity, but fundamental to our understanding of the process of capital accumulation in a free-enterprise economy and society, a process that is entrepreneur, not organisationally-based, and which operates across all size boundaries. The processes of ownership diversification may shed new light on the way we can conceptualise start-up and growth dynamics.

1.3 Definitional Issues

Definitions of the habitual entrepreneur phenomenon have evolved. Initially, there was no generally accepted definition of a habitual entrepreneur. Donckels et al. (1987: 48) suggested that:

> Multiple business starters are entrepreneurs who, after having started a first company, set up or participate in the start-up of (an) other firm(s).

Similarly, Birley and Westhead (1993: 40) focused on 'habitual' founders who had established at least one other business prior to the start-up of the current independent venture. Thorgen and Wincent (2015) defined habitual

4 *Introduction*

entrepreneurs solely with regard to entrepreneurs who own two or more start-ups (i.e., individuals who have been exposed to multiple venture engagements).

Habitual entrepreneur definitions do not solely relate to new firm formation (NFF) alone (Westhead et al., 2005a). Business ownership and a decision-making role within the firm are now widely recognized as important dimensions of entrepreneurship (Marshall, 1920). Given the prevalence of team-based entrepreneurship, this ownership may involve minority or majority equity stakes. The emerging opportunity-based conceptualization of entrepreneurship (Shane and Venkataraman, 2000) suggests that entrepreneurship involves the discovery and exploitation of at least one business opportunity. In contrast to views of entrepreneurship that focus on NFF, this approach recognizes that a business opportunity can be exploited through NFF, the purchase of an existing private firm, the discovery and creation of new opportunities in existing (family and non-family firms) (Westhead and Wright, 2013) or the discovery and creation of opportunities for self-employment. Entrepreneurs can, therefore, be viewed as having a minority or majority ownership stake in at least one business that they have either created or purchased, within which they are a key decision-maker. With regard to these key elements of entrepreneurship, a distinction between novice and habitual entrepreneurs can be made (Ucbasaran et al., 2008).

Entrepreneurship is not a single-action event because some people have careers in entrepreneurship (Westhead and Wright, 1998). Entrepreneur heterogeneity exists relating to variations in the extent and nature of entrepreneurs' PBOE. Business ownership and a decision-making role within the venture are important dimensions of entrepreneurship. *Novice entrepreneurs* are individuals without PBOE who currently own a stake in an independent firm that is either new or purchased. *Habitual entrepreneurs* hold or have held an ownership stake in two or more firms, at least one of which was established or purchased. Habitual entrepreneurs can be sub-divided into serial and portfolio entrepreneurs. *Serial entrepreneurs* have sold/closed at least one firm which they had an ownership stake in and currently have an ownership stake in a single independent firm. *Portfolio entrepreneurs* currently have ownership stakes in two or more independent firms.

A business opportunity can be exploited through new firm formation, purchase of an existing private firm, discovery and creation of new opportunities in existing firms or discovery and creation of opportunities for self-employment. This variety gives rise to a categorization of habitual entrepreneurship by the modes through which it can occur. Table 1.1 shows that habitual entrepreneurs covered by cells 1 to 5 engage in entrepreneurship sequentially, while those in cells 6 to 10 engage in concurrent entrepreneurial activities. The entrepreneurs in cells 1 and 6 found a new independent firm, while those in cells 2 and 7 are involved in new firms spun off from other organizations. Entrepreneurs in cells 3 and 8 have become owners of an established independent firm either as individuals from outside the firm undertaking a straight purchase or a management buy in (MBI), or

Introduction 5

Table 1.1 Categorization of Habitual Entrepreneurship

Nature of entrepreneurship		Serial entrepreneurs	Portfolio entrepreneurs
Involving *New* Business(es)	De Novo Business	Serial founders (1)	Portfolio founders (6)
	Spin-off (including corporate & university spin-offs)	Serial spinout entrepreneurs (2)	Portfolio spinout entrepreneurs (7)
Involving *Existing* Business(es)	Purchase (including buyouts/buy ins)	Serial acquirers (e.g. secondary MBOs / MBIs) (3)	Portfolio acquirers (e.g. leveraged buildups) (8)
	Corporate Entrepreneurship	Serial corporate entrepreneurs (4)	Portfolio corporate entrepreneurs (9)
Involving No New Legal Entity	Self-Employment	Serial self-employed (5)	Portfolio self-employed (10)

Source: Authors.

individuals from inside undertaking a management buyout (MBO). Some buyouts involve founders selling their businesses and subsequently buying them back when the acquirers find themselves unable to generate adequate performance because they do not possess the tacit knowledge of the founder. Further, some buyouts are secondary buyouts, where the same management acquires a larger stake in the firm through a financial restructuring associated with initial private equity investors selling their shares. Entrepreneurs in cells 4 and 9 are engaged as corporate entrepreneurs in existing firms and have not purchased the firm. Entrepreneurs in cells 5 and 10 are self-employed individuals who do not form a specific legal entity.

1.4 Scale of the Habitual Entrepreneur Phenomenon

Survey evidence from stratified random samples of independent private firms is now widely used to ascertain the scale of the habitual entrepreneur phenomenon (Birley and Westhead, 1993). Given the emphasis on the entrepreneur as the unit of analysis, several questionnaire surveys have been sent to a key respondent (i.e., a decision-maker) in each of the randomly selected businesses, generally a founder and/or the principal owner. Studies have confirmed habitual entrepreneurs are a widespread and substantial phenomenon.

Habitual entrepreneurs have been detected to be highly prevalent in the UK (12% to 52%), the United States (51% to 64%), Finland (50%), Australia (49%), Norway (47%), Ghana (41%), Sweden (30% to 40%) and Malaysia (39%). Some scholars studying multiple business ownership have focused on business groups relating to the set of businesses under control of the habitual entrepreneur (Rosa, 1998; Rosa and Scott, 1999). Habitual entrepreneurship may arise in settings where opportunities for growth

6 Introduction

are restricted, forcing the entrepreneurs to substitute growth of one venture with the creation of multiple firms. The following reasons for habitual entrepreneurship have been identified: tax reasons and to support the first venture established; and desire for independence, autonomy and personal wealth creation. Monetary gain may become less important in subsequent ventures, partly because they do not want to put at risk wealth generated from an earlier successful venture.

The 'correct' magnitude of the habitual entrepreneur (or business group) phenomenon is difficult to determine. Variations in the scale of the habitual entrepreneur phenomenon are, in part, shaped by the habitual entrepreneur definition operationalized, the industrial sector(s) focused upon and whether team ownership is considered. Nevertheless, the scale of the phenomenon highlighted above suggests increased academic and practitioner interest is warranted to understand the profiles, behaviour and contributions of habitual entrepreneurs and their firms.

1.5 Knowledge Gaps and Research Themes

Research relating to the habitual entrepreneur phenomenon has evolved from initial 'ground-clearing' descriptive studies of the phenomenon through qualitative studies focused on theory development to quantitative studies undertaking hypothesis testing. Birley and Westhead (1993) claimed that there was no single theory to facilitate hypothesis formation and testing relating to habitual entrepreneurs. Their exploratory study provided a 'descriptive background' surrounding the under-researched habitual entrepreneur. With reference to a large representative sample of firms their univariate analysis provided initial insights surrounding the differences (and similarities) between habitual and novice entrepreneurs with regard to the founder (i.e., personal background, work experience, reasons leading to start-up and personal attitudes towards entrepreneurship), the firm (i.e., basic business data, customer and supplier base, competitive structure, future of the business and performance) and environment (i.e., local economic environment and policy and support services).

To build theory and to provide appropriate contextualized support to address the market failures facing each 'type' of entrepreneur, there is a need for a greater understanding of the resources profiles, behaviour and contributions of each 'type' of entrepreneur relating to the extent and nature of their PBOE. Reuber and Fischer (1999) have asserted that scholars and practitioners should assess the value of founders' experience in terms of their 'stock' and 'stream' of experience. An entrepreneur's stock of experience relates to both the depth and breadth of experience accumulated over time. In contrast, an entrepreneur's stream of experience relates to the entrepreneurial process, which is associated with experimentation and learning. Reuber and Fischer argue that the entrepreneur is the appropriate unit of analysis when analysing the stock of experience. Also, Reuber and Fischer

(1999: 34) state that, "the experience of the founder / owner and the management team (if there is one) are the same as the experiences of the firm". Conversely, Reuber and Fisher assert that the venture is the appropriate unit of analysis when examining the stream of experience.

Westhead et al. (2005a) extended Reuber and Fischer's (1999) conceptual framework with regard to an individual's experience of owning an equity stake in one or more private firm(s). This framework is presented in Figure 1.1. An entrepreneur's stock of experience includes both the depth and breadth of experience accumulated at a point in time. The stream of experience relates to experience possessed over time.

Issues related to the stock of experience are discussed in Westhead et al. (2003). More limited attention has, however, been paid to the stream of experience. Westhead et al. (2005a) called for additional studies to focus upon the stream of an entrepreneur's PBOE. They suggested should focus upon the decisions and actions (i.e., stream of experience) exhibited by habitual entrepreneurs. For example, studies focusing upon the information search and opportunity recognition behaviour reported by novice, serial and portfolio entrepreneurs. Further, they asserted that studies should monitor outcomes related to the entrepreneurial process with regard to the performance of entrepreneur, rather than the surveyed independent firm(s) in which they have equity stakes. Scholars considering entrepreneurial events, processes and outputs in the contexts in which they occur are reflecting upon the following questions (Westhead and Wright, 2013):

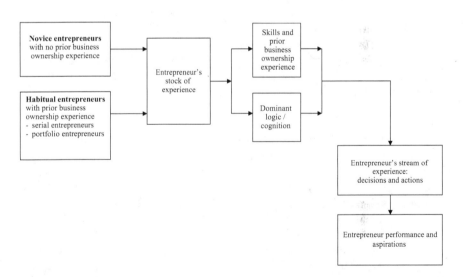

Figure 1.1 The Mediating Relationships Between Prior Business Ownership Experience and Entrepreneur Behaviour and Performance (Adapted from Reuber and Fischer, 1999, Figure 1, p.31)
Source: Authors.

8 *Introduction*

- *What is habitual entrepreneurship?*
- *Why is habitual entrepreneurship important?*
- *What is the scale of the habitual phenomenon?*
- *What do habitual and sub-types of habitual entrepreneurs do?*
- *What is distinctive about habitual entrepreneurs?*
- *Do some types of habitual entrepreneurs make greater contributions?*

1.6 Organizing Framework and Book Structure

The entrepreneurial process is at the epicentre of the debate about entrepreneurship (Moroz and Hindle, 2012). This is because it concerns what needs to take place to make entrepreneurship happen. Lack of consensus about 'what entrepreneurs do' and 'who entrepreneurs are' gives rise to several approaches to understanding entrepreneurs and the entrepreneurial process. Generally, the entrepreneurial process involves all the functions and activities associated with perceiving opportunities and pursuing them. A narrow view focuses on the emergence of new organizations, while a broader view focuses on the emergence of opportunities irrespective of whether it takes place in a new or existing firm. Accumulating (and mobilizing) resources is a key cross-cutting issue. Some see entrepreneurship as the process by which individuals pursue and exploit opportunities irrespective of the resources they currently control. Others focus on how entrepreneurs can utilize the resource they have to hand, while still others examine the process by which entrepreneurs access and co-ordinate their resources.

We discuss issues relating to the habitual entrepreneur phenomenon with reference to several themes highlighted by Gartner (1985). He presented a conceptual framework to describe the phenomenon of new venture creation. Gartner (1985) made a distinction between: the characteristics of the individual(s) starting the new venture, the organization they create, the environment surrounding the new venture and the process by which the new venture is created. Building on these insights, six themes within entrepreneurship studies (Ucbasaran et al., 2001) are highlighted in Figure 1.2. These themes will be discussed in the following chapters of this book to discuss the habitual entrepreneur phenomenon.

Theme 1 relates to *theory*. Several theories have been presented to explore the entrepreneurial process, and the behaviour and performance of entrepreneurs and their firms. These theories reflect the diversity of the nature of entrepreneurship and entrepreneurs. Entrepreneur resources are discussed in relation to human capital and cognition theory in Chapter 2.

Theme 2 relates to the *external environment for entrepreneurship*. Above, it was suggested that policy-makers and practitioners are encouraging the supply of entrepreneurs and the growth of new firms to generate economic and non-economic benefits. Governments in developed and developing economies are seeking to foster an enterprise culture. External environmental context can shape resource availability, the actions undertaken by entrepreneurs and the

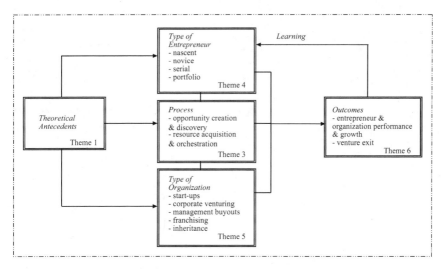

Figure 1.2 Themes Explored in Entrepreneurship Studies
Source: Authors.

performance of their firms, which is also illustrated by theme 4. In this book, the authors' studies conducted in Belgium, Scotland and the United Kingdom developed economies and the Ghana developing economy are discussed. Also, insights from studies conducted in other contexts are highlighted.

Entrepreneurship is a process that develops over time. Theme 3 relates to the *process of entrepreneurship* and focuses upon what entrepreneurs do with regard to creating and recognizing opportunities, as well as assembling and mobilizing (i.e., entrepreneurial team, organization and external environmental) resources to exploit opportunities. Entrepreneur resource profiles differences between habitual and novice entrepreneurs are highlighted in Chapter 3. Entrepreneur resource accumulation specifically in relation to finance is discussed in Chapter 4 and in relation to networking and resource orchestration in Chapter 5. Issues relating to opportunity discovery and creation are highlighted in Chapter 6. Theme 4 relates to *types of entrepreneur*. Different types of entrepreneurs exist and can be shaped by their context. Social context, such as where entrepreneurs come from, can shape aspirations, expectations and access to specific human capital resources relating to industry know-how, management know-how and entrepreneurial capabilities. Differences also relate to how entrepreneurs think (i.e., personality and cognitive mindset) and learn. Issues relating to types of habitual (i.e., serial and portfolio) and novice entrepreneurs are discussed in Chapter 1.

Theme 5 relates to *types of organizations*. We adopt a broad view of entrepreneurship. Besides the creation of new independent firms, entrepreneurship can be exhibited in family firms, corporate ventures, MBOs and MBIs,

10 *Introduction*

academic spin-offs and social enterprises. As illustrated in Section 1.3, we recognize that business ownership can occur in many formats. Presented evidence, however, generally relates to owners of private independent firms for profit.

Theme 6 relates to the *outcomes of entrepreneurial endeavours*. The economic and non-economic outcomes of entrepreneurial endeavours relate to entrepreneur and the firm. Learning from PBOE success and failure is discussed in Chapter 7. Entrepreneur and firm performance differences between habitual and novice entrepreneurs are highlighted in Chapter 8. Future research directions are raised in Chapter 9.

1.7 Summary

This chapter has highlighted that the entrepreneur and the firm can be the unit of theoretical and policy debate. With reference to the firm as the unit of analysis, we have suggested that entrepreneurs can establish, purchase and/or inherit businesses. Notably, some entrepreneurs have careers in business ownership, which we have broadly termed habitual entrepreneurs. With reference to the nature of entrepreneurship involving *new* business(es) and/or involving *existing* business(es), a categorization of habitual entrepreneurship was presented. Here, the broad habitual entrepreneur phenomenon was illustrated with reference to finer sub-types of serial and portfolio entrepreneurs. Despite no agreed widely used definition of habitual entrepreneurs (or serial and portfolio entrepreneurs), empirical studies have found that habitual entrepreneurs are highly prevalent in several national contexts. This suggests that academics, policy-makers and practitioners need to understand the backgrounds and behaviour of habitual entrepreneurs and the sub-types of serial and portfolio entrepreneurs (Carter and Ram, 2003). The movement from descriptive studies to more rigorous theory-building and theory-testing studies focusing on the habitual entrepreneur phenomenon was briefly highlighted. Knowledge gaps and research themes worthy of additional attention using qualitative and quantitative approaches were then alluded to. Several broad research questions were highlighted. The organizing structure of the book focusing upon the habitual entrepreneur phenomenon with reference to key themes relating to the entrepreneurial process was then discussed. The chapters will focus on the following entrepreneurial process issues: entrepreneur resources from a theoretical lens, entrepreneur resource profiles, entrepreneur resource accumulation relating to finance, entrepreneur resource accumulation relating to networking and orchestration, entrepreneur opportunity creation behaviour, entrepreneur opportunity discovery behaviour, entrepreneur learning, and entrepreneur and firm performance. In the final chapter, we highlight several conclusions and implications relating to the habitual entrepreneur phenomenon. Materials from articles published by the authors are utilized to illustrate key issues, findings and implications relating to the habitual entrepreneur phenomenon. In the following chapters, the discussion relates to habitual entrepreneurs, but in several instances it relates to finer sub-groups of serial and portfolio entrepreneurs with PBOE compared against novice entrepreneurs with no PBOE.

1.8 Reflection Questions

In Chapter 1, several issues relating to the nature and scale of the habitual entrepreneur phenomenon were highlighted. Please consider the following reflection questions:

- *Why should the entrepreneur be the unit of analysis?*
- *Do all entrepreneurs solely establish a single, private firm?*
- *What are the key elements when defining habitual entrepreneurs?*
- *Is the habitual entrepreneur phenomenon important for policy-makers?*
- *Should policy-makers solely support the formation of new private independent firms?*
- *Do entrepreneurs differ in relation to the stock and stream of experience?*

2 Entrepreneur Resources: Theoretical Insights

2.1 Learning Objectives and Overview

With reference to qualitative theory-building studies (i.e., proposition derivation) and quantitative (i.e., hypothesis testing) studies, several theories have been widely utilized to explore the backgrounds and behaviour of habitual (i.e., serial and portfolio) entrepreneurs and the performance of entrepreneurs and their firms. Theorists have recognized that entrepreneurs have to focus on resource accumulation to create, discover and/or exploit business opportunities.

Further, key elements of several theories relating to a resource perspective that have been used to explore the habitual entrepreneur phenomenon are briefly summarized. Key assumptions and parameters of several theories are discussed, in turn, below. These theories are utilized in the following chapters when illustrating the backgrounds and behaviour of habitual entrepreneurs (and the finer sub-groups of serial and portfolio entrepreneurs) with PBOE compared against novice entrepreneurs with no PBOE.

2.2 Human Capital Theory

2.2.1 General Human Capital

Resources are essential for the founding and development of entrepreneurial firms. Reuber and Fischer's (1999) founders' experience conceptual framework suggests that the behaviour of entrepreneurs is, in part, shaped by their human capital profiles. Entrepreneurs' human capital can, in part, shape the behaviour and performance (and their firms) (Unger et al., 2011) of businesses owned by entrepreneurs. Also, human capital theorists recognize that individuals acquire resources in particular contexts (Becker, 1993), and the resources and attitudes acquired over time may influence subsequent entrepreneur behaviour. Human capital theorists have debated how the 'inputs' accumulated by entrepreneurs relate to 'outputs' (Otani, 1996). In the context of entrepreneurship, 'outputs' can relate to the identification, pursuit and exploitation of opportunities (Shane, 2003), the 'quality' of opportunities (Fiet, 2002) relating to innovativeness (Shepherd and

DeTienne, 2005) as well as firm survival (Gimeno et al., 1997) and the performance of the firm.

We adopt a broad human capital view that recognizes that an entrepreneur's demographic characteristics, achieved attributes, accumulated work and habits, and cognitive characteristics can have a positive (or negative) impact on productivity. It is assumed that individuals with broader pools of human capital resources will report superior levels of productivity (Becker, 1975, 1993). Further, entrepreneurs with more (or higher) quality human capital 'inputs' should report superior 'outputs' (Davidsson and Honig, 2003).

Cognitive approaches offer insights into how individuals can acquire resources, skills and knowledge through experience and learning. Notably, traditional human capital approaches and cognitive approaches differ in relation to their assumptions. Traditional human capital approaches, especially those that focus on education, generally assume instrumental rationality. It is assumed that the entrepreneur (i.e., economic actor) makes a calculated decision surrounding the level of investment in human capital. The rationality assumption has been relaxed by some theorists who recognize that not all aspects of human capital are accumulated through a conscious and calculated rational process. For example, Becker (1993) has called for the inclusion of habits and other attributes of the individual into the concept of human capital that can have a positive (or negative) impact on productivity. Some human capital theorists assume bounded rationality. Following a bounded rationality view makes it easier to accommodate cognition within a broader notion of human capital. Guided by insights from a psychological paradigm cognitive theorists generally assume situated rationality. Caution is, therefore, required when integrating the concepts of human capital and cognition with reference to exploring the differences in the resource profiles and behaviour of habitual and novice entrepreneurs.

Habitual entrepreneurs following careers in business ownership have the potential to accumulate larger and more diverse pools of human capital. Novice entrepreneurs with no PBOE have more limited potential to accumulate diverse pools of human capital. A distinction is made between general and specific human capital. General human capital is generic to all types of economic activity (Castanias and Helfat, 2001). This general human capital relates to the skills and knowledge that are easily transferable across a variety of economic settings. Generally, it has been measured in terms of an individual's age, parental background, gender and education (Becker, 1975). The first three relate to demographic characteristics that are given at birth. Studies widely focus on demographic characteristics (i.e., proxies for human capital) when direct measures of human capital cannot be collected. Education is a widely monitored direct measure of human capital, which can be an important source of skills and knowledge (Cooper et al., 1994). Managerial work experience is also viewed as a key dimension of human capital. The latter experience accumulated when not being an entrepreneur

14   *Entrepreneur Resources: Theoretical Insights*

can be regarded as a dimension of general human capital (Castanias and Helfat, 2001).

2.2.2 *Specific Human Capital*

Specific human capital has a more limited scope of applicability than general human capital, and it may lose its value outside its particular domain. Direct entrepreneurial experience acquired during PBOE can generate entrepreneurship-specific human capital (Gimeno et al., 1997). Entrepreneurial (i.e., perceived ability to create, identify and exploit opportunities), managerial (i.e., ability to manage and organize people and resources) and technical skills (i.e., the focus upon technical expertise) can be accumulated and mobilized by habitual entrepreneurs with PBOE (Chandler and Hanks, 1998). Habitual entrepreneurs associated with several prior business ownership experiences may be more likely to accumulate these specific human capital skills.

An experienced habitual entrepreneur owning a business in the same sector as their previous/current venture may be able to identify what is required to earn profits in the selected market more quickly (Starr and Bygrave, 1991) than novice entrepreneurs. Further, a habitual entrepreneur's specific human capital can be enhanced though reputation and better understanding of the requirements of finance institutions. Enhanced specific human capital from PBOE may be interrelated with greater social capital associated with broader and deeper networks (Shane and Khurana, 2003). Habitual entrepreneurs with good reputations and track records of success, for example, may have business ideas sent to them from potential and current entrepreneurs. Moreover, the latter habitual entrepreneurs can mobilize their human capital to obtain predictable and uninterrupted supplies of critical resources (i.e., financial and social capital) (Cooper et al., 1994). This review suggests that habitual entrepreneurs with PBOE will be more likely to be able to accumulate (and mobilize) additional human capital and other types of resources (Ucbasaran et al., 2008).

2.3 Cognition and Heuristics

Some entrepreneurship scholars are drawing upon cognitive psychology to provide the psychological foundations for understanding the behaviour of entrepreneurs (Baron, 2004). Entrepreneurial cognition refers to: the knowledge structures used by people to make assessments, judgements or decisions involving opportunity evaluation, venture creation and growth (Mitchell et al., 2002). Cognition scholars provide insights surrounding how individuals make sense of their experiences. An individual's cognitive characteristics can shape their attitudes as well as how individuals think, process information and learn. Experience may shape an entrepreneur's cognition (Baron, 1998). By evaluating 'feedback' from PBOE exposures

(Nystrom and Starbuck, 1984), some habitual entrepreneurs may generate a dynamic cycle of learning. Experience-based knowledge can create 'cognitive pathways' promoting creativity (Amabile, 1997). PBOE may influence an individual's capacity to acquire and organize complex information. Notably, PBOE may provide a framework for processing information into recognizable patterns that allows habitual entrepreneurs to take appropriate actions (Lord and Maher, 1990).

Cognition theories can provide insights surrounding how an experienced habitual entrepreneur's cognitive profile may influence how they handle complex information in order to identify and exploit business opportunities (Ucbasaran et al., 2009). Prototype theories, expert information processing theories and heuristic information processing theories (Baron, 2004) suggest that an individual's cognition can be shaped by experience. Within the expert cognition literature, it is recognized that prior experience may improve performance, but only up to a certain point. Beyond a certain experience threshold, biases in thinking may retard subsequent entrepreneur behaviour and performance (Baron and Henry, 2006). The theoretical entrepreneurship cognition literature provides insights surrounding the effects of the nature of prior experience on behaviour. Prior failure may hinder learning and restrict the motivation to try again (Shepherd, 2003). Conversely, prior failure may stimulate learning and adaptation (McGrath, 1999). The general cognition literature suggests that the nature of prior failure needs to be considered regarding the number of failure experiences (Brunstein and Gollwitzer, 1996) and the relevance of failure experience to a person's self-identity (Schulttheiss and Brunstein, 2000).

Cognitive theories offer various tools for understanding the processes underlying business opportunity identification, many of which emphasize the role of mental frameworks that guide the process. Gaglio and Katz (2001) draw on schema theory to explain the underlying processes behind Kirzner's (1973) notion of entrepreneurial alertness and how entrepreneurs identify business opportunities. Schemas, also known as knowledge or cognitive structures, represent the content and organization of knowledge. They develop as a result of the cumulative experience, learning and meanings an individual has encountered and constructed about a specific domain (Gaglio, 1997). Schemas determine how individuals respond to new information. For example, people possessing an alertness schema are able to search for and notice change and market disequilibria, and they can respond to new information (Gaglio and Katz, 2001). Similarly, drawing upon prototype theory, Baron (2004) illustrated the role of prototypes in explaining business opportunity identification. Through experience, people acquire prototypes that serve as templates for concepts such as business opportunity identification. A prototype for an opportunity may include features such as novelty, practicality, market appeal, and the ease with which necessary resources can be obtained. New ideas can be benchmarked against prototype criteria. A new

16 Entrepreneur Resources: Theoretical Insights

idea that is closely matched against an existing prototype of an opportunity may be more likely to be identified as a business opportunity.

Gaglio and Katz (2001) assert that one of the limitations of the 'alertness' approach to business opportunity identification is that the approach ignores the heterogeneity of entrepreneurs. Variations in experience may, for example, explain why entrepreneurs differ with regard to opportunity identification behaviour. Expert information processing theory highlights that expert's process information differently from novices. Experts have more developed schema, shaped by individual experience, which allow them in a particular domain to unify superficially disparate information, and make more sophisticated critical judgements. Further, experts appreciate the relevance of information and notice patterns which may be overlooked by novices (Lord and Maher, 1990). The cognitive structure of a habitual entrepreneur's knowledge may resemble that of an expert. Experienced habitual entrepreneurs associated with higher levels of episodic knowledge (i.e., a necessary but insufficient requirement of expertise) may use their knowledge to process complex information. Habitual entrepreneurs relatively developed opportunity identification schema may direct their attention, expectations and interpretations of market stimuli, as well as enabling the generation of ideas (Gaglio, 1997). Also, habitual entrepreneurs with more developed prototypes may be able to 'connect the dots' between seemingly unrelated changes or events and detect meaningful patterns to a greater extent than inexperienced novice entrepreneurs.

Entrepreneurial cognition scholars have focused upon the use of heuristics and biases by entrepreneurs. Cognition scholars assert that entrepreneurs are particularly susceptible to the use of heuristics and biases because of the environment in which they operate (Baron, 1998). Heuristics are simplifying strategies (or mental shortcuts) used to make strategic decisions, particularly in complex situations when there is incomplete information. Greater levels of experience can be associated with 'assets' and 'liabilities' (Starr and Bygrave, 1991). Some of these liabilities may stem from the greater reliance on heuristics by habitual entrepreneurs (Ucbasaran et al., 2006). Over their entrepreneurial careers, habitual entrepreneurs may develop a repertoire of experience to draw on. Further, habitual entrepreneurs may develop heuristic principles or decision-making shortcuts. This may lead to the following biases (Tversky and Kahneman, 1974) (or liabilities associated with PBOE (Starr and Bygrave, 1991)): experienced entrepreneurs may think that they know enough (Baron, 1998), become constrained by what is familiar to them (Rabin, 1998), infer too much from limited information because they want to confirm prior beliefs, become unable to notice and react to new factors (Rerup, 2005), become overconfident (Simon et al., 2000), have an inability to consider new perspectives (Minniti and Bygrave, 2001) and adapt poorly to changing external environmental contexts. Habitual entrepreneurs prone to these biases may find it difficult to identify new business opportunities. The liabilities of PBOE may stem from attempts to repeat previously successful 'recipes' (i.e., business ideas) in changed external environmental circumstances. Constrained by the recipes, some habitual entrepreneurs may be unable to think beyond past exploited business opportunities. Some habitual entrepreneurs may be overly dependent on past contacts (Starr and Bygrave, 1991), which may hinder the ability to acquire new information and ideas. Habitual entrepreneurs with PBOE success or failure may experience hubris or denial, respectively (Simon et al., 2000). Some habitual entrepreneurs may use existing resources rather than accumulate more relevant resources (Ucbasaran et al., 2008). Moreover, some habitual entrepreneurs may only imperfectly adjust their judgement in subsequent businesses owned. Some experienced habitual entrepreneurs, however, may know when to switch from heuristic information processing to a more systematic approach (Rerup, 2005).

Heuristics, such as overconfidence (i.e., an unwarranted belief in an individual's abilities to bring about a particular outcome (Forbes, 2005), comparative optimism (i.e., over-optimism, which is the tendency of people to report that they are less likely than others to experience negative events and more likely than others to experience positive events (Helweg-Larsen and Shepperd, 2001), and representativeness (i.e., a willingness to generalize from a small number of observations (Busenitz and Barney, 1997), can encourage some people to assume that entrepreneurship is a too daunting activity.

Heuristic-based information processing has the advantage of speed. It also enables entrepreneurs to make decisions that allow them to exploit successfully brief windows of opportunity. Heuristics can reduce the burden of cognitive processing and may enable some entrepreneurs to concentrate on novel or unique material (Hillerbrand, 1989), which may lead to the creation or discovery of more innovative business opportunities (Ucbasaran et al., 2008). In contrast, novice entrepreneurs with no PBOE and fewer experience-related benchmarks to draw upon may be more likely to select analytical or systematic information processing styles (Gustafsson, 2006), which may retard opportunity creation and discovery.

Heuristic-based information processing may be less accurate than systematic processing. Habitual entrepreneurs may over-rely on heuristic principles and decision-making processes, which may not necessarily be appropriate in new and turbulent external environmental contexts. Some habitual entrepreneurs over-relying on heuristic principles may report some of the biases associated with heuristic decision-making (Bazerman, 1990).

2.4 Resource-Based View of the Firm

The resource-based view (RBV) of the firm (Barney, 1991) questions the assumed dominant power of external environmental conditions on firm and performance and competitive advantage. This perspective is widely used to explore firm and entrepreneur behaviour. In relation to the 'firm' rather than the 'entrepreneur' as the unit of analysis, Penrose (1959) identified several resources that need to be accumulated and leveraged by entrepreneurs that can ensure firm survival and profitability. Resources relate to

18 *Entrepreneur Resources: Theoretical Insights*

an entrepreneur's human capital resources as well as firm resources relating to tacit knowledge, technological resources (i.e., imagination, creativity, innovativeness etc.), finance, reputation and goodwill, organizational routines and skills. The firm is viewed as a pool of resources, the utilization of which is organized in an administrative framework. The content of the pool changes over time due to the firm's activities (i.e., external search, internal search and people within the firm learning by doing). The firm's productive opportunity relates to all the opportunities that the firm's 'managers' see and take advantage of. Each firm's opportunities depend on a combination of firm-specific advantages and/or perception of ways in which they can be profitably used. It is assumed that entrepreneurs need to accumulate appropriate resources, and to ensure firm development, they need to be efficiently used. Penrose views the firm as a 'knowledge community', and firm competitive advantage depends on the development and use of knowledge. The 'filter of knowledge' shapes how the firm's resources and capabilities can be best employed to enhance the firm's competitive advantage. Notably, Penrose (1959) recognized that entrepreneurs are not a homogeneous entity.

The RBV of the firm theorists (Barney et al., 2001) focus upon the importance of the individual firm as opposed to industry/external environmental conditions. The RBV of the firm perspective focuses upon the heterogeneous pool of idiosyncratic resources that are valuable, rare, non-imitable and non-substitutable firms that need to be accumulated by firm (and lead entrepreneurs) to ensure competitive advantage (Barney, 1991). Firms (and entrepreneurs) need to accumulate firm-specific human resources relating to the management know-how and entrepreneurial experience of the lead entrepreneur (and/or entrepreneurial team). Lead entrepreneurs can possess human capital resources important for firm development, some of which may be based on PBOE, in the case of habitual entrepreneurs. Other resources relate to legitimacy, finance, intellectual capital and technology embodied in innovation, networking and deep-bonding social capital. Social capital is the sum of actual and potential resources embedded within an entrepreneur's network of relationships. Alvarez and Busenitz (2001) link an entrepreneurship perspective to the RBV by suggesting how entrepreneurship involves the entrepreneur's unique awareness of opportunities, their ability to acquire resources to exploit an opportunity and their organizational ability to recombine homogeneous inputs into heterogeneous outputs.

Building upon insights from the RBV and the competitive strategy perspective (Porter, 1985), Spanos and Lioukas (2001) assert that a balanced view of the sources of competitive advantage can be obtained (i.e., the internal and external determinants of competitive advantages). The ability of entrepreneurs to establish and develop their firms is, therefore, seen to be shaped by their ability to deal with uncertainty and to assemble, command and leverage resources from both the internal and external environments. To exploit 'created' or 'discovered' opportunities, entrepreneurs need to draw upon their skills, experience and knowledge to make judgemental decisions about how to undertake actions that promote new firm creation to exploit identified opportunities. To ensure firm survival and to generate profits for their firms, entrepreneurs guided by their skills, experience and knowledge (and existing resources within their firms) have to acquire new resources and/or develop new competencies. Entrepreneurs have to proactively or reactively make informed judgements surrounding the ownership, management and strategic orientation of their ventures.

How entrepreneurs obtain and leverage resources to exploit new opportunities is attracting increasing attention. Resource orchestration theory is being developed as a conceptual framework to help understand the processes by which managers accumulate, combine and exploit resources to support current opportunities while developing future opportunities to achieve a competitive advantage (Sirmon and Hitt, 2003). Resource orchestration theory suggests that it is the combination of resources, capabilities and managerial action that ultimately results in superior firm performance (Sirmon et al., 2007). Existing resource orchestration theory has principally been developed in the context of strategic entrepreneurship in existing corporations, but as illustrated in Chapter 5, opportunities for its application and development relate to private firms.

2.5 Dynamic Capabilities

A distinction has been made between resources and capabilities (Amit and Schoemaker, 1993). Resources are assets that are either owned or controlled by a firm. Capabilities refer to a firm's ability to exploit and combine resources through organizational routines. Organizational development can be shaped by the leverage of a firm's existing firm-specific assets. Firms need to develop new capabilities. Consistent with the RBV, dynamic capabilities theorists analyse the sources and methods of wealth creation and capture by firms operating in rapidly changing environments. Eisenhardt and Martin (2000) make a distinction between the following three groups of dynamic capabilities: capabilities that integrate resources, those that reconfigure resources and those that gain and release resources. Firms and entrepreneurs can, therefore, accumulate and mobilize resources in relation to various dimensions of the entrepreneurial process. Firms (and entrepreneurs) can accumulate and mobilize capabilities in relation to various aspects of the entrepreneurial process.

2.6 Signalling Theory

Signalling theorists reject the assumption of perfect information held by signallers (i.e., lead entrepreneurs) and receivers (i.e., such as external resource providers). For example, information asymmetries between lead entrepreneurs and external resource provider (i.e., financier) may adversely affect the ability of entrepreneurs to obtain the requested amount of external resources (i.e., finance). Acquiring information to resolve informational asymmetries is costly because signaller attributes may not be readily observable, and the

20 *Entrepreneur Resources: Theoretical Insights*

receiver is reliant upon what the signaller is willing to share (Spence, 2002). Signalling theory focuses on the credible communication of positive information to convey positive organizational attributes.

Signal quality relates to the underlying, unobservable ability of the signaller to fulfill the demands (or needs) of an outsider observing the signal (Connelly et al., 2011). The signal highlights the unobservable quality of the signaller to potential receivers via the observable qualities of the signaller. Receivers such as external resource providers (i.e., financiers) need to distinguish between high- and low-quality signallers. Lead entrepreneurs that provide signals of quality can reduce financier doubts (Backes-Gellner and Werner, 2007) surrounding firm 'liabilities of newness and smallness' (Stinchcombe, 1965). External resource providers (i.e., financiers) may ignore lead entrepreneurs not providing adequate information about business idea quality and the management team and potential rewards and risks. To increase the likelihood of obtaining the requested amount of external resources (i.e., finance), lead entrepreneurs can provide positive costly resource signals of credibility, experience and quality to external resource providers (i.e., financiers) seeking high-quality proposals to invest in.

2.7 Learning

Entrepreneurship is a process of learning (Minniti and Bygrave, 2001) relating to a cumulative series of interdependent events (Cope, 2011; Morris et al., 2012). Learning experience is assumed to enhance exploration and exploitation of new opportunities in subsequent ventures (Wang and Chugh, 2014). Entrepreneurship specific human capital can be acquired by some entrepreneurs who have careers in sequential (i.e., serial entrepreneurs) and concurrent business ownership (i.e., portfolio entrepreneurs). The latter experimental learning from PBOE success(es) and/or closure(s) (Westhead and Wright, 2014) may generate positive alternative dimensions of entrepreneurial learning. Experimental learning theory (ELT) is a cognitive and situative learning theory that recognizes that individual's may transform (using cognitive properties) their experiences (situative) into new knowledge (Kolb, 1984). Knowledge accumulated from experience provides a framework for processing information, allowing experienced entrepreneurs to identify and exploit opportunities and new ways of creating value (Holcomb et al., 2009).

2.8 Summary

This chapter has briefly summarized the assumptions and parameters associated with several theories that have used to explore the backgrounds and behaviour of habitual, serial and portfolio entrepreneurs. In the following chapters, these theories are built upon in articles published by the authors to explore issues relating to the entrepreneurial process as well as entrepreneur and firm performance.

2.9 Reflection Questions

In Chapter 2, theories employed to explore the habitual entrepreneur phenomenon have been highlighted. Please consider the following reflection questions:

- *What is human capital?*
- *Do habitual and novice entrepreneur differ with regard to their pools of human capital?*
- *What is cognition?*
- *Do habitual and novice entrepreneurs differ with regard to their cognitive profiles?*
- *What are heuristics and biases?*
- *Are habitual entrepreneurs more susceptible to the use of heuristics and biases?*
- *What are the 'assets' and 'liabilities' of PBOE?*
- *What is the key assumption of the resource-based view of the firm?*
- *What are capabilities?*
- *What can habitual entrepreneurs 'signal' to potential external resource providers?*
- *What are the key assumptions of the experimental learning model?*

3 Entrepreneur Resource Profiles

3.1 Learning Objectives and Overview

The research discussed in Chapter 3 builds upon insights from human capital theory, cognition and heuristics theory and the RBV of the firm. The three themes in this chapter highlight differences (and similarities) between habitual (i.e., serial and portfolio) entrepreneurs with PBOE and novice entrepreneurs with no PBOE. Entrepreneur resource profiles are compared with regard to human capital as well cognition, heuristics and biases. We draw on two quantitative descriptive studies conducted in Scotland that focused upon entrepreneur human capital resources, cognition, heuristics and biases as well as a quantitative theory-testing study conducted in Great Britain that focused on the comparative optimism bias.

Some descriptive flesh relating to the habitual entrepreneur resource profile was presented by Birley and Westhead (1993). Their univariate analysis explored the differences and similarities between habitual and novice entrepreneurs in Great Britain. Profiles of entrepreneurs were compared with regard to personal background of the founder, work experience of the founder, and reasons leading to start-up. The profiles of the entrepreneur's surveyed firms were compared with regard to financial base, employment and ownership structure, customer and supplier base, competitive structure and external environmental resource elements, including the public provision of support services. Birley and Westhead (1993: 56) concluded that:

> Indeed, in some senses, the 'habituals' fit more closely to the traditional view of highly successful entrepreneurs such as Richard Branson—they start young, they have 'heroes' as role models, and they rely upon the support of family and friends for financial support. Moreover, this was sustained in their 'current' business, supporting the view that previous experience can be an asset rather than liability.

Building upon the insights relating to the growing appreciation that some entrepreneurs have entrepreneurial careers in more than business (Dyer, 1994; Ronstadt, 1982) and habitual entrepreneurs can accumulate assets and liabilities of PBOE (Starr and Bygrave, 1991); Westhead and Wright (1998) sought to provide greater clarity relating to the habitual entrepreneur phenomenon that was attracting increasing research attention. They presented a categorization of habitual (or multiple entrepreneurs) relating to two broad dimensions relating to whether entrepreneurship involves a new or existing businesses, and whether or not there is a change of ownership between ventures. Notably, they highlighted that habitual entrepreneurship involves existing firms and do novo new firms. Further, they suggested that the habitual entrepreneur phenomenon could be sub-divided into sub-sets of serial and portfolio entrepreneurs. The dataset collected by Birley and Westhead (1993) was analysed by Westhead and Wright (1998) with reference to a finer definition of habitual entrepreneurship.

The human capital resources profiles of serial, portfolio and novice entrepreneurs were compared in relation to the personal background of the founder, work experience of the founder and reasons leading to start-up. Also, the financial resource profiles of the three types of entrepreneurs were compared. Their univariate analysis explored the differences and similarities between serial, portfolio and novice entrepreneurs. Several significant differences were detected between each type of entrepreneur. Westhead and Wright (1998: 198) concluded that:

> . . . habitual entrepreneurs cannot be treated as a homogeneous group.

In this chapter, entrepreneur resource profiles are discussed. The entrepreneur human capital resource profiles of serial, portfolio and novice entrepreneurs are highlighted. As intimated above, resources are stocks of assets either owned or controlled by the entrepreneur. They are attributes of tangible and intangible assets (or capitals) that enable the entrepreneur to develop strategies to create and/or discover business opportunities and achieve competitive advantage for firms owned. Also, the cognitive profiles of serial, portfolio and novice entrepreneurs are highlighted. Assets and liabilities (i.e., biases) of PBOE experience are discussed. The comparative optimism bias is particularly highlighted.

3.2 Entrepreneur Resource Profile: General Dimensions

3.2.1 Gaps in the Knowledge Base and Research Questions

In this section, we draw on the article by Westhead et al., (2005b) who provided evidence relating to the broad characteristics, behaviour and performance contributions made by serial and portfolio entrepreneurs who can mobilize PBOE, compared with inexperienced novice entrepreneurs who have no PBOE. Although not formally stated in the article, the following broad research question was explored:

- *Do serial, portfolio and novice entrepreneurs differ in relation to their human capital, financing and organizational capabilities profiles?*

24 Profiles

3.2.2 Descriptive Analysis

This descriptive study compared the resource profiles of serial, portfolio and novice entrepreneurs. In this study, the respondents were key individuals who were the most influential decision-makers in the surveyed businesses (i.e., the founders of the business and/or the principal owner). The following definitions of novice, serial and portfolio entrepreneurs were used. Novice entrepreneurs were viewed as individuals with no prior minority or majority business ownership experience either as a business founder, an inheritor or a purchaser of an independent business, but who currently own a minority or majority equity stake in an independent business that is either new, purchased or inherited. Serial entrepreneurs were viewed as individuals who have sold / closed a business in which they had a minority or majority ownership stake, and they currently have a minority or majority ownership stake in a single independent business that is either new, purchased or inherited. While portfolio entrepreneurs were viewed as individuals who currently have minority or majority ownership stakes in two or more independent businesses that are either new, purchased and/or inherited.

3.2.3 Methodology

3.2.3.1 Data

The authors suggested that information from a representative sample of 354 private firms owned by novice, serial and portfolio entrepreneurs in Scotland had been collected. The data collection process is discussed in detail in the second section in this chapter (see Section 3.3.3.1).

3.2.3.2 Techniques

The profiles of novice, serial and portfolio entrepreneurs were compared in relation to descriptive statistics. Then, portfolio entrepreneurs were compared against novice and serial entrepreneurs. Finally, serial entrepreneurs were compared against novice and portfolio entrepreneurs. Univariate statistical analysis was conducted to identify significant differences between the types of entrepreneurs.

3.2.4 Findings

3.2.4.1 Entrepreneur and Business Ownership Profiles

In total, 200 firms (56.5%) involved novice entrepreneurs. Habitual entrepreneurs (i.e., serial and portfolio entrepreneurs) owned 43.5% of firms. The number of portfolio and serial entrepreneurs was ascertained. Sixty-six firms involved serial entrepreneurs (18.6%), and the remaining 88 firms involved portfolio entrepreneurs (24.9%).

Portfolio entrepreneurs, on average, had held equity stakes in more businesses than serial or novice entrepreneurs. Also, serial entrepreneurs had exited more businesses than portfolio entrepreneurs. Novice and serial entrepreneurs currently had equity stakes in only one independent business, whilst portfolio entrepreneurs, on average, had equity stakes in 2.8 independent businesses. No statistically significant differences were detected among the three types of entrepreneurs regarding the number of equity partners in the surveyed business when it was started, inherited or purchased.

3.2.4.2 Portfolio Entrepreneurs Compared with Novice and Serial Entrepreneurs: Human Capital

In relation to entrepreneur human capital resource profiles, serial entrepreneur firms were weakly significantly younger. No statistically significant differences, however, were recorded among the three entrepreneur types regarding their current age, or gender and educational level. A larger proportion of portfolio entrepreneurs, rather than novice or serial entrepreneurs, reported that one of their parents had experience as business owners.

As a result of PBOE, many experienced entrepreneurs may have developed skills and competencies, a network of contacts, a business reputation and a track record. The development of a portfolio of businesses suggests a need for greater managerial skills (Donckels et al., 1987). A larger proportion of portfolio entrepreneurs surveyed, compared to other entrepreneurs, reported that their last job had been a managerial position. In addition, portfolio entrepreneurs had worked in more organizations than novice entrepreneurs.

In relation to team entrepreneurship, portfolio entrepreneurs currently had more equity partners than novice or serial entrepreneurs. To avoid biases resulting from PBOE and increase their awareness in decision-making, many portfolio entrepreneurs preferred to be a 'team', rather than a 'solo' owner of a private firm. The team aspect of entrepreneurship may be important in providing the skills and resources needed to gain an equity stake in a (larger) venture, as well as to ensure business development. Portfolio entrepreneurs may use partners as a means of delegating responsibility. Partners can provide entrepreneurs with a greater depth of expertise, as well as access to wider networks.

Triggers to serial or portfolio entrepreneurship may involve a desire for independence, autonomy and wealth creation. Motivations cited by experienced entrepreneurs for owning businesses can also change over time. In line with the wealth creation expectations of policy-makers and practitioners, a larger proportion of portfolio rather than other entrepreneurs, reported 'to generate personal wealth' as the *main* reason leading to business ownership. Portfolio entrepreneurs were less likely than other entrepreneurs to suggest that they were 'unemployed / made redundant', and they were less likely than novice entrepreneurs to report that they had gained an ownership stake in the business 'to have greater flexibility for my personal and

26　*Profiles*

family life'. However, portfolio entrepreneurs were more likely than novice entrepreneurs to report 'to be challenged by the problems and opportunities of starting and growing a new business'.

3.2.4.3 *Serial Entrepreneurs Compared with Novice and Portfolio Entrepreneurs: Human Capital*

A smaller proportion of serial rather than portfolio entrepreneurs reported they had parents with PBOE. Consequently, a relatively higher proportion of serial entrepreneurs did not have access to the financial resources or the social networks generally more available to individuals drawn from business ownership parental backgrounds. However, a larger proportion of serial, rather than other entrepreneurs, indicated that they had been self-employed prior to gaining an equity stake in the surveyed business. Also, serial entrepreneurs had worked in more organizations than novice entrepreneurs. A positive interpretation of these findings is that serial entrepreneurs may have gained business experiences in a variety of settings. With regard to the main reasons leading to business ownership, serial entrepreneurs were more likely than novice entrepreneurs to cite 'to control their own time', but they were less likely than novice entrepreneurs to report that they had an equity stake in a business 'to continue a family tradition'.

3.2.4.4 *Portfolio Entrepreneurs Compared with Novice and Serial Entrepreneurs: Personal Capabilities Toward Opportunity Identification and Sources of Opportunities*

Portfolio entrepreneurs were more likely than novice entrepreneurs to agree that 'one of my greatest strengths is organizing resources and co-ordinating tasks'; 'my ability to supervise, influence and lead people'; 'my ability to delegate effectively'; 'my ability to seize high quality business opportunities'; and to have a 'special alertness or sensitivity towards spotting opportunities'. They were more likely than other entrepreneurs to agree that one of their greatest strengths is 'achieving results by organizing and motivating people' and to report they can 'usually spot a real opportunity better than professional researchers/analysts'.

3.2.4.5 *Serial Entrepreneurs Compared with Novice and Portfolio Entrepreneurs: Personal Capabilities Toward Opportunity Identification and Sources of Opportunities*

Serial entrepreneurs were less likely than other entrepreneurs to suggest that 'the business concept was developed while I was employed by another firm'. Serial entrepreneurs were more likely than novice entrepreneurs to agree that one of their greatest strengths is 'identifying goods and services that people want', and that they 'accurately perceive unmet customer needs'.

Also, serial entrepreneurs were more likely than portfolio entrepreneurs to suggest that their greatest strength was 'expertise in a technical or functional area'. In part, difficulties reported by serial entrepreneurs with regard to the identification of business opportunities may be associated with the way they identify opportunities. Serial entrepreneurs were more likely than other entrepreneurs to agree that 'the idea behind the business was the result of an accidental process. They were less likely than portfolio entrepreneurs to suggest they can 'spot a real opportunity better than professional researchers/ analysts'.

3.2.4.6 *Portfolio Entrepreneurs Compared with Novice and Serial Entrepreneurs: Financing Businesses*

An entrepreneur's background and incubator experience can have a profound influence on the amounts of initial capital, and types of finance used during the launch period of a new, acquired or inherited business. Serial and portfolio entrepreneurs with successful track records may be more credible than those who have failed first time around and may mobilize their PBOE to obtain external financial resources from banks and venture capitalists for their subsequent ventures. Portfolio entrepreneurs who have not exited from a venture(s) they have an ownership stake(s) in may be able to mobilize the internal financial resources from their existing business(es) (Alsos and Kolvereid, 1998) and may make use of finance from existing customers and suppliers. A reluctance to be involved in projects which may undermine their standing amongst the financial and business community, and a desire to invest a smaller proportion of their personal wealth the second time around may mean that some serial and portfolio entrepreneurs become risk averse over time.

Portfolio entrepreneurs, on average, invested more total initial capital to establish, inherit or purchase the surveyed businesses than novice entrepreneurs. Portfolio entrepreneurs were able to mobilize their PBOE to acquire more initial capital from banks than other entrepreneurs. However, portfolio entrepreneurs were less likely than novice entrepreneurs to report that access to bank finance and trade credit was easy. Financiers may have reservation about individuals, who are involved in multiple businesses, if there are concerns about a portfolio entrepreneur's lack of focus.

3.2.4.7 *Serial Entrepreneurs Compared with Novice and Portfolio Entrepreneurs: Financing Businesses*

On average, serial entrepreneurs invested more total initial capital to establish, inherit or purchase the surveyed businesses than novice entrepreneurs. A larger proportion of serial, rather than novice, entrepreneurs had used personal savings and/or a mortgage on their home as part of their initial capital. In terms of the proportion of initial funds contributed by each source, serial

28   *Profiles*

rather than other entrepreneurs, reported a higher proportion of initial capital was obtained from personal savings (i.e., potentially accumulated from the sale of a previous venture). This evidence may be indicative that their first (previous) venture was a financial success. On the other hand, this may be consistent with the views of venture capital firms that one of the main reasons for not funding serial entrepreneurs in a subsequent venture relates to the inability of serial entrepreneurs to identify attractive subsequent ventures. Indeed, two-thirds of serial entrepreneurs did not (or were unable to) use bank loans as part of their initial capital for the surveyed businesses.

3.2.4.8 *Portfolio Entrepreneurs Compared with Novice and Serial Entrepreneurs: Organizational Capabilities*

A firm (and entrepreneur) can gain a competitive advantage by acquiring and developing key capabilities (Teece et al., 1997). Firms and entrepreneurs may be able to learn and acquire additional organizational and intangible assets/resources (Eisenhardt and Martin, 2000) that enable them to address barriers to business development. Portfolio entrepreneurs were more likely than other entrepreneurs to report 'the need to grow the business'. Also, they were more likely than other entrepreneurs to report they 'actively recruit the most talented people'; they 'invest heavily in providing formal job related training for employees'; they use 'novel and innovative marketing techniques'; and they 'grow the business by acquiring new businesses'. Portfolio rather than novice entrepreneurs placed more emphasis upon 'strict quality control'; 'to strive to turn around performance and develop a stronger business'; to grow the 'business by using profits generated by the business'; to 'emphasize improvement in employee productivity and operations efficiency'; and to 'invest heavily in R&D'. The fact that portfolio entrepreneurs own more than one business may explain their greater focus on organizational capabilities.

3.2.4.9 *Serial Entrepreneurs Compared with Novice and Portfolio Entrepreneurs: Organizational Capabilities*

Serial entrepreneurs were more likely than novice entrepreneurs to report an emphasis on growing the 'business by using profits generated by the business'; to 'emphasize the need to grow the business'; to 'stress new products / services developments'; to 'strive to be the first to have products available'; and to 'have developed lower production costs via process innovation'. Also, serial entrepreneurs were more likely than other entrepreneurs to report that they 'strive to form alliances with other businesses'.

3.2.5 *Conclusions and Implications*

The above evidence provides insights relating to the resource profiles of serial, portfolio and novice entrepreneurs. Several differences (and similarities) were detected in relation to the resource profiles of serial, portfolio and novice entrepreneurs. Generally, the evidence suggested that the resource profiles of novice entrepreneurs may not be as appropriate as those reported by serial and portfolio entrepreneurs for careers in entrepreneurship. These findings suggest there is a need for a balanced policy agenda which encourages the supply of novice entrepreneurs but also supports the entrepreneur, rather than the firm, after the private business has been established, purchased or inherited. To broaden the entrepreneurial pool and increase the future stocks of serial and portfolio entrepreneurs, inexperienced novice entrepreneurs on the basis of this evidence could be encouraged to acquire some of the skills accumulated by experienced successful experienced entrepreneurs, particularly portfolio entrepreneurs.

3.3 Entrepreneur Resource Profile: Assets, Liabilities and Cognition

3.3.1 Gaps in the Knowledge Base and Research Questions

Although not formally stated in the article, Westhead et al., (2005c) explored the following broad research questions:

- *Do serial and portfolio and novice entrepreneurs differ in relation to the assets and liabilities of PBOE?*
- *Do serial and portfolio and novice entrepreneurs differ in relation to their cognitive profiles?*

3.3.2 Hypothesis Tested

Guided by insights from human capital theory and cognitive theory, the authors presented several speculative hypotheses relating to the asset and liabilities of serial and portfolio entrepreneurs, as well as hypotheses relating to the cognitive profiles of serial and portfolio entrepreneurs. PBOE can enable habitual entrepreneurs to accumulate several assets, which may include managerial and technical skills as well as a network of contacts that can be utilized in subsequent ventures. An experienced serial or portfolio entrepreneur owning a business in the same sector as their previous/current venture may be able to identify what is required to earn profits in the selected market more clearly than novice entrepreneurs. Some serial and portfolio entrepreneurs may, however, have accumulated several liabilities due to their business ownership experience. These liabilities may impact on the subsequent performance of firms owned by serial and portfolio entrepreneurs. For example, a number of serial and portfolio entrepreneurs may subsequently exhibit diminished motivation and reduced effort in running the subsequent venture. Previous success may, in addition, result in the success syndrome, illusion of control, blind spots and overconfidence (Simon et al., 2000). As a result of previous business 'success', some serial and

30   *Profiles*

portfolio entrepreneurs may experience hubris (i.e., replicate actions that had been previously successful), while those having experienced a 'failure' may be in denial. A liability of 'sameness' (Starr and Bygrave, 1991) may also be experienced. Several serial and portfolio entrepreneurs may continue to focus upon interpersonal interactions that hinder their ability to change, and adapt to changing external environmental conditions. Experienced serial and portfolio entrepreneurs may, therefore, attempt to repeat the same 'recipes' in changed circumstances. The assets and liabilities accumulated by a portfolio entrepreneur involved in several ventures may not be the same as those accumulated by a serial entrepreneur who has an equity stake in a single independent firm. This discussion suggested the following hypotheses:

> Hypothesis 3.1: *Serial entrepreneurs will report different assets of PBOE than portfolio entrepreneurs.*
>
> Hypothesis 3.2: *Serial entrepreneurs will report different liabilities of PBOE than portfolio entrepreneurs.*

The 'dominant logic' of the entrepreneur is an important component of his/her stock of experience. Reuber and Fischer (1999) describe a dominant logic as being an information funnel through which the entrepreneur's attention is filtered. This information funnel is akin to the entrepreneur's cognition (Baron, 1998). An entrepreneurial cognitive mindset is associated with the extensive use of heuristics and individual beliefs that impact upon decision-making. As noted earlier, heuristics are simplifying strategies that individuals use to make strategic decisions, especially in complex situations, where less complete information is available (Busenitz and Barney, 1997). There is considerable variation across individuals with regard to their reliance on heuristics. However, this observation is not fully reflected in cognitive research focusing on entrepreneurs.

The extent to which an entrepreneur relies on heuristic thinking can be shaped by the entrepreneur's level of experience. Experience provides a framework that reduces the burden of information processing, allowing the experienced individual to concentrate on novel or unique information (Hillerbrand, 1989). Conversely, novice entrepreneurs with no frame of reference can be overwhelmed by information and/or not know how to use the information. These observations would suggest that experienced serial and portfolio entrepreneurs might display cognitive characteristics that are different from those displayed by inexperienced novice entrepreneurs. Further, these differences are likely to be reflected in their attitudes to entrepreneurship.

Experienced individuals can process new information more effectively than inexperienced individuals. The authors assumed that experienced entrepreneurs would be more creative and innovative. However, serial and entrepreneurs may differ with regard to their behaviour. Serial entrepreneurs tend to focus on achieving a particular goal and exhibit attitudes and behaviour associated with reducing uncertainty. In contrast, portfolio entrepreneurs who appear to be motivated by wealth creation and who are happy to deal with the uncertainty of owning several businesses simultaneously maybe more creative and innovative. Further, some experienced entrepreneurs can gain access to more information when they are involved in a venture (McGrath, 1999; Ronstadt, 1988). The authors assumed that portfolio entreprencurs who simultaneously have equity stakes in two or more private firms would have access to wider sources of information. Portfolio entrepreneurs associated with entrepreneurial cognition and more diverse information might, therefore, display greater levels of creativity and innovation. This discussion suggested the following hypotheses:

> Hypothesis 3.3: *Novice, serial and portfolio entrepreneurs differ in relation to their attitudes to entrepreneurship.*
> Hypothesis 3.4: *Portfolio entrepreneurs will be more creative than novice or serial entrepreneurs.*
> Hypothesis 3.5: *Portfolio entrepreneurs will be more innovative than novice or serial entrepreneurs.*

3.3.3 Methodology

3.3.3.1 Data

A structured questionnaire was designed to ascertain whether entrepreneurs had ever had an equity stake in more than one independent business. The questionnaire was piloted with leading practitioners and academics, as well as with novice, serial and portfolio entrepreneurs to assess content and face validity. Suggestions made by the respondents to the pilot study, in terms of the phrasing of questions, were incorporated into the final questionnaire.

There is no comprehensive list of novice, serial and portfolio entrepreneurs who have ownership stakes in independent private businesses in Scotland. A stratified random sampling frame was constructed with regard to four broad industrial categories (i.e., agriculture, forestry and fishing, production, construction and services). Information gathered from tables detailing the population of businesses registered for value-added tax in 1999 (Office for National Statistics, 1999) was used to identify industry sampling proportions. After excluding non-independent businesses, a stratified random sample (by industry) of 3,000 independent firms was drawn up from a cleaned list of business names provided by Dun and Bradstreet. The structured questionnaire was mailed to a single key respondent (i.e., a decision-maker) in each of the randomly selected businesses, generally a founder and/or the principal owner. After a three-wave mailing covering four months, 354 valid questionnaires were obtained from a valid sample of 2,900 independent firms, representing a 12.2% valid response rate. Based on the definitions outlined earlier, 200 sampled firms (56.5%) involved novice

32 Profiles

entrepreneurs. A further 66 firms involved serial entrepreneurs (18.6%). The remaining 88 firms involved portfolio entrepreneurs (24.9%).

Chi-square and Mann-Whitney 'U' tests showed no statistically significant response bias between the respondents and non-respondents with regard to industry, legal form, age of the business and employment size. The authors concluded that a representative sample had been collected.

3.3.3.2 Techniques

Univariate non-parametric statistical tests were used to identify statistically significant differences between novice, serial and portfolio entrepreneurs. Chi-square tests were used to identify statistically significant differences between novice, serial and portfolio entrepreneurs with regard to variables measured at a nominal level. Kruskall-Wallis tests (i.e., responses reported by three types of entrepreneurs) and Mann-Whitney U tests (i.e., responses reported by two types of entrepreneurs) were used in relation to variables measured at an interval level.

3.3.4 Findings

Serial and portfolio entrepreneurs were presented with 12 statements relating to themes associated with the assets of PBOE (Starr and Bygrave, 1991). A five-point scoring system was employed, where a score of 1 suggested 'not important at all', whilst a score of 5 suggested 'very important'. There was general consensus among serial and portfolio entrepreneurs that 'building a reputation'; 'developing expertise in running an independent business'; 'being able to exploit identified opportunities more easily'; 'understanding the bank lending process more easily'; and 'obtaining finance more easily' were key assets of PBOE. No significant differences were detected between serial and portfolio entrepreneurs. Hypothesis 3.1 was not supported.

Eight statements focusing upon the liabilities of PBOE were presented to serial and portfolio respondents (Starr and Bygrave, 1991). These statements were phrased in a manner that would not result in the entrepreneur having to admit to his/her own limitations. For example, to capture the liability of sameness, the respondents were asked to indicate the extent to which they agreed with the following statement: 'I prefer relying on contacts I developed during my previous business(es) rather than developing new ones'. A five-point scoring system was employed, where a score of 1 suggested 'strongly agree', whilst a score of 5 suggested 'strongly disagree'. No significant differences between serial and portfolio entrepreneurs were detected. Serial and portfolio respondents generally agreed that 'I prefer relying on contacts I developed during my previous business(es) rather than developing new ones' and 'I am motivated less by generating personal wealth in this business compared to my previous one(s)'. Conversely, both serial and portfolio entrepreneurs generally disagreed with the following four statements:

'I am more aware about my own limitations due to my prior experience'; 'I feel I am better able to predict and adapt to changing circumstances with this business compared to my previous ones(s); 'the process of owning this business was less daunting due to my previous experience'; and 'I feel I have more control in shaping this business compared to my previous one(s)'.

Levels of overconfidence reported by entrepreneurs (Busenitz and Barney, 1997) were monitored. No significant differences were detected among the three types of entrepreneurs. Presented evidence did not support hypothesis 3.2.

Eight statements relating to attitudes to entrepreneurship were presented to the three types of entrepreneurs. A five-point scoring system was employed, where a score of 1 suggested 'strongly agree', a score of 3 suggested 'neutral', whilst a score of 5 suggested 'strongly disagree'. Significant differences among the three entrepreneur types were detected with regard to seven presented statements. Experienced entrepreneurs, particularly portfolio entrepreneurs, reported higher levels of agreement with the statement 'I find the process of starting a business very daunting' than novice entrepreneurs. Conversely, novice entrepreneurs reported higher levels of agreement with the statement 'I have a short attention span' than serial entrepreneurs. Also, novice entrepreneurs reported higher levels of agreement with the statement 'external advice is crucial for the growth of this business' than serial entrepreneurs. Serial and portfolio entrepreneurs reported higher levels of disagreement than novice entrepreneurs with the following statements: 'I feel I can predict and adapt to changing environmental circumstances'; 'I enjoy the early stages of building a business'; and 'I frequently try to establish / develop new contacts'. Further, serial entrepreneurs reported higher levels of disagreement with the statement 'I like to be aware of all the decisions made about this business and have the final say' than novice entrepreneurs. Hypothesis 3.3 was supported.

Seven statements relating to creativity and a further three statements relating to innovation (Manimala, 1992) were presented to entrepreneurs. In relation to each statement, binary 'yes' or 'no' responses were gathered from respondents. Significant differences among the three entrepreneur types were detected with regard to nine presented statements. Over two-fifths of respondents, irrespective of entrepreneur type, indicated that they 'have developed new structures, systems, or procedures in your organization'; 'have found a new source of supply'; and/or 'have introduced a new product or a new quality of an existing product'.

With regard to six out of the seven creativity statements, larger proportions of portfolio entrepreneurs than novice entrepreneurs reported they were creative. Further, larger proportions of serial entrepreneurs than novice entrepreneurs suggested they were creative with reference to two creativity statements. However, a larger proportion of portfolio entrepreneurs than serial entrepreneurs reported they were creative with reference to one creativity statement. Significantly larger proportions of both serial and portfolio entrepreneurs than novice entrepreneurs reported they had either 'used

34 *Profiles*

new ways of managing and developing personnel'; and/or 'developed new ways of managing quality control and R&D'. Also, significantly larger proportions of portfolio entrepreneurs than novice entrepreneurs had 'developed new structures, systems, or procedures in your organization'; 'found a new market or employed a new marketing strategy in an existing market'; and/or 'found new ways of dealing with government and other external agencies'. Significantly smaller proportions of novice and serial entrepreneurs than portfolio entrepreneurs indicated they had 'found new ways of managing finance'. Hypothesis 3.4 was supported with regard to portfolio and novice entrepreneurs, but only tentatively supported with regard to portfolio and serial entrepreneurs.

With reference to the three innovation statements, larger proportions of portfolio entrepreneurs than novice entrepreneurs reported they were innovative. For example, with regard to the introduction of 'a new product or a new quality of an existing product'; 'a new method of production or modified an existing method'; and/or 'a new culture especially through the induction of innovative people at the lower levels'. However, only one significant difference was detected between portfolio and serial entrepreneurs. A larger proportion of portfolio entrepreneurs than serial entrepreneurs reported they had 'introduced a new culture especially through the induction of innovative people at the lower levels'. Hypothesis 3.5 was supported with regard to portfolio and novice entrepreneurs, but not with regard to portfolio and serial entrepreneurs.

3.3.5 *Conclusions and Implications*

The authors concluded that policy-makers and practitioners might need to target separate policies towards the varying needs of novice, serial and portfolio entrepreneurs. By recognizing the resources and cognitive characteristics of different types of entrepreneurs, initiatives to encourage the supply of entrepreneurs, as well as those to encourage entrepreneur (and business) development could become more fine-tuned. The evidence also suggested that banks and venture capitalists should also take more account of the differences among types of entrepreneurs.

Portfolio entrepreneurs were more likely to be associated with experience that provides greater understanding surrounding why and how they have equity stakes in several independent businesses at the same time. In several ways, portfolio entrepreneurs highlighted the importance of specific human capital resources. Most notably, portfolio entrepreneurs gave greater importance than novice or serial entrepreneurs towards creativity and innovation. The authors speculated that portfolio entrepreneurs utilize these specific human capital resources to ensure the survival and development of independent ventures they have equity stakes in. They concluded that the provision and targeting of appropriate information towards entrepreneurs appears to be a critical resource that is required by portfolio entrepreneurs to exploit the business ideas they discover, as well as the ideas that are presented to them by other entrepreneurs.

Serial entrepreneurs often realize funds from the sale of a venture. They may also have a reverse situation with liabilities being associated with a previous business 'failure'. It is important not to lose these latter serial entrepreneurs from the entrepreneurial pool, because some of them have the potential to become successful portfolio (or serial) entrepreneurs. Support targeted towards serial entrepreneurs who have held equity stakes in businesses that have closed might encourage other serial entrepreneurs to have another (more successful) foray as equity stakeholders in private ventures. There are some who argue that individuals may learn more from 'failure' than 'success' (Sitkin, 1992).

Some serial entrepreneurs appear to have utilized skills that worked well in the past, rather than to diversify their knowledge and information bases the next time around. Serial entrepreneurs generally found business ownership a daunting experience, and they were unable to control the shape of the current business. Contrary to popular myth, both serial and portfolio entrepreneurs highlighted that business ownership was associated with obstacles and critical decisions. Both serial and portfolio entrepreneurs suggested that they did not frequently search for new contacts. Serial entrepreneurs might, therefore, require support in terms of addressing the market-related aspects of identifying business opportunities.

The experience backgrounds of some novice entrepreneurs may not be as appropriate for careers in entrepreneurship, as those reported by serial and portfolio entrepreneurs. While some novice entrepreneurs might be able to move down the experience curve and become owners of subsequent businesses, others may not have the right background to benefit from business ownership experience. In part, due to their inexperience, novice entrepreneurs seemed to be less cautious than serial and portfolio entrepreneurs surrounding the process of starting/purchasing an independent business. Many novice entrepreneurs were failing to respond to changing customer demands, and they were unable or reluctant to adapt to changing external environmental conditions. Novice entrepreneurs with more limited specific human capital might require assistance to enhance their information and knowledge bases.

3.4 Entrepreneur Resource Profile: Comparative Optimism

3.4.1 Gaps in the Knowledge Base and Research Questions

Studies have explored why entrepreneurs are associated with a greater propensity to report comparative optimism relative to non-entrepreneurs (Cooper et al., 1988; Fraser and Greene, 2006). The terms comparative optimism, overconfidence, unrealistic optimism, over-optimism and the optimistic bias are often used interchangeably. The article by Ucbasaran et al., (2010) reviewed below focused upon the comparative optimism reported by habitual

36 *Profiles*

entrepreneurs. Studies focusing upon comparative optimism reported by entrepreneurs have detected that comparative optimism can be advantageous under certain circumstances but it can also be disadvantageous (Alvarez and Busenitz, 2001; Hmieleski and Baron, 2009). Comparative optimism (and overconfidence) may positively be necessary for individuals to engage in entrepreneurship (Koellinger et al., 2007), but negatively, it may be a factor linked to business closure (i.e., poor decision-making and the establishment of under-capitalized firms) (Hayward et al., 2006).

Economists have argued that people entering entrepreneurship gradually learn about their abilities through running a business and change their behaviour in response to observing how well they do (Jovanovic, 1982). Some entrepreneurs recognizing their comparative optimism (i.e., they were initially too optimistic) may appreciate this heuristic may have contributed to the closure of their businesses. Entrepreneurs with more realistic expectations may grow their business(es) or continue their entrepreneurial career elsewhere (Fraser and Greene, 2006). Experienced entrepreneurs may, therefore, be less likely to report comparative optimism. Conversely, cognition theorists suggest that people with prior experience may infer too much from limited information, inappropriately weight information cues and become overconfident in their judgements (Brailey et al., 2001), which can retard subsequent behaviour. Experienced entrepreneurs may, therefore, be more likely to report comparative optimism than inexperienced entrepreneurs.

Experienced entrepreneurs recognizing their comparative optimism may subsequently adjust their thinking. Notably, habitual entrepreneurs may report a more realistic outlook in subsequent venture(s). Habitual entrepreneurs, particularly those with business ownership closure experience, may be less likely to subsequently report comparative optimism. However, the sub-group of portfolio entrepreneurs may accumulate biases and then be subsequently more likely to report comparative optimism.

Mixed evidence has been presented relating to the link between an entrepreneur's prior experience and reported optimism. Fraser and Greene (2006), focusing on a broad measure of optimism, detected that more experienced entrepreneurs were less likely to cite optimism. In relation to a more widely accepted measure of optimism, Cooper et al. (1988) found no significant relationship between entrepreneurial experience and reported comparative optimism. Comparing growth expectations with actual growth rates, Landier and Thesmar (2009) noted that habitual entrepreneurs who had started at least one prior business were more optimistic than novice entrepreneurs.

Ucbasaran et al. (2010) asserted that studies focusing on the *extent* of entrepreneurial experience had generally ignored the question of whether reported comparative optimism was linked to the *nature* of an entrepreneur's PBOE. They suggested a more fine-grained view of the *nature* of an entrepreneur's PBOE would provide insights surrounding how habitual entrepreneurs adjust their thinking following experience, and how experience is linked to the propensity to subsequently report comparative optimism.

Two aspects of the nature of an entrepreneur's PBOE were considered in their article: first, whether the surveyed entrepreneurs PBOE was associated with business closure (i.e., termed 'failure' in the article), and notably, if the prior business closure experience acted as a trigger, encouraging habitual entrepreneurs to reassess their judgement (McGrath, 1999) and hence adjust their comparative optimism; and second, whether the surveyed entrepreneurs' PBOE was acquired sequentially (i.e., serial entrepreneurs, which were termed sequential entrepreneurs in the article) or concurrently (i.e., portfolio entrepreneurs), and how these different kinds of experience may influence the nature of the response to business closure. In the article, the following two research questions were explored:

- *Are experienced habitual entrepreneurs with prior business ownership failure experience more or less likely to report comparative optimism than novice entrepreneurs with no prior business ownership experience?*
- *Are serial and portfolio entrepreneurs with business failure experience more or less likely to report comparative optimism than novice entrepreneurs?*

3.4.2 Hypotheses Tested

The nature of PBOE, specifically perception of an experience as a 'failure' or a 'success', can shape subsequent attitudes and behaviour (Shepherd, 2003). Business failure does not solely relate to the bankruptcy, receivership or liquidation of a venture. Gimeno et al. (1997) have asserted that business survival (and the decision to terminate a venture) is shaped by an entrepreneur's personal threshold of performance.

Evidence from other domains suggests individuals are less likely to cite optimism after a negative event experience (Van de Velde et al., 1992). Despite having been exposed to more learning opportunities, habitual entrepreneurs who have not experienced a negative event such as business failure may feel exempt from failure. The latter entrepreneurs may have limited motivation to question their thinking and decision-making because it appears to have previously yielded positive results. Entrepreneurs who have not experienced failure may be more susceptible to confirmation bias (i.e., disconfirming evidence is rejected) and misattribution of success to one's own decisions and actions (McGrath, 1999). These biases may mean that entrepreneurs not experiencing business failure report comparative optimism regarding a subsequent venture(s). Based on this discussion, the authors proposed the following hypothesis:

Hypothesis 3.6: *Habitual entrepreneurs (i.e., serial and portfolio entrepreneurs) who have not experienced business ownership failure are more likely to report comparative optimism than novice entrepreneurs.*

38 *Profiles*

Experience with business failure can be associated with cognitive/functional effects (Ucbasaran et al., 2009). Individuals are less likely to report comparative optimism after a negative event experience (Van de Velde et al., 1992). Prior experience with a negative event enables some individuals to imagine themselves in future failure situations, leading people to believe that if it happened in the past, it can happen again (Helweg-Larsen and Shepperd, 2001). Some individuals may come to overestimate the base rate of a negative event after experiencing it and then believe it is more likely to reoccur (Weinstein, 1980).

Individuals may be less likely to report comparative optimism after a failure. Failure can encourage individuals to question their attitudes and behaviours relating to the failure (Sitkin, 1992). Further, failure can facilitate learning by encouraging the individual to conduct a post-mortem to understand what led to the failure. Failure may encourage entrepreneurs to be more realistic about their own skills and their expectations with regard to a subsequent venture(s). Entrepreneurs that have learned from the experience of a negative event may, therefore, report a reduced likelihood of reporting comparative optimism. This discussion suggested the following hypothesis:

Hypothesis 3.7: *Habitual entrepreneurs (i.e., serial and portfolio entrepreneurs) who have experienced business ownership failure are less likely to report comparative optimism than novice entrepreneurs.*

Whether an entrepreneur learns from PBOE failure may be linked to the nature of their PBOE and their response to it. An entrepreneur's experience with business failure can be a traumatic event that generates negative emotions which interfere with learning (Shepherd, 2003). The context in which the failure is experienced may influence how the entrepreneur responds to failure, impacting the propensity to report comparative optimism in subsequent ventures.

Habitual entrepreneur studies suggest that PBOE can be acquired sequentially or concurrently (Ucbasaran et al., 2006). The link between PBOE failure experience and comparative optimism could differ between serial and portfolio entrepreneurs. For serial entrepreneurs, the associated (emotional) costs may be high because the serial entrepreneur is committed to a single business. Strong emotions and commitment can retard learning after a business failure experience (Shepherd, 2003). To ensure a perception of control after a business failure experience, some individuals may remain (or become) optimistic in order to reduce their sense of vulnerability. Further, to maintain self-esteem, entrepreneurs may attribute failure to external factors.

Following business failure, a serial entrepreneur who was highly committed to a failed firm may find it difficult to adjust reported comparative optimism with regard to a subsequent venture. Attribution errors and self-serving biases may dominate. To compensate for emotional loss, serial entrepreneurs may report a coping strategy of reporting comparative optimism after a business failure experience. To ensure a sense of self-worth, serial entrepreneurs that have experienced business failure may increase their propensity to report comparative optimism, suggesting the following hypothesis:

> Hypothesis 3.8: *Serial entrepreneurs who have experienced business failure will be just as likely as novice entrepreneurs to report comparative optimism.*

Conversely, portfolio entrepreneurs may reduce the emotional costs potentially associated with a single business failure by diversifying their portfolio of businesses (Rosa, 1998). When one business fails, portfolio entrepreneurs may not experience as strong an emotional reaction as serial entrepreneurs who have placed all their eggs in one basket. Portfolio entrepreneurs may wait to see how the business develops before committing additional resources. A serial entrepreneur may report more commitment to an individual venture than a portfolio entrepreneur. Due to the relative emotional costs of business failure, portfolio entrepreneurs may be less likely to report comparative optimism than serial entrepreneurs and inexperienced novice entrepreneurs. This discussion suggested the following hypothesis:

> Hypothesis 3.9: *Portfolio entrepreneurs who have experienced business failure are less likely than novice entrepreneurs to report comparative optimism.*

3.4.3 Methodology

3.4.3.1 Data

Primary information was collected to identify types of entrepreneurs relating to their PBOE and business failure experience. Information was gathered from a survey of firms to identify whether the key decision-maker in each firm was a novice, serial or portfolio entrepreneur. The questionnaire and sampling frame of firms were constructed based on the same approach as the two other studies reviewed earlier in this chapter but covering Great Britain rather than only Scotland. A structured questionnaire was mailed to a single key respondent in each business in the stratified random sampling frame of 4,307 independent firms identified. Although information was not available from multiple respondents in each firm, reliability checks on key firm-level variables such as business age, employment size and legal status detected strong correlations between the archival data provided by Dun and Bradstreet, and the survey evidence provided by key informants. The correlations ranged from 0.77 to 0.88 suggesting the data from the key informant

40 *Profiles*

was reliable. After a three-wave mailing (i.e., two reminders), 576 respondents provided complete data for the businesses that they had either created or purchased, an effective response rate of 13.4%.

The sample comprised 278 (48%) novice entrepreneurs and 298 (52%) habitual entrepreneurs. Respondents on average owned 2.2 businesses, while this figure was 3.4 businesses for habitual entrepreneurs. Some 101 habitual entrepreneurs (i.e., 34%) had experienced business failure, of which 60 (i.e., 59%) were serial entrepreneurs and 41 (i.e., 41%) were portfolio entrepreneurs.

Using Chi-square and Mann-Whitney 'U' tests, no statistically significant response bias was detected with regard to industry, standard government official region, legal form, age of the business and employment size between the respondents and non-respondents at the 0.05 level. The authors had no cause to suspect that the sample was not representative of the population of independent private firms in Great Britain. Also, the authors concluded there was no evidence to suggest that the results would be affected by common method bias.

3.4.3.2 Dependent Variables

Three dependent variables were operationalized. Guided by social psychology, which is the source of the construct, the authors highlighted that comparative optimism could be measured directly or indirectly. The direct method asks a respondent to assess whether they are more or less likely to experience an event than a specified target person. The indirect method asks a respondent to assess their own probability of experiencing an event. This question is then repeated by asking the respondent to assess the probability of an average person who is similar to the respondent experiencing the same event. The difference between the scores for each question provides an indication of the respondent's comparative optimism. Indirect measures appear to be preferred for measuring optimism in social psychology studies (Otten and Van der Pligt, 1996). While direct methods have some merit, indirect measures are generally more conservative, stable and reliable (Helweg-Larson et al., 2001).

An indirect method was selected to measure the first comparative optimism dependent variable. The two questions presented by Cooper et al. (1988) were used to construct the OPTIMISM dependent variable. Entrepreneurs were asked: "What are the odds of *this* business achieving your expectations for it in the future?" They were then asked: "What are the chances of any other business like yours succeeding?" Entrepreneurs were asked to rank their responses to both questions on zero to ten scales. No chance of success was ranked 0, whilst certain chance of success was ranked 10. The response to the first question was then subtracted from the response to the second question. Difference scores were not evenly distributed. To improve estimation, difference scores were converted into a categorical variable. A positive difference score is indicated by entrepreneurs reporting comparative optimism. The latter entrepreneurs were scored 1 for the OPTIMISM variable. Entrepreneurs reporting a negative or zero-difference score were scored 0.

Direct measures tend to focus primarily on the respondents own state rather than on the difference between themselves and their peers. Indirect measures offer greater flexibility by allowing researchers to identify the source of comparative optimism, which may stem from judgement about one's own risks, or judgements about others' risks. Further, indirect measures explicitly require respondents to think about the comparison with other peers (Covey and Davies, 2004). Indirect measures allow researchers to disentangle comparative optimism caused by entrepreneurs perceptions about themselves and their business(es) (i.e., response to the first question used to calculate the operationalized comparative optimism measure OPTIMISM) vis-à-vis comparative optimism caused by entrepreneurs ignoring (or underestimating) data on business failure rates reported by entrepreneurs who have or are exploiting similar opportunities (i.e., response to second question) (Hayward et al., 2006).

To explore whether the comparative optimism reported stemmed from assessments about one's own risk or assessments about similar others' risk, two more fine-grained optimism dependent variables were operationalized. An 'optimism relating to own business' dependent variable was operationalized. Entrepreneurs were presented with the following question: "What are the odds of this business achieving your expectations for it in the future?" Respondents could rank this question on a 0 to 10 scale. No chance of success was ranked 0, whilst certain chance of success was ranked 10.

An 'optimism relating to similar other peoples' businesses' dependent variable was operationalized. Entrepreneurs were presented with the following question: "What are the chances of any other business like yours succeeding?". Respondents could rank this question on a 0 to 10 scale. No chance of success was ranked 0, whilst certain chance of success was ranked 10.

3.4.3.3 Independent Variables

Each entrepreneur reported the total number of failed businesses they had owned. Business failure was deemed to have taken place if the respondent had closed or sold a business due to bankruptcy, liquidation or receivership, or if the business had been closed or sold because it had failed to meet the expectations of the entrepreneur (Gimeno et al., 1997). By definition, novice entrepreneurs had no PBOE at the time of the survey, and hence had not experienced business failure. A distinction was made between habitual entrepreneurs who had experienced failure and habitual entrepreneurs who had not experienced failure. The two types of habitual entrepreneurs were compared with novice entrepreneurs, which was the reference category.

42 Profiles

A distinction was also made between serial entrepreneurs who had experienced business failure and portfolio entrepreneurs who had experienced business failure. They were compared with novice entrepreneurs, which was the reference category.

As highlighted in Section 3.4.2, business closure (i.e., termed 'failure' in this article) is not solely a function of economic performance because it can relate to performance relative to an entrepreneurs critical threshold (Gimeno et al., 1997). An entrepreneur may choose to close or sell a business that may not be a total economic failure. A distinction can be made between economic business failure (i.e., firm bankruptcy) and failure because the business did not meet expectations (i.e., closure/sale of a business whose performance was too low in relation to the entrepreneur's expectations). To explore whether the results were sensitive to a selected business failure definition the following more fine-grained business failure definitions were operationalized: habitual entrepreneurs who had experienced the failure of at least one business solely due to economic reasons (i.e., firm bankruptcy, liquidation or receivership); habitual entrepreneurs who experienced failure of at least one business because it failed to meet their expectations; sequential entrepreneurs who had experienced the failure of at least one business due to bankruptcy, liquidation or receivership; serial entrepreneurs who experienced failure of at least one business because it failed to meet their expectations; portfolio entrepreneurs who had experienced failure of at least one business due to bankruptcy, liquidation or receivership; and portfolio entrepreneurs who experienced the failure of at least one business because it failed to meet their expectations. They were compared with novice entrepreneurs, which was the reference category.

The *number* of failed businesses previously owned by habitual entrepreneurs was incorporated. The following independent variables were operationalized: habitual entrepreneurs who had experienced one business failure; habitual entrepreneurs who had experienced two or more business failures; serial entrepreneurs who had experienced one business failure; serial entrepreneurs who had experienced two or more business failures; portfolio entrepreneurs who had experienced one business failure; and portfolio entrepreneurs who had experienced two or more business failures. They were compared with novice entrepreneurs, which was the reference category.

3.4.3.4 Techniques

Probit regression analysis was used to explore the independent variables linked with OPTIMISM. Ordered probit and ordinary least squares (OLS) regression analysis were used to test hypotheses relating to the categorical dependent variables (i.e., optimism relating to own business and optimism relating to similar other people's businesses).

3.4.4 Findings

With regard to the OPTIMISM dependent variable and a broad measure of business failure, the probit regression analysis detected that habitual entrepreneurs who had not experienced failure were significantly more likely to report comparative optimism than novice entrepreneurs. Hypothesis 3.6 was supported. While habitual entrepreneurs who had experienced failure were less likely than novice entrepreneurs to report comparative optimism, the likelihood was not statistically significant. Hypothesis 3.7 was not supported. No significant difference was detected between the serial entrepreneur group who had experienced failure and the novice entrepreneur reference group. Hypothesis 3.8 was supported. The portfolio entrepreneur group who had experienced failure was significantly less likely to report comparative optimism than novice entrepreneurs. Hypothesis 3.9 was supported.

Additional analyses were conducted to explore the robustness of the results and their sensitivity to the operationalization of the business failure and optimism measures. With regard to the OPTIMISM dependent variable and finer measures of business failure, several probit regression models were computed. When an economic definition of business failure was operationalized (i.e., fail-economic), the sensitivity analysis suggested that portfolio entrepreneurs who had experienced failure were less likely to report comparative optimism than novice entrepreneurs, but the likelihood was no longer significantly different. However, when an expectations definition of business failure was operationalized (i.e., fail-expectations), the evidence provided support for hypothesis 3.9.

In total, 197 (66%) habitual entrepreneurs reported no experience of business failure, whilst 101 (34%) habitual entrepreneurs reported economic or failure to meet expectations prior business failure, of which 67 (23%) reported one failure and a further 34 (11%) reported two or more failures. The authors explored whether the initial results were sensitive to the *number* of business failures previously owned by habitual entrepreneurs. With regard to the OPTIMISM dependent variable and finer measures relating to the number of business failures, several probit regression models were computed. The probit models confirmed the initial results. Both portfolio entrepreneurs who had experienced one business failure and portfolio entrepreneurs who had experienced two or more business failures were significantly less likely to report comparative optimism than novice entrepreneurs.

Sensitivity analysis was also conducted with regard to the selected dependent variable. The initial models relating to the OPTIMISM dependent variable were re-run with regard to the 'optimism relating to own business' dependent variable, and then the 'optimism relating to similar other peoples' businesses' dependent variable. Ordered probit and OLS regression analysis were used to test hypotheses relating to the categorical dependent variables.

44 Profiles

Hypothesis 3.7 was supported with regard to the 'optimism relating to own business' dependent variable. Habitual entrepreneurs who had prior business failure experience were significantly less likely than novice entrepreneurs to have reported 'optimism relating to own business'. However, the latter significant relationship was not detected with regard to 'optimism relating to similar other peoples' businesses' dependent variable. Results relating to the testing of hypothesis 3.7 were being driven by assessments of risk about similar others and that the experience of failure did not dampen this latter form of optimism.

3.4.5 Conclusions and Implications

Entrepreneurs are frequently described as suffering from an optimism bias. High new business closure rates can be attributed to this bias. It is not clear whether all entrepreneurs are equally prone to this potential bias. The authors argued in the article that an entrepreneur's PBOE and business failure experience were linked to the likelihood of reporting comparative optimism. Their findings supported the validity of opposing views relating to the potential learning benefits associated with entrepreneurial experience and specifically business failure experience. The authors found that entrepreneurial experience offered opportunities to reduce the likelihood of subsequently reported comparative optimism but this depended on the nature of the entrepreneurial experience.

Despite exposure to more learning opportunities through multiple business ownership experiences, habitual entrepreneurs who had not experienced business failure were *more* likely than novice entrepreneurs to have reported comparative optimism. This finding questions the ability of entrepreneurs to learn solely from positive experiences. Some experienced habitual entrepreneurs may be prone to the liabilities of success discussed in Section 3.3.4 (McGrath, 1999).

Experience with business failure represents an opportunity to temper the likelihood of comparative optimism for some types of experienced entrepreneurs. Assuming entrepreneurs learned from business failure the authors expected that habitual entrepreneurs who had experienced a business failure would be less likely to report comparative optimism than novice entrepreneurs with no business failure experience. The authors detected that only portfolio entrepreneurs (and not serial entrepreneurs) who had experienced business failure were less likely than novice entrepreneurs to report comparative optimism. Serial entrepreneurs appeared to be immune to the potential learning effects of business failure.

The circumstances under which business failure was experienced appeared to be linked to how the entrepreneur responded to and learned from that experience. The study highlighted significant differences in how serial and portfolio entrepreneurs made sense of their experience of business failure. While portfolio entrepreneurs reported a lower likelihood of comparative optimism following business failure experience, serial entrepreneurs appeared to maintain their comparative optimism. Entrepreneurs who have experienced business failure were found to be heterogeneous. The authors concluded that entrepreneurs having experienced business failure should not be aggregated into a single crude business failure group that does not differentiate economic business failure from failure to meet an entrepreneur's expectations.

The authors claimed that their findings provided new insights into an emerging debate relating to business failure. While some scholars view failure as representing an opportunity for learning (McGrath, 1999), others have argued that it may be difficult to learn from business failure (Shepherd, 2003). The authors' findings suggest that both views have some validity. Experience of business failure offers opportunities for learning, but only under certain conditions. Emotional costs of business failure may be 'diluted' for portfolio entrepreneurs because they have other businesses to fall back on. Portfolio entrepreneurs may adopt an experimental approach which often results in them making smaller and incremental investments into new ventures. They, therefore, may strategically seek to minimize the emotional and financial costs of business failure. Relative to serial entrepreneurs, portfolio entrepreneurs may be more able to distance themselves from their ventures and adopt a more objective evaluation of each business owned.

The authors' findings supported the view that serial entrepreneurs are unable to revise the likelihood of comparative optimism downwards. Additional analysis, however, suggested that serial entrepreneurs with prior business failure experience were significantly less likely to have reported 'optimism relating to own business'. Their comparative optimism appeared to have been driven by their assessment of risks about similar others. The authors suggested that portfolio entrepreneurs seeking to minimize their exposure to risk and to lower their personal and financial commitment to a single venture may select a diversification strategy associated with two or more firms. These conditions might minimize the costs of failure and make learning more likely. The authors claimed that this kind of entrepreneurial experience was a necessary but not sufficient condition for tempering optimistic expectations. Notably, the authors concluded that portfolio experience has to be coupled with business failure experience to trigger the adoption of more realistic expectations with regard to subsequent ventures owned.

3.5 Summary

The evidence in this chapter indicates that entrepreneur resource profiles shape the subsequent behaviour and performance of serial and portfolio entrepreneurs. The 'assets' accumulated from PBOE may enhance the subsequent entrepreneurial behaviour of serial and portfolio entrepreneurs. Conversely, the 'liabilities' or biases may impair the subsequent entrepreneurial

46 *Profiles*

behaviour of serial and portfolio entrepreneurs. The chapter also explored whether serial and portfolio entrepreneurs were more likely than novice entrepreneurs to report the comparative optimism bias and whether serial and portfolio entrepreneurs with business closure (i.e., termed 'failure') experience were more likely to report comparative optimism than novice entrepreneurs with no business closure experience.

3.6 Reflection Questions

In Chapter 3, serial, portfolio and novice entrepreneur resource profiles were compared in relation to human capital, cognition, heuristics and biases. 'Assets' and 'liabilities' accumulated by serial and portfolio entrepreneurs were summarized that may shape the subsequent entrepreneurial behaviour of serial and portfolio entrepreneurs. Please consider the following reflection questions:

- *What entrepreneurial resource assets do serial entrepreneurs exhibit?*
- *What entrepreneurial resource assets do portfolio entrepreneurs exhibit?*
- *Are the entrepreneurial resource assets reported by portfolio entrepreneurs the same as those reported by serial entrepreneurs?*
- *What entrepreneurial resource deficiencies do novice entrepreneurs exhibit more than serial and portfolio entrepreneurs?*
- *Are the cognitive profiles reported by portfolio entrepreneurs the same as those reported by serial entrepreneurs?*
- *What are the 'assets' and 'liabilities' of PBOE reported by serial and/or portfolio entrepreneurs?*
- *What is comparative optimism?*
- *Is there an agreed definition of comparative optimism?*
- *What are the upside advantages for entrepreneurs with comparative optimism, and what are downside disadvantages for entrepreneurs with comparative optimism?*
- *Are serial or portfolio entrepreneurs more likely to report comparative optimism than novice entrepreneurs?*
- *Are serial or portfolio entrepreneurs with business closure (i.e., failure) experience more likely to report comparative optimism than novice entrepreneurs with no closure experience?*

4 Entrepreneur Resource Accumulation: Finance

4.1 Learning Objectives and Overview

Entrepreneurs can face resource, operational and strategic barriers to NFF and development. They face major challenges in assembling and configuring the resources they need to exploit opportunities to become revenue generating products or services. The challenges arise partly because some entrepreneurs, particularly novice entrepreneurs, may possess very limited pools of resources. Entrepreneurs need to obtain resources from their external environments. The external environment shapes the ability of entrepreneurs to discover or create opportunities, and their subsequent ability to exploit these opportunities for competitive success. Further, the external environment (or locality) can contain a pool of scarce and valued resources. Entrepreneurs with limited experience and legitimacy (Hannan and Carroll, 1992) may find it challenging to persuade outsiders in the external environment like financiers to contribute resources when an opportunity involves a product that may be little more than an idea to serve a market that does not yet exist.

Accessing external finance poses a particularly major challenge (Colombo and Grilli, 2005). Financial capital concerns both the amount of funds and the specialist skills that finance providers bring to help develop the venture. Finance can be crucial for acquiring or creating other resources necessary to exploit opportunities, such as the recruitment of specialist personnel and conducting product trials. Firms with strong financial resources have slack, which can facilitate the development of innovations. Entrepreneurs have to address market resource barriers to firm formation and development (Robson and Obeng, 2008). Finance is a primary constraint, specifically the difficulty of accessing affordable credit over a reasonable period (Tagoe et al., 2005). Various contributory factors relate to the entrepreneur demand-side and the financier supply-side.

In line with the 'pecking order hypothesis' adapted for entrepreneurial firms (Vanacker and Manigart, 2010) to ensure they retain independent ownership and control of their private firms, many entrepreneurs solely use internal finance (Martin et al., 2005). High information costs and risk aversion due to an unproven market-readiness are likely to prevent lenders

48 *Entrepreneur Resource Accumulation: Finance*

investing in some new and small firms, particularly those providing innovative products or services. The reluctance, or inability, to accumulate mobilize external debt finance may retard firm development, and firm survival may be put in jeopardy.

Serial and portfolio entrepreneurs can accumulate 'assets' due to their track record in business ownership. Habitual entrepreneurs may mobilize their pool of internal entrepreneur resources (Villanueva et al., 2012) to send credible quality signals to outsiders (i.e., receivers of signals) to increase their likelihood of accessing external finance required for firm development. Serial and portfolio entrepreneurs may 'signal' the assets of PBOE (i.e., entrepreneurial, managerial and technical skills (Ucbasaran et al., 2008)) to potential external resource providers such as financiers concerned with reducing information asymmetries between themselves and potential targets for assistance. PBOE may be viewed as a positive 'high-quality signal' sought and favourably received by external resource providers.

In Chapter 4, the role of the entrepreneurs' resource profiles in relation to obtaining external finance is discussed. Three themes that build upon insights from human capital theory, RBV of the firm, recontracting theory and/or signalling theory are reviewed. The first theme focuses on the link between the asset of serial and portfolio entrepreneur PBOE experience in relation to their ability to obtain debt finance in the Ghana developing economy context. In the latter context, firm development may be retarded by chronic credit-rationing by financiers. The second theme explores whether university spin-outs (USO) associated with the presence of the 'high quality' signal of a habitual entrepreneur increased their likelihood of obtaining first formal venture capital investment (FFVCI). The accumulation of the latter type of finance is assumed to enhance firm development. The third theme explores the screening process involved in financing serial entrepreneurs including issues relating to recontracting with entrepreneurs that the venture capital firm had previously invested in compared with investing in entrepreneurs that previously received funding from a different venture capital firm in their earlier venture.

4.2 Finance: Debt

4.2.1 *Gaps in the Knowledge Base and Research Questions*

The article by Robson et al., (2013) focused on whether habitual entrepreneurs were less likely to be credit-rationed entrepreneurs. Previous studies have failed to consider whether the ability to secure the requested amount of external finance in resource deficit developing economy contexts is shaped by the *nature* of PBOE reported by serial and portfolio entrepreneurs who may respond differently to the finance barrier. The authors explored issues relating to credit-rationing in the Ghana resource deficit context. This context, based on business risks arising from a specific set of demand and supply conditions may differentiate the ability of entrepreneurs to obtain external capital, and raises the possibility that the risk can be potentially reduced by habitual entrepreneurs who mobilize their PBOE to send quality signals that are favourably sought and received by local financiers with skills and knowledge deficiencies. The authors asserted that lead entrepreneurs that invest in costly observable quality signals can highlight unobservable quality of the signaller to potential receivers (i.e., external financiers) via the observable qualities of the signaller (i.e., lead entrepreneurs' human capital). Relative to inexperienced novice entrepreneurs with no PBOE signals to mobilize, experienced entrepreneurs with PBOE can mobilize their broader specific human capital (and social capital generated by experience and legitimacy) to obtain the requested amount of debt finance. Although the issue of the timing of the debt finance gap has previously been considered, its time length has been explored with reference to varying time periods. The authors explored the profiles of credit-rationed entrepreneurs by considering the length of the debt finance gap with reference to temporary (over one year), major (over two years) (Cavalluzo et al., 2002) and chronic (over three years) (Crook, 1996) debt finance gaps.

The authors explored the link between an entrepreneurs PBOE experience and ability to obtain debt finance in the African context, where a need to explore links between local resource endowments and the exploitation of opportunities has been identified. Guided by insights from signalling, resource-based view of the firm and human capital theory, the following research question was explored in a developing context with resource deficiencies:

- *Do attributes relating to the resources and signals of lead entrepreneurs, particularly PBOE quality signals, reduce the probability that entrepreneurs will be chronic credit-rationed in a developing economy context with resource deficiencies?*

4.2.2 Hypotheses Tested

Building upon the insights from signalling theory, it was suggested that the resource profiles of entrepreneurs, particularly the observable quality signal of PBOE, can be a mechanism for financiers to overcome informational asymmetries and reduce the prevalence of credit rationing over time to smaller firms. Lead entrepreneurs that fail to provide adequate quality signals relating to their credibility and expertise, as well as the market potential associated with their business opportunities, may be unable to obtain the requested amount of external finance. Conversely, lead entrepreneurs that have invested in human capital resources (Colombo and Grilli, 2005), and provide observable signals of quality relating to the unobservable quality of their firms will be more likely to obtain the requested amount of external finance. PBOE can contribute to entrepreneurship-specific human capital (Gimeno et al., 1997) and is a resource investment signal sought and

50 *Entrepreneur Resource Accumulation: Finance*

favourably received by financiers. Experienced lead entrepreneurs may have an enhanced reputation and a better understanding of the requirements of financiers. Further, experienced lead entrepreneurs may have tested alternative approaches with regard to obtaining debt finance, and they may have learnt the 'tricks of the trade' relating to the observable signals of quality sought and favourably received by financiers. Entrepreneurs reporting long durations of PBOE may have had more opportunities to accumulate and mobilize their entrepreneurship-specific human capital. Human capital from PBOE may be interrelated with the accumulation and mobilization of social capital via networking in relation to strong and weak ties to mobilize additional resources (Ozgen and Baron, 2007). This discussion suggested the following hypothesis:

> Hypothesis 4.1: *Entrepreneurs with longer durations of PBOE are less likely to report being chronic credit-rationed entrepreneurs.*

Lead novice entrepreneurs lacking an established track record may have to rely upon internal sources of initial capital to obtain ownership stakes. Successful lead experienced habitual entrepreneurs may have larger amounts of personal capital than novice entrepreneurs. Habitual entrepreneurs may invest funds from private business sales in subsequent ventures. In addition, they may have learnt from the feedback associated with PBOE successes (and mistakes). Habitual entrepreneurs may have honed their ability to acquire and organize complex information (Nystrom and Starbuck, 1984). Moreover, habitual entrepreneurs may have developed a better understanding of the information requirements and processes of debt finance institutions, enabling them to obtain funds more easily and on better terms (Westhead et al., 2003). This discussion suggested the following hypothesis:

> Hypothesis 4.2: *Habitual entrepreneurs are less likely than novice entrepreneurs to report being chronic credit-rationed entrepreneurs.*

The goals, resource assets and liabilities reported by portfolio entrepreneurs, who own multiple firms concurrently, can differ from those reported by serial entrepreneurs, who own multiple firms sequentially (Ucbasaran et al., 2008), each of which may differ from those of novice entrepreneurs. Portfolio entrepreneurs with broader resource pools may find it easier than novice entrepreneurs to circumvent barriers relating to the securing of the requested amount of debt finance. Novice entrepreneurs generally do not have broad pools of experience, and they may not fully appreciate the relative benefits associated with mobilizing debt finance.

Entrepreneurs that obtain debt finance increase their exposure to risk. Portfolio entrepreneurs may be willing to bear risk. Notably, they have other firms in their portfolio to fall back on if one of their debt financed firms is not successful. Portfolio entrepreneurs who have not exited from a venture(s) in which they have an ownership stake(s) may be able to mobilize the internal financial resources from their existing business(es), and may use finance from existing customers and suppliers. Some portfolio and serial entrepreneurs may have accumulated funds from the sale of a previous business. However, a reluctance to be involved in projects which may undermine their standing amongst the financial and business community and a desire to invest a smaller proportion of their personal wealth the second time around may mean that some experienced entrepreneurs become risk averse over time.

Some habitual entrepreneurs may display an over-reliance on heuristic principles and decision-making processes, which may not necessarily be appropriate in new situations, especially in changing environments. The accumulation of liabilities associated with PBOE by some lead serial entrepreneurs may generate skills, capabilities and knowledge deficiencies that retard their ability to secure subsequent debt finance. Serial entrepreneurs associated with a track record of business(es) 'closure' may be reluctant to seek debt finance or unable to secure the requested amount of debt. This discussion suggested the following hypotheses:

> Hypothesis 4.3: *Portfolio entrepreneurs are less likely than novice entrepreneurs to report being chronic credit-rationed entrepreneurs.*
> Hypothesis 4.4: *Serial entrepreneurs are less likely than novice entrepreneurs to report being chronic credit-rationed entrepreneurs.*
> Hypothesis 4.5: *Portfolio entrepreneurs are less likely than serial entrepreneurs to report being chronic credit-rationed entrepreneurs.*

Lead entrepreneurs associated with new innovative products and services, as well as work practices and production process innovation, may face scepticism by debt financiers who are unable to understand the technology and the innovative practices. However, financiers that understand the technology and the size of the potential market can view investment in innovation as a high-quality signal. To address the reluctance by some financiers to invest in innovative firms, lead entrepreneurs who have invested in resources relating to innovation may seek to mobilize resources accumulated in PBOE exposures. As intimated above, serial and portfolio entrepreneurs can mobilize their financial resources (from former and/or current ventures in the case of portfolio entrepreneurs), experience, knowledge, credibility, established track record, web of previous and existing suppliers and customers, and network bridge contacts accumulated in PBOE exposures to exploit their new innovative products and services, or innovative strategic renewal practices relating to their current surveyed venture. The compounded credible high-quality signals relating to the interactions (Mueller et al., 2012) between type of innovation and type of PBOE may provide signals more favourably sought and received by financiers seeking to maximize up-side gains of investments, but at the same time seeking to minimize the downside losses.

52   *Entrepreneur Resource Accumulation: Finance*

By definition, innovative novice entrepreneurs with no PBOE resources to mobilize are unable to provide the compounded credible high-quality signals exhibited by innovative serial and portfolio entrepreneur. This discussion suggested the following hypotheses:

> Hypothesis 4.6: *Lead entrepreneurs reporting the compounded credible high-quality signal of innovative and serial entrepreneurs will be less likely than novice entrepreneurs to report being chronic credit-rationed entrepreneurs.*
>
> Hypothesis 4.7: *Lead entrepreneurs reporting the compounded credible high-quality signal of innovative and portfolio entrepreneurs will be less likely than novice entrepreneurs to report being chronic credit-rationed entrepreneurs.*

4.2.3 Methodology

4.2.3.1 Data

Primary information was collected to identify the human capital profiles of entrepreneurs who have applied for debt finance and who have obtained the requested amount of debt finance. Information was gathered from a survey of firms to identify whether the lead entrepreneur in each firm was a novice, serial or portfolio entrepreneur. In developing the sample frame of independent firms for the survey, several organizations provided data. The Ghanaian government is seeking to promote the development of firms that employ between four and 50 employees. Participants were selected based on the following criteria: the business must have at least four employees and at most 50 employees; the business must be in operation for at least one year; the respondent must be the owner/founder or major partner in the case of a co-investment; the business must be independently or privately owned; the business must be engaged in activities within the agricultural, manufacturing and servicing sectors; and the business must be located within the six districts of the Greater Accra Region, which is the main economic hub of entrepreneurship and innovation activity. Industry and standard region sampling proportions were identified for a stratified random sample of independent private firms.

The structured questionnaire was administered in face-to-face interviews with lead entrepreneurs as key informants by one of the authors and three trained researchers from Accra University. From an effective cleaned sample frame of 750 businesses, a total of 496 respondents provided complete data for the selected variables explored, yielding an effective response rate of 66%.

In total, 198 respondents were habitual entrepreneurs (40%), among whom 61 (12%) were serial entrepreneurs, and a further 137 respondents (28%) were portfolio entrepreneurs. These proportions are comparable to

Entitlement Resource Accumulation: Finance   53

those reported in developed country studies (Ucbasaran et al., 2008). In total, 280 (56%) respondents indicated they were credit-rationed entrepreneurs (166 (33%), 90 (18%) and 24 (5%) were temporary, major or chronic, respectively).

Parametric (i.e., Bonferroni test) and non-parametric tests (i.e., Mann-Whitney and Chi-square tests) confirmed that there was no statistically significant response bias between the respondents and non-respondents with regard to industry, government official region, legal form, age of the business and employment size at the 0.05 level. On these criteria, there was no cause to suspect the sample was not representative of the population of private firms. Also, the authors concluded there was no evidence to suggest that the results would be affected by common method bias.

4.2.3.2 Dependent Variable

Following Cosh and Hughes (2003), lead entrepreneurs in each firm were asked, "With regard to debt finance, in the last three years which of the following has occurred: successful (full amount); successful, but amount reduced; not successful; did not apply for debt finance?" The question was followed by three grid boxes, which enabled respondents to indicate their answer for each of the three previous years relating to temporary (over one year), major (over two years) and chronic (over three years). Respondents who indicated that they had applied for debt finance in the previous three years and gave a 'successful, but amount reduced' response were coded as credit-rationed entrepreneurs. Chronic credit-rationed over three years entrepreneurs were scored 3, major credit-rationed over two years entrepreneurs were scored 2 and temporary credit-rationed over one year entrepreneurs were scored 1, whilst respondents reporting no credit-rationing were scored 0.

4.2.3.3 Independent Variables

Respondents were asked to report the number of years they had owned and run a business (Experience). Also, they were asked to indicate the total number of businesses they had established and/or purchased in which they had minority or majority ownership stakes. Four binary variables were operationalized: habitual entrepreneurs (Habitual), serial entrepreneurs (Serial), portfolio entrepreneurs (Portfolio) and novice entrepreneurs (Novice). The Serial and Portfolio variables were included in the regression models, and the reference category was Novice entrepreneurs.

A broad definition of innovation was operationalized (Becheikh et al., 2006; Cosh and Wood, 1998). Respondents were asked, "In the last three years, has your firm undertaken any form of innovation as regard to seven statements relating to the following"—product or services, production processes (including storage), work practices or workforce organization, supply

54 Entrepreneur Resource Accumulation: Finance

and supplier relations, markets and marketing, administration and office systems, and product or service distribution were presented. For each statement, respondents had to select one of the four following responses: innovation not tried (scored 1), innovation tried and failed (scored 2), innovation new to firm but not new to the industry (scored 3) and innovation new to industry (scored 4). Respondents who reported they had introduced product or service innovation (tried and introduced (options 3 and 4)) were allocated a value of value of 1, whilst other entrepreneurs (options 1 and 2) were allocated a value of 0 (ProductI). Further, respondents reporting innovative strategic renewal practices relating to the introduction of at least one out of the six types of work practices and/or production process innovation (tried and introduced (options 3 and 4) with regard to at least one of the six types of work practices and production process innovation) were allocated a value of value of 1, whilst other entrepreneurs (options 1 and 2 with regard to all six types of work practices and production process innovation) were allocated a value of 0 (RenewalI).

4.2.3.4 Technique

Ordered logistic regression analysis (Hamilton, 2003) was used to detect the combination of variables associated with the ordinal dependent variable that ranged from 0 to 3. A base model focusing upon the control variables relating to the firm and the domestic external environment was presented. Alternative measures of PBOE were then added to the base model (i.e., model relating to control variables and Experience; model relating to control variables and Serial and Portfolio; and model relating to control variables, Serial, Portfolio, Product x Serial, ProductI x Portfolio, RenewalI x Serial and RenewalI x Portfolio). The change in Nagelkerke R^2 associated with the sequential inclusion of the alternative PBOE variables was monitored. All presented models were significant at the 0.01 level or lower.

4.2.4 Findings

The length of the debt finance gap was ascertained. Table 4.1 summarizes the length of the debt finance gap by type of PBOE.

Entrepreneurs who cited more years of experience (Experience) were significantly less likely to have reported being chronic credit-rationed entrepreneurs at the 0.01 significance level. Hypothesis 4.1 was supported.

Habitual entrepreneurs were significantly less likely to have reported being chronic credit-rationed entrepreneurs at the 0.05 significance level. Hypothesis 4.2 was supported.

Portfolio and serial entrepreneurs were both less likely to have reported being chronic credit-rationed entrepreneurs at the 0.01 significance level. Hypotheses 4.3 and 4.4 were supported.

Entrepreneur Resource Accumulation: Finance   55

Table 4.1 Length of the Debt Finance Gap by Lead Entrepreneur Type of Prior Business Ownership Experience

Type of prior business ownership experience	Length of debt finance gap				
	None Number %	Temporary (over one year) Number %	Major (over two years) Number %	Chronic (over three years) Number %	Total Number %
Novice	110	36.9	114	38.3	57	19.1	17	5.7	298	100.0
Serial	37	60.6	14	23.0	8	13.1	2	3.3	61	100.0
Portfolio	69	50.4	38	27.7	25	18.2	5	3.6	137	99.9
Total	216	43.5	166	33.5	90	18.1	24	4.8	496	99.9

Source: Authors.

Portfolio entrepreneurs were not significantly less likely than serial entrepreneurs to have reported being chronic credit-rationed entrepreneurs. Hypothesis 4.5 was not supported.

The interaction between innovation type and PBOE type was considered. Serial entrepreneurs involved in work practices and production processes innovation (RenewalI x Serial) were less likely to have reported being chronic credit-rationed entrepreneurs. Portfolio entrepreneurs involved in new innovative product or service innovation (ProductI x Portfolio) and work practices and production processes innovation (RenewalI x Portfolio) were less likely to have reported being chronic credit-rationed entrepreneurs. Hypothesis 4.6 was partially supported. However, hypothesis 4.7 was supported.

4.2.5 Conclusions and Implications

Irrespective of the length (i.e., Experience) or type (i.e., Habitual, Serial or Portfolio) of PBOE, experienced entrepreneurs were consistently less likely to have reported being chronic credit-rationed entrepreneurs. Entrepreneurs with longer periods of PBOE were less likely to have reported being chronic credit-rationed entrepreneurs. Habitual entrepreneurs and the sub-types of serial and portfolio entrepreneurs were less likely to have reported being chronic credit-rationed entrepreneurs. Portfolio and serial entrepreneurs provided 'signals' that are sought and positively received by debt financiers.

A novel finding was the detection of an interaction effect between a focus on product innovation and/or renewal innovation and entrepreneurs' type of PBOE, and the reported lower likelihood of entrepreneurs being credit-rationed entrepreneurs. This suggests that debt financier perception of risk

56 *Entrepreneur Resource Accumulation: Finance*

with any form of innovation can be reduced if lead entrepreneurs have PBOE to mobilize. Portfolio entrepreneurs involved in new innovative products or services and/or work practices and production processes innovation were less likely to have report being chronic credit-rationed entrepreneurs. Further, serial entrepreneurs involved in work practices and production processes innovation were less likely to have reported being chronic credit-rationed entrepreneurs.

Presented evidence suggested that portfolio entrepreneurs were less likely to be credit-rationed. Portfolio entrepreneurs appear to benefit from entrepreneurial learning associated with PBOE successes (and or failures) by developing practices to tackle barriers to the provision of debt finance. To facilitate economic development, there is a need to encourage the formation and development of 'quality' new firms, particularly engaged in renewal innovation from the outset. In a developing economy context, advisors and government agencies promoting the take-up of technical and innovative capabilities may maximize the returns from their investments by targeting support to 'winning' portfolio entrepreneurs, who are markedly more likely than novice entrepreneurs to obtain the requested amount of debt finance required to exploit product and innovative work practice innovations. Also, findings suggested that novice entrepreneurs, particularly those engaged in innovation, would benefit from developing links with portfolio entrepreneurs. In a resource-deficit developing economy context, this may provide an important 'mentoring' role. Network bridging schemes that encourage inexperienced entrepreneurs to learn how to build relationships with experienced entrepreneurs, debt financiers and potential equity investors could be introduced to address network gaps. Schemes could be introduced to establish sponsored incubators (Tötterman and Sten, 2005) that encourage networking and information exchange between novice entrepreneurs and successful portfolio entrepreneurs, and social capital accumulation by all types of entrepreneurs.

Risk-averse debt financiers may decide to target debt finance to portfolio entrepreneurs who have collateral in two or more firms and who have more diverse ownership teams with increased legitimacy, which are seeking wealth creation, rapid growth and job generation. In a resource-deficit developing economy context, where informational asymmetries are likely to be highly problematical and debt finance is scarce, and where lending decision-makers are less likely to be experienced, portfolio entrepreneurs may be especially attractive.

4.3 Finance: Venture Capital

4.3.1 *Gaps in the Knowledge Base and Research Questions*

The article by Mueller et al., (2012) focused on whether habitual entrepreneurs engaged in USOs would be more likely to obtain FFVCI. USOs that attract formal venture capital (VC) are assumed to report superior firm performance (Zhang, 2009). Formal VC investment is defined as equity investments and non-collateral forms of investments made by formal VC investors to invest in unquoted private firms in which they have no family connection. The inability of most USOs to generate substantial jobs (Garnsey and Heffernan, 2005) and wealth creation may be due to the reluctance and/or inability of entrepreneurs to obtain formal VC (Martin et al., 2005). Some USOs obtain finance from government schemes and/or business angel informal finance, and then are reluctant and/or unable to obtain additional external formal VC, which can partially retard product development and business growth. Formal VC may be required to ensure a strong commercial drive leading to a shorter time to market in product development, which will subsequently generate significant local jobs and wealth (Colombo and Grilli, 2005). Formal VC backing of innovative firms involves a higher level of risk relative to funding more traditional equity arrangements because, oftentimes, it is not backed by collateral (Babcock-Lumish, 2009).

'Star' universities in the United Kingdom such as Oxford, Cambridge, Imperial College and University College London report the highest research income and the largest numbers of USOs, patents and licences (Lawton Smith, 2007). USOs drawn from 'star universities' located in the 'golden triangle' (i.e., Cambridge, Oxford, Imperial College, King's College London and University College London) in the United Kingdom are assumed to possess spatial proximity benefits (Martin et al., 2005), which may increase their ability to obtain FFVCI relative to USOs located elsewhere. USOs not drawn from 'star' universities have to compensate for institutional disadvantages by accumulating and combining resources from diverse actors in novel ways to ensure business development.

USO profiles more likely to obtain formal VC are poorly understood. Additional studies integrating theoretical insights concerning the USO and the founder are warranted to explore whether USOs that provide particular firm (Lockett and Wright, 2005) and founder resource 'signals' increase their likelihood of obtaining formal VC. There may be increased onus on academic entrepreneurs outside 'golden triangle' universities to understand investment criteria used by formal VC firms and to clearly signal investment readiness (i.e., existing USO resource pools send observable (and unobservable) positive signals of quality) of their USOs. Information asymmetries between academic entrepreneurs and formal VC firms may have negative consequences for VC provision. Entrepreneurs not providing adequate positive 'signals' of credibility and expertise, as well as the market potential of their business opportunities may be unable to obtain the formal VC they require. With reference to the habitual entrepreneur phenomenon, they explored the following research question:

- *Do USOs located outside 'golden triangle' universities that are unable to leverage the proximity benefits associated with 'golden triangle' university entrepreneurial systems have to combine resources to increase the likelihood that first formal VC (FFVCI) is obtained, whilst controlling for cyclical variations in VC supply and deal flow?*

58 *Entrepreneur Resource Accumulation: Finance*

4.3.2 Hypothesis Tested

Guided by the resource-based view of the firm and signalling theory, the authors explored whether USOs located outside 'golden triangle' universities that are unable to mobilize the proximity benefits associated with 'golden triangle' university entrepreneurial systems have to combine resources to increase the likelihood that FFVCI is obtained, whilst controlling for cyclical variations in VC supply and deal flow. To overcome information asymmetry problems in the provision of formal VC, USOs (i.e., signallers) seeking finance from formal VC firms (i.e., receivers) need to internally assemble and manage costly resource bases (i.e., human, firm and social capital) that signal USO observable (and unobservable) credible quality to formal VC firms. Notably, USOs assemble and combine resources (i.e., provide credible interactive signals that are sought and favourably received by formal VC firms) to increase the likelihood that FFVCI is obtained. High-quality signals are sought by formal VC firms seeking to reduce exposure to risk when financing USOs.

Formal VC firms look for experienced entrepreneurs who have already made costly investments in honing their entrepreneurial skills and expertise. These entrepreneurs may have broader and more developed technical, industry and management know-how, and entrepreneurial capabilities. Experienced entrepreneurs with established skills, networks and reputations may be better able to cope with liabilities of newness. Human capital from PBOE may be interrelated with greater social capital associated with diverse networks (Ozgen and Baron, 2007). Experienced founders may have tested alternative approaches to obtain finance and learnt approaches that are more likely to work. Founders with PBOE more likely have greater knowledge for understanding their technology, market and customers, which enables VC investors to reduce and control operational risks.

USOs located outside 'golden triangle' universities can compensate for 'golden triangle' proximity benefits by sending compounded clear, credible and costly observable human capital signals, which can reduce information asymmetry perceived by potential formal VC investors. The interaction effect between USO's region of origin and USO demand-side signal of habitual entrepreneur PBOE experience was analysed with reference to the following hypothesis:

Hypothesis 4.8: *USOs located outside 'golden triangle' universities that signal the presence of a habitual entrepreneur key founder that had started a business before will be more likely to obtain FFVCI.*

4.3.3 Methodology

4.3.3.1 Data

Contrasting with previous USO studies using cross-sectional databases (Rothaermel et al., 2007), the authors explored a panel database with annual observations for the period of USO formations and formal VC funding events between 1st January 1990 and 31st December 2007. This unique longitudinal dataset combined archival and survey data. USOs were identified from the Library House (now Dow Jones) database not widely available to the general public. Library House defines USOs as start-ups dependent on the formal transfer of IP rights from the university (Wright et al., 2006), but the university still holds an equity stake. The population of 579 USOs in the United Kingdom founded during 1990 to 2007, the most active period in USO formation, was identified.

Library House, Companies House, FAME and the Annual Business Inquiry (ABI) databases were explored to identify information relating to each USO's status, market size, industry context and prior take-up of external financing. The esp@cenet database was used to identify the annual number of patents filed by each USO. As no information was publicly available on human capital profiles of USO founders and the USOs networks, an online survey of key founders was used to collect this information. Returns were obtained from 134 respondents with a response rate of 23%. A firm was defined as surviving if still in business by the start of 2008. In total, 125 USOs had survived, whilst nine had closed. The 93.3% survival rate was in line with a study of USOs in the United States over the 1990 to 2001 period (94.4%) (Zhang, 2009). No USOs had been taken over by another organization.

Mann-Whitney 'U' and Chi-square tests confirmed no statistically significant response bias between respondents and non-respondents regarding firm age, total disclosed funding, funding events, year of most recent investment, total average of years until first external investment, number of previous USOs from the university of origin, region of origin, industry, university of origin, whether the university was a member of the leading Russell Group and whether the USO was drawn from a 'golden triangle' university. The authors concluded that the sample was representative of the population of USOs in the United Kingdom.

To assess content validity, the online questionnaire was tested during a pilot survey. Practitioner conferences relating to USOs and start-up financing were attended to ensure understanding of USO financing needs. An early version was revised in line with comments from two academic entrepreneurs. To check face validity, ten academic entrepreneurs were contacted and comments from this pilot were incorporated in a revised questionnaire. Common method bias was minimized. Responses from one data source were validated with responses from an alternative source.

Mann-Whitney 'U' and Chi-square tests failed to detect significant differences between the 517 USO survivors and the 62 closed USOs up to the 31st December 2007 in terms of firm age, number of funding events, amount of formal VC, USO region, sector, university Russell Group membership and survival of surveyed respondents. In all reported models, firm survival was consistently not found to be significant. There was no evidence to suggest that the presented results were distorted by firm survivor bias.

60   *Entrepreneur Resource Accumulation: Finance*

4.3.3.2 Dependent Variable

Key founders were asked for the percentage distribution of equity owner-ship in their USOs relating to the following categories: your share, man-agement, university, other companies, venture capitalists, business angels, public funds, hybrid public and private equity funds, IPO (public shares) and other. For USOs obtaining VC finance, the timing of VC investment was cross-checked with information held by Library House. Key founders reporting that 1% or more of their USOs equity was owned by formal VCs were scored 1, and 0 otherwise (FFVCI).

4.3.3.3 Independent Variables

The databases were used to identify each USO's main operational premises. USOs located in the 'golden triangle' were scored 1, and 0 otherwise (GTL). Also, following Yip and Tsang (2007), a variable relating to 'non-golden-triangle' location was computed. USOs not located in the 'golden triangle' were scored 1, and 0 otherwise (NGTL). Key founders indicated whether they had started at least one firm before the surveyed USO (Shane and Stu-art, 2002). Founders indicating they had started a firm before were scored 1, and 0 otherwise (Habitual).

4.3.3.4 Technique

Event history analysis models were computed (Blossfeld et al., 2007) to identify factors significantly related to the USOs' ability to obtain FFVCI (Shane and Stuart, 2002). A base model relating to the control variables was presented followed by a model relating to NGTL and control vari-ables. Then, a full model, including NGTL, NGTL interaction variables and control variables, was presented. Sensitivity analysis was also conducted relating to a full model that included GTL, GTL interaction variables and control variables.

4.3.4 Findings

In total, 72 USOs (54%) had obtained FFVCI. NGTL, NGTL interaction variables and control variables were explored in an event history analy-sis model. A positive significant interaction was found between USOs not located in the 'golden triangle' (NGTL) and habitual founder experi-ence (NGTL x Habitual). USOs located outside the 'golden triangle' with habitual founders were significantly more likely to have obtained FFVCI. Hypothesis 4.8 was supported.

4.3.5 Conclusions and Implications

Issues relating to key founders are generally neglected within innovation policy (Bodas Freitas and von Tunzelmann, 2008). The study's findings have implications for policy addressing the locational disadvantages of USOs not located in the 'golden triangle' (NGTL). The authors extended recent prior research on spatial mismatches between investors and investees (Babcock-Lumish, 2009). They provided fresh evidence on the adaptive resource mobilization and signalling, which can be encouraged by practitioners to enable more USOs to obtain VC backing. The authors showed how USOs located outside the 'golden triangle' can compensate for the absence of 'spatial proximity benefits' (Martin et al., 2005).

Event history analysis identified, consistent with a spatial mismatch view between investors and investees, that USOs located outside 'golden triangle' universities (NGTL) were not significantly less likely to have obtained FFVCI. USO signallers located outside 'golden triangle' universities (NGTL) in the United Kingdom can compensate for the weaker reputation of their localities and universities by sending observable, credible and costly high-quality founder and firm resource signals to reduce information asymmetry to increase the likelihood that their USOs obtained FFVCI. The credible signal of quality relating to habitual founder PBOE was sought by VC investors looking to address risk and information asymmetry problems.

Practitioners have a role in encouraging USOs not located in the 'golden triangle' (NGTL) to consider strategies that combine resources to facilitate more USOs to provide the positive credible signals, which can reduce the asymmetric information problems faced by potential formal VC investors. However, resource combinations promoted in NGTL entrepreneurial systems (i.e., habitual entrepreneurs) may not be the same as those promoted in USOs located in the 'golden triangle' (GTL) entrepreneurial systems. In the latter context, technology transfer officers (TTOs) could facilitate USOs to have reputable management teams.

4.4 Finance: Venture Capital Reinvestment in Serial Entrepreneurs

4.4.1 Gaps in the Knowledge Base and Research Questions

Previously backed entrepreneurs are assumed to be important in generating VC deal flow. Entrepreneur PBOE is viewed as an element of the deal-screening process. Scant attention has been directed towards the process by which venture capitalists screen serial entrepreneurs that have exited from a previous venture, and the criteria they use to make their financing selection decisions. While there is some evidence concerning the extent to which founders of new businesses have previously started a venture, there is little evidence concerning the extent to which serial entrepreneurs existing from one venture are backed a second or subsequent time by their financial partner. This issue assumes increasing importance as a VC industry matures and exits from existing investments increase. For the formal VC industry, the funding of exiting entrepreneurs in the acquisition of existing businesses through a secondary management buyout or management buy in may be as

62   *Entrepreneur Resource Accumulation: Finance*

important in terms of the volume of investments, and possibly, even more important in value terms. Hence, the article by Wright et al., (1997) focused on the links between venture capitalists and serial entrepreneurs.

4.4.2 Hypotheses Tested

This article adopted a framework relating to the stages in the VC process. In relation to serial entrepreneurs, this can be conceptualized as involving the following: exit of the serial entrepreneur at the time of venture capitalist exit or afterwards with assessment by the venture capitalist for potential reinvestment; post-exit contact by the venture capitalist if reinvestment does not occur on exit; screening of serial entrepreneurs, together with first-time novice entrepreneurs and entrepreneurs exited from other venture capitalists' portfolios, with a view to investment; and deal negotiation and completion. This study particularly focused on the benefits associated with serial entrepreneurs acquiring human capital resources and capabilities from owning prior ventures. The study drew upon insights from contracting theory. This study explored how first-time novice entrepreneurs who subsequently become serial entrepreneurs learnt from the initial VC deals when they were novice entrepreneurs. Notably, it is assumed that the initial VC deal experience can shape novice entrepreneurs' ability to negotiate a better contract with regard to a subsequent deal when they become serial entrepreneurs.

Traditionally, the investment proposals of entrepreneurs were generally screened by venture capitalists in relation to entrepreneur personality and experience. To a lesser extent, issues relating to a firm's market, product, and strategy were considered. To reduce the potential of adverse selection issues, venture capitalists particularly focus on an entrepreneur's track record of past experience. It is assumed that the pool of human capital resources and capabilities accumulated can be mobilized to successfully create, discover and exploit business opportunities with significant wealth and growth potential. Experience directly related to entrepreneurial activity is assumed to be of particular value. This discussion suggested the following hypotheses:

> Hypothesis 4.9: *Venture capitalists who express a preference for investing in experienced entrepreneurs will place greater emphasis on previous entrepreneurial experience than those who do not have such a preference.*
>
> Hypothesis 4.10: *Venture capitalists will evaluate novice entrepreneurs and serial entrepreneurs differently.*

It may be expected that if the screening process is working effectively, venture capitalists will assess both the assets and the liabilities of an individual entrepreneur's previous experience. It can be assumed that venture capitalists will only invest in entrepreneurs whose assets are more than their liabilities. This discussion suggested the following hypothesis:

Entrepreneur Resource Accumulation: Finance   63

Hypothesis 4.11: *Venture capitalists will assess the net benefits of previous experience and target those entrepreneurs where the assets of previous experience exceed liabilities.*

In recontracting with entrepreneurs who have exited from their own firm's portfolio, venture capitalists are potentially faced with a situation where the entrepreneur is more aware than previously of the effectiveness of the venture capitalist's monitoring and support and of how (dis)advantageous the initial VC contract was. With respect to entrepreneurs who have exited from other venture capitalists' portfolios, the contracting problem is more complicated, as the entrepreneur now has knowledge about the VC negotiating process in general, though not of the venture capitalist to whom an approach is being made for the first time. Moreover, while venture capitalists may know the entrepreneurs who have exited from their own portfolios, they are still faced by potential adverse selection problems in respect of entrepreneurs who have exited from other venture capitalists' portfolios. This discussion suggested the following hypotheses:

Hypothesis 4.12: *As a result of the potential for recontracting problems, venture capitalists will be cautious about reinvesting in experienced entrepreneurs from their own portfolios.*

Hypothesis 4.13: *Venture capitalists will be cautious about investing in entrepreneurs who have exited from other venture capitalists' portfolios because of recontracting problems relating to both asymmetric information and the entrepreneurs' knowledge of the negotiation process.*

During the screening process venture capitalists will need, and be more able, to satisfy themselves that experienced serial entrepreneurs still have the motivation to perform, and that experienced serial entrepreneurs will perform at least as well as they did before and at least as well as inexperienced novice entrepreneurs. This led to the derivation of the following hypothesis:

Hypothesis 4.14: *Venture-backed serial entrepreneurs are expected to perform both at least as well as they did in their own first venture and as well as novice entrepreneurs.*

4.4.3 Methodology

4.4.3.1 Data

The study involved two questionnaires that were administered to venture capitalists. In relation to the first questionnaire, a pilot study was initially conducted. The pilot questionnaire survey instrument was sent to several venture capitalists, advisors and academics. Evidence from previous studies relating to how venture capitalists access entrepreneur VC proposals was

64 *Entrepreneur Resource Accumulation: Finance*

used to derive the questions reported on the questionnaire. The revised questionnaire was sent to the 113 venture capital institutions who were full members of the British Venture Capital Association. A consistent key informant approached was used. The questionnaire was sent to the Chief Executive in each of the 113 venture capital institutions, or senior colleagues in these institutions whom the Centre for Management Buyout Research (CMBOR) had regular contact with in relation to its buy-out and buy-in surveys. The questionnaire was administered, and then a follow-up reminder was sent. In total, 55 responses were returned with a response rate of 48.7%.

Subsequently, a second questionnaire was designed and sent to the 40 (out of the 55 respondents to the first survey) respondents who had indicated during the first survey that they had either invested in an entrepreneur who had exited from their own and/or another venture capitalist's portfolio. The second survey yielded 23 usable responses with a response rate of 57.5%. This second survey was administered to gather further information about the process of contracting with entrepreneurs from their own or from other VC firms' portfolios.

4.4.3.2 *Techniques*

Univariate tests (i.e., student's t-tests) and multivariate analysis of variance (i.e., multivariate analysis of variance (MANOVA)) were conducted to test the presented hypotheses. The testing of Hypothesis 4.9 required a comparison of two groups of venture capitalists, notably, a group of venture capitalists who preferred to invest in experienced entrepreneurs and a group of venture capitalists who did not across a set of screening criteria. The criteria used in investment appraisal are not independent. Relationships between some, if not all, criteria were expected. Consequently, simple univariate tests on each criterion were not viewed to be appropriate. Accordingly, a multivariate statistical approach that accommodated the effects of interdependence between criteria was selected. Principal Components Analysis (PCA) was conducted in relation to all investment appraisal statements. The PCA was conducted to identify underlying dimensions/relationships between the investment appraisal statements and the identification of groups of investment appraisal statements. Notably, the PCA identified five components that accounted for 70% of the variance. A varimax rotation was conducted. The following five components were identified. Component 1 related to entrepreneur track record, relating to ownership experience. Component 2 related to entrepreneur track record of management experience. Component 3 related to entrepreneur personal attributes such as age, knowledge and family background. Component 4 related to links to the funding institution. Component 5 related to financial commitment (i.e., a single variable component). Respondent responses relating to variations in the five investment appraisal components were then compared using MANOVA. Preference for use of a serial entrepreneur was an independent variable.

4.4.4 Findings

With respect to testing Hypothesis 4.9, in most instances, there was no evidence of any significant differences in the rating applied to each component across the two groups of venture capitalists (Table 4.2). However, in relation to previous ownership experience, some weak statistically significant differences were detected at the 0.1 level of significance. Previous ownership experience, length of ownership career and number of previous ventures all obtained significantly higher ratings from those venture capitalists that preferred to invest in serial entrepreneurs. Evidence to support Hypothesis 4.9 was weak.

To test Hypothesis 4.10, respondents were asked to score factors relating to their importance in assessing an investment potential of novice and serial entrepreneurs. The study found that venture capitalists reported a high degree of similarity in the ways in which the two types of entrepreneur were assessed. Only management skills (i.e., at the 0.05 level) and ability to cope with stress (i.e., at the 0.1 level) were found to be significantly more important in the assessment of novice entrepreneurs than in the assessment of serial entrepreneurs. Relating to both novice and serial entrepreneurs the three most important factors were leadership skills, management skills, and the achievement of sales/finance targets. Evidence for Hypothesis 4.10 was weak. The emphasis on different screening criteria did not differ significantly between novice and serial entrepreneurs, despite the potential for adverse selection problems to be lower for serial entrepreneurs.

Responses relating to serial entrepreneurs in whom venture capitalists had invested suggested awareness by them of the positive and negative aspects of experience, with those with negative attributes not receiving subsequent backing. Hypothesis 4.11 was supported. Further, there was tentative support for Hypothesis 4.12 in relation to the descriptive statistics relating to the low level of use of previously funded entrepreneurs. Compared to usage of entrepreneurs from the venture capitalists' own portfolio, there is evidence of a substantial difference, which would tend to suggest that venture capitalists see recontracting as less problematic with entrepreneurs previously funded by a different venture capitalist.

Major differences were found in the second survey between first-time and serial entrepreneurs with regard to negotiations. The data from the second survey provided some support for recontracting problems when venture capitalists dealt with entrepreneurs from their own portfolios. Hypothesis 4.12 was supported. However, the extent of such difficulties seemed rather less in the case of entrepreneurs from the portfolios of other venture capitalists. Hypothesis 4.13 was not supported. The results of the second survey suggested that in terms of performance in the second venture in comparison to that in the first, there was little evidence of much difference. Hypothesis 4.14 was supported.

Table 4.2 Multivariate Analysis of Variance for Investment Appraisal Criteria

	Means tests				
	Prefer serial entrepreneur	*Do not prefer*	*Multivariate F-ratio*	*Univariate F-ratio*	*Significance*
Ownership			2.45	–	0.074
Previous ownership experience	2.85	2.14	–	2.48	0.098
Length of ownership career	2.58	1.79	–	4.09	0.048
Number of previous ventures	2.5	1.79	–	5.69	0.021
Management			1.10	–	0.340
Managerial experience	4.53	4.71	–	0.84	0.362
Managerial success	4.85	4.79	–	0.19	0.661
Personal background			1.07	–	0.389
Qualifications	2.53	2.86	–	1.10	0.297
Knowledge of industry	4.35	4.79	–	2.88	0.095
Stable family background	2.28	2.76	–	2.49	0.120
Age	2.78	3.07	–	1.18	0.281
Motivation	4.62	4.71	–	0.12	0.732
Institutional links			1.15	–	0.323
Level of funding sought	2.60	2.43	–	0.20	0.656
Previous relationship with manager	2.90	2.28	–	2.30	0.135
				0.43	0.67
Financial commitment[*]	3.80	3.93	–	0.43	0.67
N	40	14	–	–	–

[*] Reported test statistic is T-ratio because financial commitment is a univariate measure.

Source: Authors.

4.4.5 Conclusions and Implications

The study suggested that the extent to which venture capitalists use previously funded entrepreneurs is relatively low compared to the number of investments harvested. Although entrepreneur PBOE was of some importance, it was not in itself a critical factor. Notably, venture capitalists needed to be satisfied that that experienced entrepreneurs still had the motivation, ambition, and managerial skills to succeed in a subsequent venture. Presented evidence suggested that future studies should consider the views of venture capitalists in relation to the characteristics and motivations of the serial entrepreneurs seek external VC finance. Examination of issues concerning the processes by which serial entrepreneurs enter into subsequent ventures, from the perspective of the entrepreneurs, may help in understanding the phenomenon. The results of the study have implications for practitioners. First, the findings emphasize the importance of not considering PBOE in isolation but in the context of other key investment criteria. Second, the lack of strongly greater performance from serial, versus novice, entrepreneurs further emphasizes the care to be taken in assessing experienced entrepreneurs. Third, the relatively low degree of formal and rigorous post-exit assessment and monitoring by venture capitalists suggests that important opportunities to invest in experienced entrepreneurs may be missed.

4.5 Summary

This chapter has reviewed three themes relating to financial resources and habitual entrepreneurs. The first, related to debt finance, was conducted in the developing context of Ghana, whilst the second and third related to VC and were conducted in the developed economy context of the United Kingdom. In the first article, the entrepreneur positive signal of PBOE was assumed to be linked to entrepreneurs being less likely to have reported being chronic credit-rationed. Irrespective of the length of PBOE or type (i.e., habitual, serial or portfolio) of PBOE, experienced entrepreneurs were consistently found to have been less likely to have reported being chronic credit-rationed entrepreneurs. In the second article, it was assumed that USOs with habitual entrepreneurs would send a positive signal that was sought and favourably received by formal VC firms. The study found that USOs located outside the 'golden triangle' could compensate for the absence of 'spatial proximity benefits'. Notably, USOs located outside the 'golden triangle' that signalled a habitual entrepreneur significantly increased the likelihood of obtaining FFVCI required for venture development. The third article summarized focused on the perspectives of venture capital firms investing in serial entrepreneurs. The basis for the article was that entrepreneurs had exited from an initial VC investment before considering a further investment with a VC firm. This study considered serial entrepreneurs

68   *Entrepreneur Resource Accumulation: Finance*

but excluded portfolio entrepreneurs. It was assumed that VC firms would assess novice and experienced serial entrepreneurs differently. Notably, VC firms would take into account the assets and liabilities of prior experience. It was also assumed that venture capitalists would be cautious regarding recontracting with experienced serial entrepreneurs. This study highlighted that there was little difference in how novice and experienced serial entrepreneurs were assessed. The study highlighted that experienced serial entrepreneurs were not assessed solely on the basis that they had prior experience. However, somewhat surprisingly, the study highlighted that venture capitalists see recontracting as less problematic with entrepreneurs previously funded by a different venture capitalist than with those from their own portfolio.

4.6 Reflection Questions

In Chapter 4, entrepreneur PBOE was assumed to be a 'positive signal' sought and favourably received by external finance providers. Please consider the following reflection questions:

- *Why do entrepreneurs need external finance?*
- *Who are chronic credit-rationed entrepreneurs?*
- *What 'signals' can entrepreneurs send to reduce the likelihood of being chronic credit-rationed entrepreneurs?*
- *Why do USO entrepreneurs require FFVCI?*
- *What theories have been presented to explain the take-up of finance by USO entrepreneurs?*
- *What 'signals' can USO entrepreneurs send to increase the likelihood of obtaining FFVCI?*
- *Why might VC firms be reluctant to reinvest in entrepreneurs who have exited from their own portfolio?*
- *Why might the balance of power in negotiating a deal between an entrepreneur and a VC firm change between the first and the second deal?*
- *To what extent might entrepreneurs who have exited from a first deal be able to play useful subsequent roles for VC firms and other entrepreneurs?*

5 Entrepreneur Resource Accumulation: Networking and Resource Orchestration

5.1 Learning Objectives and Overview

Entrepreneurs have to obtain resources from external actors through networking to ensure the sustained competitive advantage of their firms. These resources constitute an entrepreneur's social capital. A major issue in entrepreneurship research generally concerns the mechanisms through which entrepreneurs' networks and relationships develop and help create social capital (Gedajlovic et al., 2013). Entrepreneurs may develop networks that involve repeated interactions, creating strong ties and bonding social capital, or occasional interactions with less familiar actors, creating weak ties and bridging social capital (Adler and Kwon, 2002). While the former may be helpful to entrepreneurs initially, they can lead to rigidity in the identification and exploitation of entrepreneurial opportunities. The latter can help entrepreneurs to make new connections that open up the identification and exploitation of new opportunities. Of particular concern here are the potential differences between the networks of habitual entrepreneurs and novice entrepreneurs with no PBOE to mobilize. While habitual entrepreneurs may have developed the ability to build stronger and more effective networks than novice entrepreneurs (Wiklund and Shepherd, 2008), there is limited analysis of how this process occurs, and of the variety in the elements of these networks.

Entrepreneurs also have to co-ordinate or orchestrate the resources they assemble in order to both recognize and exploit opportunities. They need to develop the capabilities to do this. PBOE may provide learning that helps them to perform this process better than novice entrepreneurs. But PBOE in the form of portfolio entrepreneurship especially may provide opportunities to leverage experiences from existing parts of a portfolio for the successful development of new ventures, yet understanding of this process is limited. In the following sections, the asset of PBOE is discussed with regard to the networking behaviour of academic entrepreneurs and the orchestration of resources by portfolio entrepreneurs.

70 Networking and Resource Orchestration

5.2 Networking

5.2.1 Gaps in the Knowledge Base and Research Questions

The article by Mosey and Wright (2007) explored the social capital accumulation by academic entrepreneurs with different levels of PBOE. Technology-based academic entrepreneurs face a number of significant barriers in creating and sustaining new ventures (Vohora et al., 2004). First, the venture is generally based upon a technological breakthrough that may have multiple commercial applications (Shane, 2000). Second, the entrepreneur may not have the skills or knowledge to recognize opportunities (Venkataraman, 1997). Third, the entrepreneur is unlikely to possess the skills or knowledge required to exploit an opportunity (Franklin et al., 2001). Fourth, the traditionally non-commercial environment of universities poses serious issues regarding the level of support available to create and develop such ventures (Lockett and Wright, 2005). The debate about how to overcome these barriers has focused on the human capital shortages of the entrepreneurs. Typologies of academic entrepreneurs have typically not considered the heterogeneity of the entrepreneurs' experience as an entrepreneur (Mustar et al., 2006), the implicit assumption being that they are creating a venture for the first time. There is an absence of systematic studies that identify the extent to which habitual entrepreneurs exist in universities.

In contrast to entrepreneurs in commercial environments, the traditionally non-commercial environment of universities likely means that academic entrepreneurs face major challenges in developing social capital, especially if they remain within the university (Mustar et al., 2006). However, we know little about the development of social capital by academic entrepreneurs with different human capital derived from entrepreneurial experience. Understanding these differences is important, since unlike the private sector context, the process of developing greater social capital from ownership experience may not be straightforward in an academic entrepreneurship context. The following broad research question was explored:

- *How do differences in the human capital derived from the entrepreneurial experience of academic entrepreneurs influence their ability to develop social capital?*

To explore this question, the study utilized a longitudinal study of academic entrepreneurs. A group of technology based nascent, novice and habitual academic entrepreneurs were observed in relation to the development of their social capital over an academic year. The study drew upon two separate literatures. First, it drew on the literature relating to the link between the human capital derived from entrepreneurs' PBOE and their behaviour. Leading academic researchers may be entrepreneurial in identifying new research areas and sources of funds, but they may have difficulties identifying opportunities with commercial market applications (Lockett et al., 2003). It is an empirical question whether leading scientists are homogeneous with regard to their ability to identify commercial opportunities (Wright et al., 2004). Second, to gain an insight into barriers faced by nascent academic entrepreneurs, this study also drew upon the social capital literature. Social capital is important for the creation of ventures based upon university research. The social network of academics is typically constrained to a narrow scientific research network. However, academics may have close or strong ties with team members in their department, leading to the creation of bonding social capital. Weak ties between an academic actor and industrial actors may lead to bridging social capital (Adler and Kwon, 2002).

The human capital profiles of academics may be enhanced by focusing on weak ties with industry actors (Davidsson and Honig, 2003), which can sometimes develop into strong ones. Hoang and Antoncic (2003) have highlighted three aspects of social networks. First, the network structure relates to the patterns of relationships between actors in the network. Second, the network content relates to the nature of the resources exchanged between actors. Third, the network governance relates to the mechanisms that govern relationships between actors. These three aspects provided a framework within which to explore more specific elements relating to the presented broad research question.

Academic entrepreneurs may be heterogeneous with respect to their previous entrepreneurial experience. The traditional university environment raises questions about 'whether' and 'how' the human capital of inexperienced and experienced academic entrepreneurs is related to the development of social capital. As little is known about these relationships, the following specific research questions were explored:

> *RQ1: What structural social capital is in place at the start of new venture development for academic entrepreneurs with different levels of PBOE?*
>
> *RQ2: What new ties are developed during the early stages of new venture development by academic entrepreneurs with different levels of PBOE?*

Considering social network content, experienced entrepreneurs in a commercial environment are likely to have access to more diverse resources through their social network (Callon et al., 1997). By contrast, less experienced entrepreneurs with more limited social networks may lack access to seed finance, industry knowledge to recognize opportunities or access to investment finance. This discussion suggested the following specific research question that was explored:

> *RQ3: What is the nature of the resources gained through the social networks of academic entrepreneurs with different levels of PBOE at the early stages of venture development?*

72　Networking and Resource Orchestration

Considering network governance, experienced entrepreneurs in a commercial environment likely will have built relationships based upon trust that may enhance the quality of resource flows through social networks (Larson and Starr, 1993). Through PBOE, entrepreneurs can establish such relationships and have a positive reputation and credibility with key actors (Delmar and Shane, 2004). Less experienced entrepreneurs are less likely to have an established reputation and may be unsure how to build one. Universities may offer a context where the development of trust relationships and reputation are different and problematical. However, prior research has not established how different levels of PBOE by academic entrepreneurs can address these challenges. This discussion suggested the following specific research question that was explored:

> *RQ4: What governance mechanisms are utilized by academic entrepreneurs with different levels of PBOE to access resources through social networks at the early stages of venture development?*

There may be an important contribution to human capital from the discipline base of education and research. Industrial experience may contribute to human capital and enable access to social networks for the identification and exploitation of opportunities. The degree of success of PBOE may, in addition, be linked to the development of social capital. The university incubator environments in which academic entrepreneurs find themselves differ in terms of providing access to commercial social networks (Lockett and Wright, 2005). This discussion suggested the following specific research question that was explored:

> *RQ5: What is the influence of discipline-based and industrial experience aspects of human capital, the degree of success of previous ventures and the nature of the university incubator environment on the ability of academic entrepreneurs with different levels of PBOE to develop social networks and access resources through social networks at the early stages of venture development?*

5.2.2　Methodology and Data

A multiple inductive case study approach was adopted, using a system of replication logic, with each case treated as an independent experiment (Yin, 1993). Within each case, the level of analysis is the entrepreneur, and the unit of analysis is the social capital developed by the entrepreneur. Forty-four interviews were conducted with academics, business development officers and heads of school involved in the process of new venture creation.

In total, 24 academics were selected, exhibiting a variance in terms of PBOE as follows: six nascent entrepreneurs, twelve novice entrepreneurs and six habitual entrepreneurs. Following the stages in the university spin-out process identified by Vohora et al., (2004), nascent entrepreneurs were defined as those entrepreneurs in the process of addressing the opportunity recognition juncture between research and the framing of an opportunity at the start of the period. Novice entrepreneurs were defined as those that had already crossed the opportunity recognition juncture and were addressing the entrepreneurial commitment juncture at the start of the period. Habitual entrepreneurs were defined as having previously formed at least one other business at the start of the period.

The respondents were based within ten schools of engineering or applied science in six universities in the United Kingdom. The different schools and universities were selected to exhibit a diversity of prior commercialization performance (Mustar et al., 2006). Ten business development officers and ten heads of school were also interviewed to provide a different perspective.

The academics were identified through their participation in intervention schemes to stimulate academic entrepreneurship. Notably, the development of their social capital was observed over the academic year 2002 to 2003. The academics were engaged with business plan competitions, proof-of-concept funding and fellowship schemes. Focus on this set of entrepreneurs provided a degree of homogeneity that helped control for other factors outside the study's focus. Academics were interviewed at the start and end of the academic year, during which the intervention schemes were in place.

Construct validity was considered by comparing the views of the academics with the views of TTOs, heads of school and the examination of sources of secondary data. Sources included records of commercialization performance of the participating schools, curriculum vitae of the academics and evaluation reports from the various intervention schemes. Time sequences relating to certain key events were observed directly by one researcher during attendance at workshops and informal meetings. The interview transcripts, documentary evidence and notes on opinions of potential causality were read and re-read as data were collected. Emerging themes were refined as this process progressed.

5.2.3 Findings

5.2.3.1 Patterns of Social Capital Development

There were consistent differences in human and social capital between entrepreneurs that managed to progress their ventures during the year and those that did not, irrespective of the entrepreneurial environment. Specific human capital, such as PBOE, appeared to relate to differences in social capital and venture development. At the start of the study, nascent entrepreneurs had, on average, only developed two types of network ties. In contrast, novice entrepreneurs had developed nine types of network ties, and habitual entrepreneurs had developed thirteen types of network ties. An analogous pattern was observed when comparing network structure and governance between different types of entrepreneurs.

74   *Networking and Resource Orchestration*

In contrast to PBOE, prior industrial experience did not appear to relate to venture growth. A notable observation emerged in comparing entrepreneurs with similar levels of PBOE; the academic discipline of the entrepreneur was related to venture development rate.

5.2.3.2   *Nascent Entrepreneurs: Network Structure, Content and Governance*

In relation to network structure, for nascent academic entrepreneurs, the two most commonly used categories of actor were research colleagues and IP/legal firms. A greater diversity of ties was developed during the course of the year, including university proof-of-concept funds and business angels.

With regard to network content, the nascent academic entrepreneurs perceived all of the categories of actors they used to be useful, with the exception of the TTO. Advice received from the TTO was perceived to have less value than that received from other sources. In contrast, nascent academic entrepreneurs were more complimentary regarding the opportunity recognition advice they received from academic colleagues who had direct commercialization experience. Relating to network governance, nascent academic entrepreneurs appeared inspired by more experienced colleagues but frustrated by the lack of assistance provided by the TTO.

5.2.3.3   *Novice Entrepreneurs: Network Structure, Content and Governance*

In relation to network structure, the novice entrepreneurs had in place a greater number and variety of network ties at the start of the year of study than the nascent entrepreneurs. They were seen to develop a greater number of ties during the year of study. The most commonly used actors with whom new ties were developed were large firms. Further, the next most popular were finance providers in the form of government grants and equity investment.

With regard to network content, novice entrepreneurs supported the views of the nascent entrepreneurs in relation to the perceived high value of advice received from research colleagues. However, novice entrepreneurs also saw value in resources gained from a wider diversity of resources than the nascent entrepreneurs. Novice entrepreneurs gave greater credence to the assistance provided by the TTO than the nascent entrepreneurs. Further, novice entrepreneurs were consistently positive regarding providers of proof of concept funding resources they gained from actors within large firms, but they were less positive regarding the advice received from regional business advisors.

Relating to network governance, all novice entrepreneurs had built a relationship with the TTO by the start of the year. However, entrepreneurs who had developed their ventures from entrepreneurial commitment to gaining credibility then used the established relationship with the TTO to help connect them to new network ties. These entrepreneurs also utilized their research contacts to appropriate business resources. The novice entrepreneurs' broader social networks enabled them to reap rewards in terms of critical resources for their ventures. They all built effective relationships and credibility with the TTO. The latter relationship was utilized to gain access to legal advice and additional resources through the TTO extended network. Through this 'brokering' role, the TTO helped bridge a structural hole by drafting formal partnership agreements with potential industry partners, from whom novice entrepreneurs gained proof of concept funding, facilities and industry knowledge. Discipline of study was important. The seven novice entrepreneurs progressing to the stage of gaining credibility for their ventures were situated in schools of mechanical engineering, electronic engineering, food science and chemistry. Those who did not progress beyond entrepreneurial commitment were situated in schools of bioscience and pharmacy.

5.2.3.4 Habitual Entrepreneurs: Network Structure, Content and Governance

In relation to network structure, the habitual entrepreneurs exhibited the greatest number of ties at the start of the year. During the year, habitual entrepreneurs were surprisingly focused and consistent regarding the new ties they built. They were all engaged in building ties to large firms, and three of them were also building ties to SMEs. Equally, they were all developing new ties to equity investors, either business angels or venture capitalists. However, they were active in seeking professional venture growth advice, with three habitual entrepreneurs seeking surrogate entrepreneurs, two seeking professional venture management firms and two building ties to science parks.

With regard to network content, habitual entrepreneurs proposed that their most valuable ties were those to the providers of industry knowledge, business development knowledge and technical knowledge. Surrogate entrepreneurs were rated the most highly by the two habitual entrepreneurs engaged with them. A surprising result was the continued value seen in research colleagues by habitual entrepreneurs. These ties were seen to provide credibility to the venture through the reputation of academia and also through providing a source of new technologies to retain its competitive position. Yet, habitual entrepreneurs were scathing of local government advisors and government support initiatives. The habitual entrepreneurs interviewed from universities where the TTO had a strong track record argued that they succeeded despite of rather than because of the TTO.

Relating to network governance, habitual entrepreneurs were prolific networkers. They were active in maintaining their established relationships. In addition, they were engaged with building new ties with providers of business development knowledge, equity finance and industry knowledge/ potential customers.

Habitual entrepreneurs appeared to have broader social networks than their less experienced colleagues. However, it was the nature of such ties that was important. Habitual entrepreneurs appeared to focus upon ties to gain

76 Networking and Resource Orchestration

equity finance and venture development knowledge to rapidly grow their early stage ventures. They also built new ties to researchers to identify new opportunities and match technologies to their knowledge of industry needs.

5.2.3.5 Development of Propositions

Based upon the evidence presented in the previous section, the paper set out a framework (see Table 5.1), and developed propositions to guide future research. Propositions are presented below relating to network structure, content and governance.

5.2.3.5.1. NETWORK STRUCTURE

The evidence gathered indicated that habitual entrepreneurs with a successful track record of raising equity investment overcame discipline-related barriers to raising finance. This suggested that PBOE can help gain credibility within industries that have such limitations regarding time to market and appropriability regime. These findings suggested the following propositions:

> *Proposition 5.1: Nascent and novice academic entrepreneurs from engineering and material science disciplines are more likely to build new ties outside the scientific research network than those based in biological sciences and pharmacy [see Table 5.1, column 1, rows 1 and 2].*
>
> *Proposition 5.2: Technology-based academic entrepreneurs with PBOE are more likely to build new ties outside the scientific research network regardless of their academic discipline [see Table 5.1, column 1. row 3].*

5.2.3.5.2. NETWORK CONTENT

Different types of entrepreneurs typically gained different types of resources from their network ties during the year of study (see Table 5.1, column 2). Nascent entrepreneurs exhibited an inability to conceptualize how their technologies can be best applied to satisfy a real industry need, finding it difficult to engage with the TTO, let alone actors external to the university. In contrast, novice entrepreneurs were typically engaged at the next stage of venture development, where they were seeking proof of concept funding and industry knowledge regarding potential customers and their unmet needs (see Table 5, column 2, cell 2). Here, a lack of PBOE posed problems in gaining credibility outside the university. Different again, habitual entrepreneurs were typically engaged in raising equity finance and gaining management knowledge to help grow their ventures, thereby overcoming the potential barrier of reorientation (see Table 5.1, column 2, cell 3). The authors proposed that different types of entrepreneurs reported differing efficacy at gaining resources. Habitual entrepreneurs appeared more likely to

Table 5.1 Summary Findings of Social Capital Development Between Different Types of Entrepreneurs

Type of Entrepreneur	Focus of Social Network Structure Developed (Column 1)	Network Content Gained (Column 2)	Network Governance Issues (Column 3)	Typical Stage of Venture Development After One Year (Column 4)
Nascent Entrepreneur (row 1)	More experienced academic colleagues Engineering & materials science more able to build ties outside scientific network	Advice on recognizing opportunities and IP protection but difficulties in engaging with TTO	Experienced structural holes to industry networks Links with more experienced academic entrepreneurs & TTO	Opportunity recognition Entrepreneurial commitment
Novice Entrepreneur (row 2)	TTO Industry networks Engineering & materials science more able to build outside ties	Proof of concept funding Market knowledge Identification of potential customers Materials science & engineering disciplines use TTO & broker deals with industry contacts	TTO acts as broker managing formal legal agreements to funding bodies and industry contacts especially for engineering and materials science	Entrepreneurial commitment Gaining credibility
Habitual Entrepreneur (row 3)	Academic colleagues Equity funders Professional managers Not discipline constrained	New technologies Equity finance building on prior success Venture management knowledge Going beyond TTO	Developing direct 'open-ended' relationships based upon trust to replace TTO & government advisers	Gaining credibility Venture growth

Source: Authors.

78   *Networking and Resource Orchestration*

gain initial equity finance than nascent entrepreneurs. This is possibly due to prior experience or established social capital. Equally, habitual entrepreneurs appeared more likely to gain management knowledge from surrogate entrepreneurs than novice entrepreneurs. Another observed distinction between different types of entrepreneurs was in relation to the perceived value of the TTO. The different types of entrepreneurs shared similar views of the value of one type of actor, their research colleagues. These findings suggested the following propositions:

> *Proposition 5.3: Novice academic entrepreneurs from engineering and the material sciences are more likely to gain proof of concept funding and market and industry knowledge using the university technology transfer office than habitual and nascent entrepreneurs [see Table 5.1, column 2, rows 1 and 2].*
>
> *Proposition 5.4: Nascent and novice academic entrepreneurs are more likely to gain management resources from their research colleagues than are habitual academic entrepreneurs [see Table 5.1, column 2, rows 1 and 2].*
>
> *Proposition 5.5: Academic entrepreneur PBOE is more important than more generic industrial experience in gaining management knowledge and equity finance from network actors external to the university [see Table 5.1, column 2, row 3].*
>
> *Proposition 5.6: Habitual academic entrepreneurs are more likely to gain technical resources from their research colleagues than are nascent and novice academic entrepreneurs [see Table 5.1, column 2, row 3].*

5.2.3.5.3. NETWORK GOVERNANCE

Clear differences were observed between the methods used by different types of entrepreneurs to maintain existing ties, and to build new ones. Nascent entrepreneurs were typically limited to building ties within the university network, with more experienced academic entrepreneurs and TTOs. Novice entrepreneurs were more effective at building ties outside the university through attending networking events held by local government agencies, and through brokerage activities managed by the TTO. Habitual entrepreneurs built relationships very differently. They tended to have already worked closely with research colleagues, TTOs, local government advisors and proof of concept funders. Through this interaction, they were active in strengthening useful relationships and finding alternatives to less effective ones. For instance, because some habitual entrepreneurs had found TTO and government advisors to be obstructive, they had built new relationships with professional legal advisors, to replace the TTO, and with large and small firms, to replace the government advisors. Habitual entrepreneurs were, in addition, more strategic regarding the new ties they wished to build.

They were in a better position to understand their partners' needs, and to identify new providers to meet their goals. These relationships were typified by the parties agreeing to share the risks and rewards. These findings suggested the following propositions:

> *Proposition 5.7: Nascent and novice academic entrepreneurs from engineering and material sciences are more likely to develop joint ventures with large and small firms, brokered by the university TTO than those based in biological sciences or pharmacy [see Table 5.1, column 3, rows 1 and 2].*
> *Proposition 5.8: Habitual academic entrepreneurs are more likely to build open-ended relationships based on trust with equity financiers through repeated interactions than novice or nascent academic entrepreneurs [see Table 5.1, column 3, row 3].*

5.2.3.5.4. VENTURE DEVELOPMENT

The authors observed significant differences in the stage of venture development typically attained by the different types of academic entrepreneur during the year. Further, the authors proposed that differences in social capital developed by habitual entrepreneurs with actors external to the university helped them to gain credibility for their ventures. This finding suggested the following proposition:

> *Proposition 5.9: Habitual academic entrepreneurs are more likely to overcome the critical juncture of gaining credibility for their new ventures than novice or nascent academic entrepreneurs.*

5.2.4 Conclusions and Implications

A number of structural holes (Burt, 1982, 1992) were identified that appeared to constrain the development of nascent and novice entrepreneurs. First, a structural hole existed between scientific research networks and industry networks that constrained opportunity recognition. Second, structural holes between academics and financiers and professional managers appeared to constrain novice entrepreneurs' ability to gain entrepreneurial commitment, venture credibility and venture reorientation. Here, there appeared to be no obvious substitute for direct business ownership experience. Habitual entrepreneurs were found to have gained this knowledge though building network ties with equity financiers, professional managers, industry partners and potential customers. Yet, it appeared that few nascent and novice entrepreneurs had built these relationships.

A surprising commonality was the consistently high value in which all entrepreneurs regarded their relationships with their research colleagues. Less experienced entrepreneurs valued their research colleagues as potential role models. However, more experienced entrepreneurs valued their colleagues as potential sources of technological opportunities.

For policy-makers and practitioners, the authors suggested there may need to be development of focused policies that meet the needs of the different types of entrepreneur, and entrepreneurs from different academic disciplines. Presented case evidence regarding the role of experienced colleagues provided a distinctive policy insight in the context of academic habitual entrepreneurs in contrast to habitual entrepreneurs from a commercial environment. The authors suggested that TTOs seeking to stimulate academic entrepreneurship might usefully attempt to develop systematic ways of drawing on this experience.

5.3 Resource Orchestration

5.3.1 Gaps in the Knowledge Base and Research Questions

While the motivations of portfolio entrepreneurs to engage in small business group formation have been extensively researched, the micro-processes by which they obtain and leverage resources and capabilities across a portfolio of ventures to exploit new opportunities over time have been a black box. Resource orchestration theory explores the processes by which managers accumulate, combine and exploit resources to support current opportunities, while developing future opportunities to achieve a competitive advantage (Sirmon and Hitt, 2003). Different processes may be involved in orchestrating resources across a portfolio of ventures to develop portfolio-level capabilities and synergies when pursuing opportunities. Accordingly, Baerts et al., (2016) explored the following research question:

• *What are specific processes of resource orchestration across a portfolio of ventures aimed at exploring and exploiting new opportunities?*

Baerts et al. used a single interpretive case study approach to build a theory. An iterative process was employed, involving rich narrative accounts of both successful and failed activities of a portfolio male entrepreneur in the digital web industry.

5.3.2 Theoretical Background

Resource orchestration practices include the processes of structuring the portfolio of resources (i.e., acquiring, accumulating and divesting), bundling resources to build capabilities (i.e., stabilizing, enriching and pioneering) and leveraging capabilities in the marketplace (i.e., mobilizing, co-ordinating and deploying) to create value (Sirmon et al., 2007). Resource orchestration poses specific challenges for entrepreneurial firms. Emergent entrepreneurial firms need to orchestrate resources to support their nascent business model under conditions of uncertainty (Rutherford et al., 2003). During exploration attempts, experimental resource allocation patterns are frequently used to identify valuable and potentially rare operational and product configurations to obtain a competitive advantage. As the firm starts to grow, resource orchestration activities will shift towards structuring the organization, such as implementing formalized procedures, and adding a managerial hierarchy in order to facilitate exploitation.

Resource orchestration theory has mostly focused on within firm processes that enable firms to explore and exploit opportunities. However, different processes may apply across a group of ventures being developed by a portfolio entrepreneur.

5.3.3 Methodology and Data

Baerts et al. adopted a longitudinal single-case study approach based on the narrative of a portfolio entrepreneur to be able to develop an understanding of how resource orchestration processes unfold as the entrepreneur's portfolio of ventures developed. The case involved the growth of a Belgian entrepreneur's portfolio of firms, including the development of a digital web agency and related ventures starting in 2006. Between 2006 and 2013, the entrepreneur was simultaneously involved in nine independent ventures, of which two ceased to exist. One venture is a holding company supporting a network of eight small independent ventures.

Data collection was conducted over 2.5 years. From early 2011 to mid-2013, data was collected on developments between 2006 and 2013 in the entrepreneur's portfolio and the digital industry. Initial desk research started in 2011, concentrating on developing understanding of the evolution of the web development industry and the identification of market players. To gain additional information, seven industry experts were also interviewed. The primary data collection method involved semi-structured interviews with the entrepreneur and his three business partners, conducted in three interview rounds between early 2011 and mid-2013. All interviews were conducted by at least two individuals, increasing confidence in the reliability of interpretation. The interviews lasted approximately one to 2.5 hours and were recorded and subsequently transcribed verbatim. This information was complemented with secondary data from company reports, almost 2,500 blogs, financial accounting data, press articles, company presentations and the websites of each venture.

Moving back and forth in an iterative fashion between the qualitative data and relevant theoretical arguments, a data structure was developed and translated into a theoretical model. Using Nvivo to code the interview transcripts, the analysis was conducted in three major steps following the guidelines by Gioia et al. (2013) relating to creating categories and first-order codes, integrating first-order codes and creating second-order constructs and building a grounded theoretical framework.

82 Networking and Resource Orchestration

5.3.4 Findings

Exploring the processes underlying resource orchestration and capability development across a portfolio of ventures enabled the identification of eight resource orchestration sub-processes (i.e., accessing, multiplying, redeploying, incubating, decoupling, aligning, complementing and pruning) that are distinct, yet complementary, to the resource orchestration sub-processes (i.e., acquiring, accumulating, divesting, stabilizing, enriching, pioneering, mobilizing, co-ordinating and deploying) discussed in prior literature on value creation through resource management. Because of a lack of fit between these sub-processes and existing theoretical constructs on resource orchestration, they were grouped into three aggregate dimensions or general resource orchestration processes new to resource orchestration theory (i.e., sharing, transforming and harmonizing). All single-firm resource orchestration sub-processes previously identified by Sirmon et al. (2007) were also identified.

5.3.4.1 Sharing Resources and Capabilities

Analysis showed that three of the across-portfolio sub-processes identified referred to sharing existing resources and capabilities across the portfolio. By sharing resources and capabilities, the entrepreneur brought about synergies across the portfolio of ventures when setting up new business activities. Specifically, the entrepreneur engaged in accessing, multiplying and redeploying resources and capabilities across ventures. First, when sharing resources and capabilities, the entrepreneur engaged in the sub-process of accessing a pool of existing resources and capabilities across the portfolio. This process occurred by documenting and archiving information with the intent to share such information across the portfolio of ventures. Second, in order to be able to diffuse resources and capabilities across his portfolio, the entrepreneur engaged in a sub-process of multiplying (i.e., creating fungible resources and capabilities).

The entrepreneur developed resources or capabilities so that they could be accessed by multiple ventures. First, the entrepreneur created an umbrella of support services. Second, by developing fungible resources and capabilities, the entrepreneur was able to reproduce and transfer resources and capabilities to make them accessible across the portfolio. To engage in the sub-process of multiplying, the entrepreneur learned to make sure that the resources and capabilities s/he wished to diffuse across his portfolio could actually be repurposed from one venture to another. Third, when sharing the resource and capability set available across his portfolio, the entrepreneur engaged in the sub-process of redeploying certain resources or capabilities across ventures depending on the specific needs of these ventures. In particular, three types of resource orchestration actions were used to effect redeployment (i.e., exchanging customer portfolios, moving champions and employees around and moving financial resources around).

5.3.4.2 Transforming Resources and Capabilities

Two of the eight resource orchestration sub-processes, incubating and decoupling, refer to nurturing resource and capability configurations to prepare for the exploration of new market opportunities. Notably, the entrepreneur engaged in the process of transforming heterogeneous resources and capabilities from across the portfolio into independent, self-sufficient ventures.

The entrepreneur engaged in a process of supporting and testing configurations of heterogeneous resources and capabilities from across the portfolio (i.e., the sub-process of incubating a new venture). For instance, after having selected a new business idea that emerged from within his ventures, the entrepreneur infused the necessary knowledge and allocated the necessary resources and capabilities to support its transformation in a new venture. This enabled testing of the new capability configuration to prove its potential to become a new venture by independently generating revenues. The champion developing the new activity received resources involving support processes and structures from the entrepreneur at the portfolio level.

Second, when the entrepreneur felt s/he had found a profitable resource and capability configuration to exploit a new market opportunity, s/he decoupled the self-sufficient configuration from the supporting firm (i.e., the incubator). Subsequently, the entrepreneur invested additional resources so that the venture could independently develop its core capabilities to fully exploit the market.

Incubating complemented the previously identified process of pioneering (Sirmon et al., 2007) a new capability within a single firm. This incubation allowed a new venture to develop its core capability. However, whereas pioneering relates to the development of a specific capability in a single-firm context, incubating refers to the development of an entire configuration to tackle a market opportunity using heterogeneous resources and capabilities from across the portfolio. Also, decoupling represents an essential part of incubating, although it is different from the divesting process identified by Sirmon et al. (2007). This is because the newly developed capability configuration remains part of the portfolio and ultimately has the potential to strengthen the competitive positioning of the overall portfolio.

5.3.4.3 Harmonizing Resource and Capability Configurations

A resource orchestration process helps to balance resource and capability configurations across the portfolio of ventures in order to create value for customers and owners (i.e., the process of harmonizing configurations across the portfolio). Through three specific sub-processes, aligning, complementing and pruning, the entrepreneur was able to design a value-creating portfolio of resource and capability configurations.

First, the entrepreneur engaged in the sub-process of aligning. This related to adjusting configurations using the resources and capabilities available from elsewhere in the portfolio according to the needs of particular growing ventures at different stages of their development in line with his experience of what other ventures required at that stage. The entrepreneur created synergies and facilitated the transfer of knowledge and practices in a timely manner. Fine-grained analysis revealed the following three types of resource orchestration actions through which aligning took place. They were balancing entrepreneurial and managerial capabilities, aligning corporate structures and processes with growth and adjusting financial resources to growth. The aligning process extended theory on resource orchestration by showing how a portfolio entrepreneur can realize synergies across the portfolio by readjusting the capability configurations within a specific venture in line with his experience of the configurations available in ventures ahead in the growth curve elsewhere in the portfolio.

Second, the entrepreneur harmonized configurations of resources and capabilities across the portfolio to explore and exploit market opportunities, through the sub-process of complementing. The sub-process of complementing entailed the exploitation of value-creating synergies across the portfolio using complementary capability configurations. Two types of resource orchestration actions facilitated complementing. The entrepreneur integrated complementary capability configurations from across the portfolio on a temporary basis to explore and exploit complex market opportunities. By adopting a long-term perspective, this juxtaposition of complementary capability configurations across the portfolio also led to value creation. Doing so allowed the entrepreneur to explore and exploit more and different market opportunities simultaneously. Complementing allowed the entrepreneur to effectively and flexibly pursue an entrepreneurial strategy by responding to multiple market opportunities using the same resources and capability configurations available to him.

Third, an important element of the entrepreneur's efforts to harmonize configurations of resources and capabilities across the portfolio was exhibited by pruning resources and capabilities. Such a pruning sub-process consisted of disentangling poorly fitting resource and capability configurations, with the aim to recover resources and capabilities across the portfolio. The entrepreneur engaged in two specific resource orchestration actions. First, when a specific resource and capability configuration displayed a lack of fit, the entrepreneur could decide to discontinue the venture. Pruning also includes a further distinctive sub-process that occurred across the portfolio consisting of releasing capabilities and resources tied up in a venture, back into the portfolio of firms, with the intent to reuse them and create value across the portfolio. Whereas the divesting aspect of pruning consisted of the irreversible liquidation of a resource or capability from the firm, and hence the portfolio, the second aspect of pruning referred to the extraction of resources and capabilities from failed ventures, with the aim of recuperating them as much as possible elsewhere in the portfolio.

5.3.5 Conclusions and Implications

This analysis contributed to theory on portfolio entrepreneurship in several ways. First, the study identified new insights that portfolio entrepreneurship requires the continuing generation of entrepreneurial opportunities to be complemented by the development of synergies across the portfolio of ventures for those new opportunities to be explored and exploited. Second, the findings suggested that simply extending existing resource orchestration theory to across firms/portfolio entrepreneurship contexts would miss important distinctive mechanisms in the resource orchestration process. This study extended theory beyond resource orchestration within firms by identifying eight sub-processes that occur across firms and which lead to the development of synergies among the existing resources and capabilities available in an entire venture portfolio. These synergies are important because the new markets that the portfolio entrepreneur was entering were characterized by uncertainty. The portfolio entrepreneur tried to reduce this uncertainty by drawing on the resources and capabilities from his previous ventures. Third, the results highlighted the central role of the portfolio entrepreneur in diffusing resources and capabilities across a portfolio of ventures. As a portfolio entrepreneur's ability to steer resource orchestration evolves, s/he may develop an ability to identify, create and facilitate the diffusion of knowledge and capabilities. The ability to steer resource orchestration processes across ventures may, therefore, be viewed as a critical boundary condition to explain the successful exploitation of a portfolio of ventures, and may be an important factor in explaining organizational outcomes (Wales et al., 2013).

Additional research might usefully explore how the co-ordination processes examined operate with portfolio entrepreneurs in other contexts. Research might also explore the optimal size and scope of a portfolio of ventures in relation to capabilities for orchestration. Further research is needed to empirically determine and quantify the economic benefits of resource orchestration across firms in dynamic environments.

5.4 Summary

This chapter has summarized two theory-building themes. With respect to their networks, the research identified important differences between nascent, novice and habitual academic entrepreneurs regarding their network structure, content and governance. Habitual academic entrepreneurs demonstrated more ties in their networks than nascent or novice entrepreneurs. With respect to network content, habitual entrepreneurs were more likely than the other two types of entrepreneur to have built valuable ties with the providers of industry knowledge, business development knowledge and technical knowledge, notably with surrogate entrepreneurs. Regarding network governance, habitual entrepreneurs were both more active in maintaining established relationships as well as being engaged with building new

86 *Networking and Resource Orchestration*

ties with providers of business development knowledge, equity finance and industry knowledge/potential customers than nascent or novice entrepreneurs. With respect to resource orchestration, the research shows that there are important differences between these processes within large corporations compared with those that take place across a portfolio of ventures.

5.5 Reflection Questions

In Chapter 5, entrepreneur PBOE was assumed to be a resource that could be mobilized, shaped and orchestrated. Please consider the following reflection questions:

- *Compare and contrast the networks of novice and experienced academic entrepreneurs.*
- *Why might the academic discipline affect the networks of novice and experienced academic entrepreneurs?*
- *Why are universities' technology transfer officers highly limited in their ability to provide network links for habitual academic entrepreneurs?*
- *To what extent is it the depth rather than breadth of the networks of habitual academic entrepreneurs that are more important?*
- *What differences might be expected in the resource orchestration processes of novice, serial and portfolio entrepreneurs?*
- *What different challenges in resource orchestration might you expect portfolio entrepreneurs to encounter in sectors outside fast-moving IT industries?*

6 Opportunity Discovery and Creation

6.1 Learning Objectives and Overview

In this chapter, key elements of opportunity 'discovery theory' and 'creation theory' are briefly summarized. Themes relating to innovation and opportunity creation are then highlighted. A brief summary of the opportunity-based conceptualization of entrepreneurship is then presented. This chapter reviews two quantitative theory-testing studies relating to opportunity discovery, and one quantitative theory-testing study relating to opportunity discovery.

The first article focusing upon opportunity discovery behaviour relates to the Scotland context. This study builds upon insights from human capital theory, Reuber and Fischer's (1999) 'stock' and 'streams' of entrepreneur experience perspective, and Schein's (1978) career anchor views. The article explored whether serial and portfolio entrepreneurs with PBOE and the 'entrepreneurship career anchor' would report different opportunity identification activities than novice entrepreneurs with no PBOE and the 'autonomy career anchor'. Further, it was assumed that portfolio entrepreneurs involved in multiple ventures simultaneously and engaged in a process of dynamic and fluid entrepreneurial churn would identify more business opportunities than serial or novice entrepreneurs. Non-parametric statistical analysis was conducted to identify differences between types of entrepreneurs.

The second article relates to the Great Britain context. This study builds upon insights from cognition and motivation theories as well as schema theory, prototype theory and expert information processing theory. This article explored within a multivariate statistical framework the link between the nature and extent of an entrepreneurs PBOE and the number of business opportunities identified, in a given period. Further, it explored the link between the nature and extent of entrepreneurs PBOE in relation to the innovativeness of the latest business opportunities exploited.

The third article focuses on opportunity creation and relates to the Ghana context. Entrepreneurs can create business opportunities by investing in innovation. This study builds upon insights from the RBV of the firm and human capital theory in relation to private firms introducing several types

88 *Opportunity Discovery*

of innovation. A broad definition of innovation was employed that considered technological innovations, as well as new work practices and workforce organization, new sources of supply or materials, the exploitation of new markets or means of reaching these markets and new administration and office systems. This article explored within a multivariate statistical framework whether experienced entrepreneurs measured in relation to four measures of PBOE (i.e., duration of PBOE, habitual entrepreneur, serial entrepreneur and portfolio entrepreneur) were more likely to engage in innovation activity.

6.2 Opportunity Discovery and Creation Theories

6.2.1 *Key Elements of Opportunity Discovery and Creation Theories*

Key elements of the discovery and creation opportunity theory perspectives are summarized in Table 6.1. Opportunity-based conceptualizations of entrepreneurship (Ardichvili et al., 2003; Davidsson, 2006; Shane, 2003; Shane and Venkataraman, 2000) have been developed. The importance of

Table 6.1 Opportunity Discovery Versus Opportunity Creation

	Discovery Theory	*Creation Theory*
Nature of opportunities	Opportunities exist independent of the entrepreneur [exogenous; objective]	Opportunities do not exist independently of the entrepreneur [endogenous; socially constructed]
Nature of entrepreneur	Differs in some important ways from non-entrepreneurs, ex ante	May or may not differ from non-entrepreneurs ex ante; differences may emerge ex post dependent on path taken
Nature of decision-making context	Risky [can collect information to estimate probability of outcomes]	Uncertain [cannot collect information to estimate probability of outcomes]
Typical questions	Are entrepreneurs that form and exploit opportunities really different than individuals who do not? How do entrepreneurs estimate the riskiness of their decisions?	How does action by entrepreneurs create opportunities? Are there differences between entrepreneurs who form and exploit opportunities and those that do not cause or effect entrepreneurial action? How can entrepreneurs use incremental, iterative and inductive processes to make decisions?

Source: Alvarez and Barney (2007)

Opportunity Discovery 89

the entrepreneur 'alertness' skill was highlighted in the pioneering work of Kirzner (1973). According to Kirzner, the prospect of monopoly profits motivates people to search for information, and the collection and processing of information by an entrepreneur enables them to 'spot' business opportunities (Casson, 1990). Kirzner does not explain where change comes from in an economy (i.e., disequilibrium—the gap in the market). Some entrepreneurs, therefore, discover business opportunities by being 'alert' to gaps in the market. Such alertness involves noticing opportunities that previously have been ignored or not noticed. Alertness to business opportunities can be exhibited without searching for them. An entrepreneur's mindset can be composed of alertness which is supported by information that facilitates the rapid discovery and exploitation of business opportunities, even those that are highly uncertain relating to innovative products or services. Imaginative and innovative entrepreneurs can mobilize their experience, subjective understanding and current information to identify business opportunities (Witt, 1998).

Kirzner (1973) recognized that there are constant shifts in the demand and supply for products/services. By engaging in an information search, some entrepreneurs can enhance their alertness to 'gaps in the market' (i.e., market disequilibrium) relating to products demanded by consumers not being supplied, or not being supplied at an appropriate price. Notably, Kirzner (1973) recognized that some people accumulate experience and knowledge. He suggested that the possession of additional knowledge by some people provides opportunities for creative business opportunity discovery. Kirzner claimed that entrepreneurs engaged in information search may 'notice' how to exploit the gap in the market, for example, through arbitrage. Entrepreneurs can collect and join information together, which can lead to the 'developmental approach' to opportunity identification. The identification and pursuit of an opportunity can also lead to the collection and analysis of additional data and business opportunities (i.e., shadow options) (McGrath, 1999). People who have the ability to collect and process information may record a spiral of opportunity identification and exploitation.

6.2.2 *Innovation and Opportunity Creation*

Schumpeter (1934) recognized the importance of entrepreneur imagination and creativity in relation to the creation of business opportunities. He suggested that entrepreneurs are the creators and catalysts of dynamic discrete change due to the introduction of radically new technological processes or products. Schumpeterian innovations are discrete and substantial and are linked to the following five sources of significant change (i.e., new combinations):

- The introduction of a new good (or an improvement in the quality of an existing good);
- The opening of a new market, in particular, an export market in a new territory;

90   *Opportunity Discovery*

- The conquest of a new source of supply of raw materials or half-manufactured goods;
- New method of production as yet unproven; and
- The creation of a new type of industrial organization, particularly, the formation of a trust or some other type of monopoly.

Radical innovation can lead to formation of new firms as well as the closure of out-of-date firms. This productive churn was termed 'creative destruction'. Schumpeter (1934) has provided a useful concept of entrepreneurship focusing on 'quality' business ideas that can act as a catalyst fostering economic development.

Marshall (1920) also recognized that the entrepreneur is central to the promotion of economic progress. He suggested that a key function of the entrepreneur is knowledge accumulation, co-ordination and leverage that can promote novelty and discontinuity. Knowledge can be leveraged to introduce 'incremental innovation' (i.e., less resistance to incremental change such as application or extensions of established routines) rather than radical innovation.

There is a need for studies to specifically focus on the 'quality' of opportunities—particularly those with potentially wider societal contributions (i.e., wealth creation and taxation and job generation potential) (Zahra, 1993). The innovativeness of an opportunity is viewed as a surrogate measure of potential value (or wealth creating potential) (Fiet, 2002; Shane, 2000).

6.2.3 *Opportunity-Based Conceptualization of Entrepreneurship*

Shane and Venkataraman (2000) developed an opportunity-based conceptualization of entrepreneurship relating to the identification and exploitation of opportunities. Their approach differs from other frameworks. Notably, they focus on the existence, discovery and exploitation of opportunities; they examine the influence of individuals and opportunities, rather than environmental antecedents and consequences; and they consider a broader framework than firm creation. They focus upon the actions of individuals and the insights from individuals to firms and institutions via modes of exploitation.

6.3 Opportunity Discovery: Nature of Experience

6.3.1 *Gaps in the Knowledge Base and Research Questions*

The article by Westhead et al., (2005a) extended Reuber and Fischer's (1999) entrepreneurs 'stock' and 'stream' of experience conceptual framework with regard to an individual's experience of owning an equity stake in one or more private firm(s). This framework was summarized in Chapter 1 (see Figure 1.1). The 'stock' of entrepreneur experience relates to both the depth and breadth of experience accumulated at a point in time, whilst the 'stream' of entrepreneur experience relates to experience possessed over time. Previous studies have generally assumed that entrepreneurs are a homogeneous entity, and they have generally ignored issues relating to the 'stream' of entrepreneur experience. To address this gap, Westhead et al., (2005a) focused on the entrepreneur as the unit of analysis and focused upon the 'stream' of an entrepreneur's PBOE. They assumed that serial and portfolio entrepreneurs would exhibit different streams of experience relative to novice entrepreneurs. The authors extended Reuber and Fischer's (1999) conceptual framework by specifically focusing upon the role of PBOE reported by serial and portfolio entrepreneurs. Specifically, they explored differences in the decisions and actions (i.e., stream of experience) related to information search behaviour reported by novice, serial and portfolio entrepreneurs. The study was conducted in Scotland. Issues relating to the data collection process have been summarized in Section 3.3.3.1. Survey data was analysed using univariate statistical techniques. The following research question was explored:

- *What decisions and actions distinguish novice, serial and portfolio entrepreneurs from one another?*

6.3.2 Hypotheses Tested

The authors suggested that experienced entrepreneurs, drawing upon their specific human capital relating to PBOE, would have accumulated skills and experience that enables them to discover additional business opportunities. Schein (1978) raised the notion of a career anchor, which is the pattern of self-perceived talents, motives and values that guide, constrain, stabilize and integrate a person's career. Building on Schein's work, Katz (1994) suggests that entrepreneurs with an autonomy anchor are more likely to be driven by the desire to have freedom from control by others and to be involved in a venture one at a time. These serial entrepreneurs typically prefer sole proprietorships, which generally do not demonstrate substantial business growth. Conversely, individuals with an entrepreneurship anchor are more likely to be driven by the opportunity recognition process or wealth creation, as well as seeking business growth. They tend to be portfolio entrepreneurs who are involved in multiple ventures simultaneously. Rosa (1998) asserts that portfolio entrepreneurs engage in a process of dynamic and fluid entrepreneurial churn, which leads to the creation of new venture opportunities linked to their existing businesses. The authors assumed that in any given time period, portfolio entrepreneurs would identify more business opportunities than serial entrepreneurs. This discussion suggested the following hypotheses:

Hypothesis 6.1: *Novice, serial and portfolio entrepreneurs will report different opportunity identification activities.*

92   *Opportunity Discovery*

Hypothesis 6.2: *Portfolio entrepreneurs will identify more opportunities than novice or serial entrepreneurs.*

6.3.3 Findings

Seven statements relating to opportunity identification behaviour were presented to entrepreneurs. A five-point scoring system was employed, where a score of 1 suggested 'strongly agree', a score of 3 suggested 'neutral', whilst a score of 5 suggested 'strongly disagree'. Differences were detected between the responses made by the three types of entrepreneurs. Novice entrepreneurs reported significantly lower levels of agreement with the statement that 'new business opportunities often arise in connection with a solution to a specific problem' than serial or portfolio entrepreneurs. However, portfolio rather novice entrepreneurs were significantly more likely to report that 'I have special alertness or sensitivity towards spotting opportunities', and 'I enjoy just thinking about and/or looking for new business opportunities'. In addition, portfolio entrepreneurs were significantly more likely than novice or serial entrepreneurs to suggest that 'I would describe myself as opportunistic', and 'I can usually spot a real opportunity better than professional researchers/analysts'. Hypothesis 6.1 was supported.

Significant difference was detected between the three types of entrepreneurs with regard to the number of opportunities identified for creating or purchasing a business over the last five years. A larger proportion of novice entrepreneurs, compared with serial or portfolio entrepreneurs, had failed to identify (i.e., spot) any opportunities for creating or purchasing a business. Moreover, a larger proportion of serial entrepreneurs, rather than portfolio entrepreneurs, had failed to spot an opportunity. A larger proportion of portfolio entrepreneurs, rather than serial or novice entrepreneurs, had identified two or more opportunities. Hypothesis 6.2 was supported.

6.3.4 Conclusions and Implications

This article highlighted that the experience backgrounds of novice entrepreneurs may not be as appropriate as those reported by habitual entrepreneurs. Portfolio entrepreneurs were more likely than other types of entrepreneurs to express dimensions of entrepreneurial behaviour. This behaviour manifested itself in several ways. Portfolio entrepreneurs had the ability to spot more than one business opportunity. A larger proportion of portfolio entrepreneurs rather than serial or novice entrepreneurs had identified two or more business opportunities. Portfolio entrepreneurs were more likely than novice or serial entrepreneurs to report that they were 'opportunistic'. Moreover, portfolio entrepreneurs were more likely than other entrepreneurs to suggest that they could spot a real opportunity better than a professional analyst/researcher. Portfolio entrepreneurs, therefore, generally exhibited more proactive opportunity search behaviour.

6.4 Opportunity Discovery: Extent and Nature of Experience

6.4.1 Gaps in the Knowledge Base and Research Questions

Studies exploring the relationship between business ownership experience and outcomes have tended to focus on whether or not the entrepreneur has experience and/or the amount of experience (Baron and Ensley, 2006; Westhead and Wright, 1998). These studies have generally assumed that the *extent* of experience will be associated with superior outcomes. Experience can facilitate learning by providing an opportunity for feedback about past decisions (Bazerman, 1990). Due to delays or bias in feedback, however, individuals may be prone to errors when seeking to learning from experience (Northcraft and Neale, 1987). Studies have neglected to consider whether a there is a threshold of PBOE associated with superior opportunity identification and exploitation. The possibility of an optimal level of PBOE associated with superior business opportunity identification and exploitation outcomes has been ignored. Previous studies have also generally failed to make an explicit distinction between the *extent* and *nature* of PBOE. Studies have generally ignored how the nature of experience (i.e., whether past experience is associated with business failure or success) may impact on business opportunity identification and exploitation.

The article by Ucbasaran et al. (2009) reviewed below builds on cognitive and motivation theories that explore the role of experience in shaping individual cognition and subsequent behaviour. An individual's cognitive profile can shape how they handle complex information in order to identify and exploit business opportunities. This article was guided by insights from prototypes theories, expert information processing theories and heuristic information processing theories (Baron, 2004) that suggest an individual's cognitive profile can be shaped by experience. Moreover, the expert cognition literature recognizes that prior experience may improve performance but only up to a certain point. Notably, beyond a certain experience threshold, biases in thinking can retard subsequent entrepreneur behaviour (Baron and Henry, 2006). The general cognition literature suggests that the nature of the failure experience and the number of failure experiences (Brunstein and Gollwitzer, 1996) can shape subsequent behaviour. Consequently, this article also

94   *Opportunity Discovery*

considered how the success or failure of past business ownership experience (i.e., the nature of experience) influenced subsequent behaviour. Guided by insights from cognitive and motivation theories, the authors argue that opposing views on the effects of business failure experience may be reconciled by considering intervening factors such as whether failure relates to self-definitional goals, and the number of failures in an entrepreneur's business ownership portfolio. This article explored gaps in the research and policy knowledge base with regard to the two following research questions:

- *What is the nature of the relationship between an entrepreneur's business ownership experience (i.e., extent and nature of experience) and the number of opportunities for creating or purchasing a business identified in a given period?*
- *How does an entrepreneur's business ownership experience relate to the innovativeness of the opportunity exploited?*

6.4.2 Hypothesis Tested

Building upon insights from schema theory (Gaglio and Katz, 2001), prototype theory (Baron, 2004) and expert information processing theory (Lord and Maher, 1990), the authors suggested that habitual entrepreneurs relatively developed opportunity identification schema could direct their attention, expectations and interpretations of market stimuli. This could lead to the generation of business ideas (Gaglio, 1997) by habitual entrepreneurs who can 'connect the dots' relating to problems and solutions better than inexperienced novice entrepreneurs (Baron and Ensley, 2006).

Despite the assets of PBOE highlighted in Section 2.3 in Chapter 2, the relationship between experience and performance may plateau (Baron and Henry, 2006). Experienced individuals may perform no better or even worse than novices. The expertise literature suggests that performance plateaus unless individuals engage in deliberate practice. This is consistent with the domain of entrepreneurship, where some studies have failed to detect that habitual entrepreneurs perform better than novice entrepreneurs (Westhead and Wright, 1998).

Experienced habitual entrepreneurs, over their careers in business ownership, can accumulate several 'liabilities'. These liabilities may impair the subsequent behaviour of some habitual entrepreneurs. Guided by these insights, the authors assumed that at a low level of experience, entrepreneurs will identify few business opportunities. The number of business opportunities identified was expected first to increase as ownership experience increases and opportunity identification schemas develop. However, as the level of business ownership experience increases further, it was assumed that habitual entrepreneurs may become increasingly prone to decision-making biases that could retard business opportunity identification. A linear relationship between business ownership experience and subsequent business opportunity identification should not be assumed. This discussion suggested the following hypothesis:

Hypothesis 6.3: *There will be an inverse U-shaped relationship between an entrepreneur's business ownership experience and the number of opportunities identified in a given period.*

The innovativeness of an opportunity is viewed as an indicator of its potential value (or wealth creating potential) (Fiet, 2002; Shane, 2000). Innovation is viewed as an important feature of entrepreneurial opportunities (Schumpeter, 1934), but the innovativeness of an opportunity can vary. At the individual level of analysis, there is scant evidence relating to why and how some individuals identify more innovative opportunities than others. This study provided fresh evidence relating to the link between an entrepreneur's experience and the nature of the latest opportunity exploited.

Scholars argue that creativity is the result of the convergence of multiple forces, with knowledge being an important factor. The content (or amount) of knowledge as well as the structure and organization of that knowledge can be important. As discussed above, experience contributes to the development of schemas. These schemas provide a framework for recognizing and evaluating information relevant to an opportunity. When schemas become richer with experience, they facilitate quicker and more effective information processing (Lord and Maher, 1990). This, in turn, reduces the burden on cognitive processing, allowing greater concentration on novel and unique information. Habitual entrepreneurs with relatively more developed knowledge structures may identify more innovative opportunities.

The liabilities of experience should not be ignored. Schema of experienced individuals may allow them to process information in an effortless and automatic manner. The latter schemas may be useful for routine activities, but they may not encourage novel activities. By directing the individual's attention to information relevant to their underlying knowledge, a well-developed schema can allow an entrepreneur to identify opportunities related to their knowledge base (Baron, 2004). On the downside, some individuals solely drawing upon existing schema will fail to notice, encode and remember information that is inconsistent with the existing schema. Experienced individuals who become mechanical can miss new pieces of information or ignore new connections (Rabin, 1998). PBOE beyond a certain level may encourage entrepreneurs to exploit less innovative opportunities. This discussion suggested the following hypothesis:

Hypothesis 6.4: *There will be an inverse U-shaped relationship between an entrepreneur's PBOE and the innovativeness of the latest opportunity exploited.*

96   *Opportunity Discovery*

The nature (or quality) of PBOE needs to be considered. One aspect of prior experience relates to whether that experience was associated with success or failure. People who have failed in the past may be become less motivated, which may influence the number of business opportunities identified and the innovativeness of the latest exploited opportunities.

There is no widely agreed definition of business failure, and it can be defined in a number of ways. In financial terms, business failure occurs when a fall in revenues and/or rise in expenses are of such magnitude that the firm becomes insolvent and is unable to attract new debt or equity funding; consequently, the firm cannot continue to operate under the current ownership and management (Shepherd, 2003). McGrath (1999) defined failure more broadly as the termination of an initiative that fell short of its goals. The latter business failure definition was employed in this study because it generally encapsulates the former definition.

Conflicting evidence has been presented relating to the links between an individual's propensity to report prior failure and subsequent behaviour (Brunstein and Gollwitzer, 1996). Failure can dampen an individual's motivation to try again. Shepherd (2003) suggests that business failure is a traumatic event. Moreover, failure can generate negative emotions (e.g., grief) among entrepreneurs, which can interfere with both learning and the motivation to try again. Failure to previously undertake a specific task can reduce an individual's belief in their ability to successfully undertake that task in the future (Bandura, 1995). Also, failure relating to a task can create a sense of helplessness (or lack of control), which can lower the likelihood of an individual subsequently successfully undertaking that task (Wood and Bandura, 1989). Conversely, failure has been found to be associated with a number of benefits. Sitkin (1992) has asserted that failure represents a 'clear signal' which facilitates the recognition and interpretation of otherwise ambiguous outcomes. A business failure signal can encourage learning because the individual is forced to examine the causes of failure. To take advantage of the potential learning benefits associated with business failure, an individual must want to re-enter the activity he/she has withdrawn from. Entrepreneurs who have experienced failure may seek to put into practice what they have learned. Habitual entrepreneurs who have experienced failure may be motivated to identify more opportunities.

Business failure experience may moderate the relationship between experience and opportunity identification because of its effect on motivation. Doubts surround the direction of this relationship. One way of resolving this ambiguity is to measure the number of business failures reported by an entrepreneur relative to the total number of businesses owned over their lifetime. Entrepreneurs may be confident in their own ability to deal with business failure if has occurred among a set of perceived business successes. An entrepreneur may maintain confidence in his/her own ability if the latter business failure is viewed as an anomaly (i.e., external attribution). McGrath (1999) has asserted that a single failure may lead to reactance, a process whereby a person becomes more motivated to overcome setbacks after experiencing one. In contrast, repeated failures have been found to produce motivation deficits that translate into weak performance (Brunstein and Gollwitzer, 1996). Multiple failures in the absence of successes may result in a loss of faith and an inability to conquer adversity.

The negative 'hit' to an entrepreneur's confidence can be rebuilt reasonably quickly if the business failure experience is a relatively isolated incidence within a general set of business success. If, on the other hand, failure is reported in a context of few successes, then the negative 'hit' to confidence is expected to persist. Negative emotions and doubts surrounding personal abilities can also reduce motivation to subsequently re-enter a particular activity. This discussion suggested the following hypothesis:

> Hypothesis 6.5: *There will be an inverse U-shaped relationship between the proportion of failed businesses relative to the number of businesses owned by entrepreneurs and the number of identified business opportunities in a given period.*

The nature of experience (i.e., success or failure) can either promote (or retard) the cognitive processes associated with creativity (Ward, 2004). Prior success (and failure) experiences may shape the way in which current situations/problems are framed. Experience of success may encourage individuals to focus more narrowly on cognitive processes (or heuristics) that worked well in the past. Further, individuals may refine well-known ways of combining knowledge (i.e., sticking to a well-developed schema) rather than exploring for new knowledge. This kind of 'mental block' can thwart novelty and creativity in a variety of settings. Conversely, experience of failure can generate behavioural abandonment and the search for new knowledge. This is because those who have experienced failure are more likely to be searching for an adequate or superior outcome/solution.

Habitual entrepreneurs reporting prior business failure experience who appreciate that their prior business strategies were ineffective may search for new information and knowledge. Conversely, habitual entrepreneurs reporting prior business success may be more likely to stick to knowledge and activities that have proved effective in the past. The latter entrepreneurs may be less to exhibit behaviour that diverges from the status quo. This view is consistent with the assertion that the creative process is path dependent. Once an individual generates a creative idea, future creative ideas will be framed from the perspective of the initial idea. These arguments suggest that habitual entrepreneurs who have experienced business failure will subsequently seek to exploit more innovative opportunities. This latter discussion ignores the emotional consequences associated with failure such as reduced motivation. As discussed above, the number of business failures needs to be compared against the number of business successes. Entrepreneurs associated with a limited number of business failures

98 *Opportunity Discovery*

relative to the total number of businesses owned (i.e., a small number of failures among a run of successes) may be less likely to view failure as a 'clear signal' suggesting the need for change. As earlier intimated, some entrepreneurs would regard the latter failures as anomalies. The need for change reported by entrepreneurs might become stronger if the proportion of business failures increases. However, entrepreneurs associated with high proportions of business failures may become risk averse, and they may only exploit less innovative opportunities. This discussion suggested the following hypothesis:

> Hypothesis 6.6: *There will be an inverse U-shaped relationship between the proportion of failed businesses relative to the number of businesses owned by entrepreneurs and the innovativeness of the latest opportunity exploited.*

6.4.3 Methodology

6.4.3.1 Data

Issues relating to the data collection process in Great Britain were summarized in Section 3.4.3.1. The sample analysed in this article related to 637 entrepreneurs who provided complete data for the selected variables explored. Seven habitual entrepreneurs indicated that they had owned ten or more businesses. As outliers can have a distorting effect on regression models containing power polynomials, they were removed from any further analysis (Cohen et al., 2003). Their exclusion did not alter the strength or the direction of the reported relationships. The exclusion of outliers, however, altered the inflection points when curvilinear relationships were examined. The final sample included 630 entrepreneurs, yielding an effective response rate of 14.6%. Fifty-three percent (i.e., 336) of respondents were habitual entrepreneurs. The average number of businesses owned by the whole sample was 2.1 businesses, while habitual entrepreneurs, on average, owned three businesses. Thirty-two percent of habitual entrepreneurs (i.e., 114) reported that at least one of their prior businesses had failed (i.e., the firm had been sold or closed because it had not met expectations or it had closed due to bankruptcy, receivership or liquidation). The authors concluded there was no evidence to suggest that the results would be affected by common method bias.

6.4.3.2 Dependent Variables

Two dependent variables were operationalized. The first dependent variable related to the *number of opportunities identified* (Hills et al., 1997; Shepherd and DeTienne, 2005). A conservative definition of business opportunities was selected. Entrepreneurs were presented with a statement asking them, 'How many opportunities for creating or purchasing a business have you *identified* ('spotted') within the last five years?' They were presented with eight opportunity identification outcomes (i.e., 0, 1, 2, 3, 4, 5, 6 to 10, or more than 10 opportunities). The authors detected that some categories had few respondents. The eight opportunity identification outcomes were collapsed into three broader categories. The resulting categorization ensured that an acceptable number of entrepreneurs were allocated to each category. Entrepreneurs who reported that they had failed to identify an opportunity were scored 1, those who reported that they had identified one or two opportunities were scored 2, whilst those who had identified three or more opportunities were scored 3.

A second dependent variable relating to innovation was operationalized. Debate surrounds the definition of innovation. The following issues were considered in the operationalization of the 'innovativeness' dependent variable. First, the full range of innovative activities (Schumpeter, 1934) were taken into account rather than focusing solely on product innovation. Second, given the scope of the study, a measure of innovativeness that was applicable to firms in several industries (i.e., not just high-technology industries) was selected. Third, a measure of innovativeness should not solely emphasize the inputs into the innovation process. Commonly used measures such as R&D expenditure and patents failed to meet these criteria. These measures emphasize the inputs into the innovation process rather than the outcomes. Further, these measures tend to favour high-technology firms and product innovation, the latter representing only one dimension of innovation. Patents in particular may not be an appropriate gauge of process innovation. A self-report measure of innovation was utilized (DeTienne and Koberg, 2002).

The innovation measure operationalized related to the scale proposed by Manimala (1992) and the cross-cutting theme of 'newness' was considered (Schumpeter, 1934). Entrepreneurs were asked to indicate if they had:

- introduced a new product or a new quality of an existing product
- introduced a new method of production or modified an existing method
- found a new market or employed a new marketing strategy in an existing market
- found a new source of supply
- found new ways of managing finance
- developed new structures, systems, or procedures
- introduced a new culture especially through the introduction of innovative people
- found new ways of managing and developing personnel
- used new ways of managing quality control and R&D
- found new ways of dealing with government and other external agencies.

With reference to each question, respondents could have awarded a score of 1 if they answered 'yes' or a score of 0 if they answered 'no'. These ten scores were summated. The authors examined the distribution of responses to the innovation questions and found an even distribution in each category

100 *Opportunity Discovery*

from 0 to 10. Respondents were asked to report whether or not they undertook a particular innovative activity rather than an attitudinal response based on a Likert-type scale. Social desirability bias was assumed to be lesser in the former case than the latter.

6.4.3.3 *Independent Variables*

The independent variable TOTAL was operationalized. Entrepreneurs were asked to indicate the total number of businesses they had established and/ or purchased in which they had minority or majority ownership stakes. TOTAL is a continuous variable. Curvilinear relationships between PBOE and the dependent variables were hypothesized. A polynomial approach was used to test for curvilinearity. Cohen et al., (2003) has suggested that theory should guide the selection of power polynomials with a meaningful zero value. However, most social science theories suggest quadratic relationships. Following the arguments leading to the derivation of the hypotheses in the article, a quadratic term of the TOTAL variable was operationalized. $TOTAL^2$ represents TOTAL squared.

Because each entrepreneur owned at least one business, the TOTAL variable could not be equal to zero. A centring procedure was conducted, whereby the sample mean was subtracted from the variable (Cohen et al., 2003). Both TOTAL (mean value of uncentred TOTAL is 2.1 businesses) and $TOTAL^2$ were centred. Robustness checks relating to a cubic relationship ($TOTAL^3$) were conducted and no significant relationship was detected. Reported models related to the hypothesized quadratic relationships.

The independent variable FAILURE was operationalized. Each entrepreneur reported the total number of failed businesses they had owned as a percentage of the total number of businesses they had owned up to the time of the survey (FAILURE). Business failure was deemed to have taken place if the respondent had closed or sold a business due to bankruptcy, liquidation or receivership, or because the business had been closed or sold because it failed to meet the expectations of the entrepreneur (McGrath, 1999). To test the hypothesized curvilinear relationship, the quadratic term of the FAILURE variable was operationalized. Because the FAILURE variable had a meaningful zero value (i.e., some entrepreneurs may not have reported a business failure), both FAILURE and $FAILURE^2$ were not centred.

6.4.3.4 *Technique*

Ordered probit regression analysis and negative binomial regression were used to test the hypotheses. Due to the ordinal nature of the opportunity identification dependent variable, ordered probit regression analysis was used to hypotheses 6.7 and 6.8. Similar results were detected with regard to an ordered logit regression analysis. The innovation dependent variable related to count data. A negative binomial regression approach was used to test hypotheses 6.9 and 6.10.

6.4.4 Findings

The extent of experience variable, TOTAL, was positively and significantly associated with the number of business opportunities identified. However, the TOTAL^2 variable was negatively and significantly associated with the number of business opportunities identified. A non-linear relationship between the extent of experience and the number of business opportunities identified was detected. Specifically, for entrepreneurs owning up to 4.5 businesses, PBOE was positively associated with the number of business opportunities identified. Conversely, for entrepreneurs owning more than 4.5 businesses, greater PBOE was associated with the identification of fewer business opportunities. Hypothesis 6.3 was supported.

The extent of experience variable, TOTAL, was positively and significantly associated with the innovativeness of the latest opportunity exploited. The TOTAL^2 variable was not found to be significant. There was no evidence to suggest a non-linear relationship between the extent of PBOE and the innovativeness of the latest opportunity exploited. Hypothesis 6.4 was partially supported, whereby an entrepreneurs' PBOE was positively associated with the innovativeness of the latest opportunity exploited, but not a diminishing rate.

The proportion of business failure experience to all business ownership experience (i.e., the FAILURE variable) was positively and significantly associated with the number of business opportunities identified. The FAILURE^2 variable was negatively and significantly associated with the number of business opportunities identified. Specifically, business failure experience was positively associated with more business opportunities identified as long as the proportion of failures did not exceed 20% of the entrepreneur's total stock of businesses. For entrepreneurs who cited that more than 20% of their total stock of businesses had failed, failure experience was negatively associated with the number of business opportunities identified. Hypothesis 6.5 was supported.

Both the FAILURE and FAILURE^2 variables were not significantly associated with the innovativeness of the latest opportunity exploited. Hypothesis 6.6 was not supported.

6.4.5 Conclusions and Implications

Cognitive theorists suggest that experienced entrepreneurs can mobilize their prior experience and knowledge to process information more efficiently. Further, entrepreneurs who can process information efficiently generally have more cognitive resources at their disposal, which can allow them to concentrate on more unique and novel material (Hillerbrand, 1989). Consistent with these views, the authors detected that experienced habitual entrepreneurs identified more business opportunities and the latest exploited opportunity was more innovative with wealth creation potential. However, beyond a certain level, the benefits associated with PBOE can be

102   *Opportunity Discovery*

outweighed by the biases that can be accumulated by habitual entrepreneurs from PBOE. As hypothesized, an inverse U-shaped relationship between entrepreneur PBOE and the number of business opportunities identified was found. Up to 4.5 business ownership experience, PBOE was positively associated with the number of business opportunities identified. However, above 4.5 business ownership experience, PBOE was negatively associated with the number of business opportunities identified.

The cognitive and motivation effects of PBOE associated with failure have been the subject of growing debate. Entrepreneur business ownership failure is viewed as demotivating and can lead to a preoccupation with the failure, reducing cognitive effectiveness. Conversely, the failure may aid cognitive development by introducing greater diversity into an entrepreneur's schema. Failure at a task that is deemed to be central to an entrepreneur's self-definition could motivate the entrepreneur to try harder. The validity of these opposing views may depend on the total number of business failure experiences reported by an entrepreneur relative to the total number of all businesses owned. Business failure experience does not necessarily lead to more cautious and risk-averse habitual entrepreneurs. As hypothesized, however, some habitual entrepreneurs were only able to 'stomach' a certain level of business failure. Most notably, entrepreneurs who cited that 20% or more of their businesses had failed identified fewer business opportunities. Contrary to expectation, an entrepreneur's prior business failure experience was not significantly associated with the innovativeness of the latest exploited opportunities; habitual entrepreneurs with proportionally more business failures did not subsequently exploit more innovative latest business opportunities.

The authors suggested that their findings should alert entrepreneurs to the potential problems associated with an over-reliance on personal PBOE alone. This study highlighted that beyond a certain level of PBOE, the 'liabilities' of experience can outweigh the potential 'assets' with regard to the identification of additional business opportunities. Business ownership experience need not peak and end up becoming a barrier to business opportunity identification if the entrepreneur engages in deliberate practice, that is, activities designed by a teacher (or mentor) to improve an entrepreneur's performance.

6.5 Opportunity Creation

6.5.1 *Gaps in the Knowledge Base and Research Question*

The article by Robson et al., (2012a) summarized below explored the link between an entrepreneur's PBOE and their propensity to engage in innovation opportunity pursuit. Links between the clustering of innovative firms and hard economic development measures have been explored (Acs et al., 1992; Rocha, 2004), but there is a relative dearth of studies that focus on entrepreneurs that generate and exploit new innovative ideas. The profiles of successful private firm innovators are poorly understood, and conflicting evidence relates to several factors (Wright et al., 2007). Many studies have generally simply explored whether or not innovation relating to new products and services or new production processes have been introduced. Yet, innovation process outcomes may be important including new work practices and workforce organization, new sources of supply or materials, new markets or means of reaching these markets and new administration and office systems (Cosh and Wood, 1998; Hausman, 2005).

Attitudinal and resource barriers to innovation may vary according to the type of innovation. Barriers to product or service innovation and production process innovation may be different from barriers to innovation relating to work practices and workforce organization. Resource barriers to innovation may be more pronounced in regional contexts associated with low levels of resource munificence, which is widespread in many developing country contexts. Entrepreneurs in regions with resource deficits may strategically decide not to focus on innovation at all. Those that do may focus on less resource-demanding innovation relating to work practices, which can provide a competitive platform for future, more resource-demanding product or services innovation and production process innovation.

An entrepreneur's human capital resources relating to skills, expertise and knowledge (i.e., PBOE) can be mobilized to address attitudinal and resource barriers to innovation. Currently, there is limited knowledge surrounding the resource profiles of entrepreneurs and firms that are more likely to address attitudinal barriers to specific types of innovation. Also, there is a gap in the knowledge base relating to the profiles of entrepreneurs that attempt to circumvent attitudinal and resource barriers to innovation, particularly those who are successful compared to those who are not. A firm's environmental context, notably its industrial activity and geographical location, can shape access to and competition for resources that can influence innovation. Entrepreneurs need to embed themselves with other actors in the external environment to ensure appropriate resources are accumulated and mobilized to enhance a firm's technical and entrepreneurial capabilities to generate innovative ideas. An entrepreneur's human capital profile can shape opportunity exploitation (Shrader and Siegel, 2007). Experienced entrepreneurs with PBOE experience may utilize their absorptive capacity (Zahra and George, 2002) and superior platform of knowledge (Lazaric et al., 2008) to enhance the probability that innovation is tried and introduced.

Some experienced entrepreneurs can mobilize their own knowledge and the knowledge accumulated by other local and non-local individuals to raise their capacity to innovate and their ability to exploit an innovation. Further, some entrepreneurs have careers in entrepreneurship, and habitual entrepreneurs exploit more than one business opportunity (Ucbasaran et al., 2008). Entrepreneurs who acquire their business ownership experience sequentially (i.e., serial entrepreneurs) may have different skills and knowledge to mobilize than those that acquire experience concurrently (i.e., portfolio entrepreneurs) (Westhead and Wright, 1998). Yet, the extent and nature of

104   *Opportunity Discovery*

an entrepreneur's specific human capital, particularly PBOE, in relation to other entrepreneur, firm and external environmental factors are generally ignored, particularly outside developed country contexts.

In an emerging region context, where there are possible resource deficits, habitual entrepreneurs may have a disproportionately important role to play in stimulating innovative activity, which can contribute to local and national economic competitiveness. Habitual entrepreneurs can act as role models, and they may be better placed due to their experience to identify novel opportunities. To maximize the returns from policy investments, a case to target assistance to experienced habitual entrepreneurs, particularly portfolio entrepreneurs, has been made (Westhead et al., 2003). This study provided new insights into these relationships. The following research question was explored:

- *Do entrepreneurs' human capital profiles, particularly PBOE, increase the probability that they will engage in innovation activity, as well as increase the probability of the introduction of particular types of innovation in a developing region context?*

A broad definition of innovation was operationalized that considered technological innovations (Becheikh et al., 2006), as well as new work practices and workforce organization, new sources of supply or materials, the exploitation of new markets or means of reaching these markets, and new administration and office systems (Cosh and Wood, 1998). The latter types of innovation are particularly relevant within a developing regional economy context. The authors also distinguished between a range of innovation outcomes, ranging from whether or not innovation was tried, whether innovation was tried and introduced or tried and failed and the frequency that all types of innovation were always introduced. Very few studies have gathered information from large samples of entrepreneurs in Africa. There is no prior evidence relating to the scale, nature and behaviour of novice, serial and portfolio entrepreneurs in Africa, particularly with regard to their ability to engage in innovative activity. The lead entrepreneur who shapes resource allocation and strategy in smaller private firms was the unit of analysis. Ghana is a particularly important context to explore the presented research question for the following reasons: recent economic transformation policies have enabled Ghana to be recognized as one of only seven emerging economies in sub-Saharan Africa, and the inadequate market support institutions and weak enforcement capacity of regulatory and legal institutions create business uncertainty that can be potentially reduced by entrepreneurs who can mobilize their PBOE.

This study sought to add to the theoretical and empirical foundations of innovation theory, which are generally grounded within North American and European contexts. Developed economy findings may not be equally applicable in an emerging region. Although some studies have explored the innovation process in developing regions, they have not explored the links between the entrepreneur's human capital, the firm's resource profile and innovation type outcomes in a developing regional economy context. Also, this study sought to provide new insights relating to the contributions made by habitual entrepreneurs who can mobilize PBOE relative to novice entrepreneurs.

6.5.2 Hypotheses Tested

The study was guided by insights from the RBV of the firm perspective and human capital theory. Reuber and Fischer (1999) highlighted that a founder's experience can impact upon entrepreneur and firm behaviour but failed to make a distinction between the *extent* and *nature* of PBOE. Entrepreneurs who acquire their business ownership experience sequentially (i.e., serial entrepreneurs) may have different skills and knowledge to mobilize than those that acquire experience concurrently (i.e., portfolio entrepreneurs) (Westhead and Wright, 1998). This study provides fresh evidence relating to the contributions made by habitual entrepreneurs who can mobilize PBOE relative to novice entrepreneurs. Both the *extent* and *nature* of entrepreneurs' PBOE were considered with regard to three dimensions: years of business ownership experience, habitual entrepreneurs compared with novice entrepreneurs and portfolio entrepreneurs compared with serial entrepreneurs.

Experiential knowledge can shape the propensity to innovate. PBOE can contribute to entrepreneurship-specific human capital (Gimeno et al., 1997). Entrepreneurs with PBOE can accumulate entrepreneurial, managerial and technical skills (Chandler and Hanks, 1998). Entrepreneurial skills focus upon the perceived ability to create, identify and exploit opportunities. Managerial skills relate to the ability to manage and organize people and resources, while technical skills focus upon technical expertise. PBOE can add to human capital through enhanced reputation and better understanding of the requirements of financial institutions. Experienced entrepreneurs with established skills, networks and reputations may be better able to cope with the liabilities of newness (Politis, 2005). Human capital from PBOE may be interrelated with greater social capital associated with diverse networks (Shane and Khurana, 2003). Experienced entrepreneurs can mobilize their human capital to access resources that are critical for innovation exploitation. Entrepreneurs reporting long durations of PBOE may have had more opportunities to accumulate and mobilize their specific human capital. This specific human capital may be especially important in the risky and complex context of innovation, particularly product or service innovation. Longer durations of PBOE can provide the time to build up routines for innovation, which encode entrepreneurs' tacit knowledge and sophisticated heuristics to guide action. Experienced entrepreneurs may have tested alternative approaches to innovation, and identified approaches that are more likely to work. More efficient, experienced entrepreneurs can ensure that each type of innovation pursued is introduced. Over time, experienced

106 *Opportunity Discovery*

entrepreneurs can also develop their human capital profiles. Entrepreneurs can learn from their prior successes and mistakes, and they can mobilize this know-how to identify and pursue the types of innovations (and innovative work practices) being sought in the market. This discussion suggested the following hypothesis:

Hypothesis 6.7: *Entrepreneurs with longer durations of PBOE are more likely to engage in innovation activity.*

The extent and nature of PBOE can shape opportunity identification, pursuit and exploitation behaviour. Experience can increase the flow of creative ideas that become innovative opportunities (Shepherd and DeTienne, 2005). Habitual entrepreneurs may have learnt from the feedback associated with PBOE successes (and mistakes). Conversely, novice entrepreneurs with no PBOE do not have any entrepreneurial capability feedback to draw upon (Ucbasaran et al., 2008, 2009). Further, habitual entrepreneurs that recognize their own innovation capacity deficiencies may proactively seek (and/or attract) knowledge from local and non-local entrepreneurs to circumvent barriers to innovation. PBOE may develop human capital that enables habitual entrepreneurs to transfer learning from an initial firm to a subsequent new firm. PBOE does this by enhancing an individual's absorptive capacity (Zahra and George, 2002), which is the ability to build and improve the routines for processing information relevant to identify, pursue and exploit an opportunity. This allows entrepreneurs to focus more upon novel information associated with the identification, pursuit and exploitation of innovations. This discussion suggested the following hypothesis:

Hypothesis 6.8: *Habitual entrepreneurs are more likely than novice entrepreneurs to engage in innovation activity.*

The goals, resources and liabilities reported by portfolio entrepreneurs, who own multiple firms concurrently, can differ from those reported by serial entrepreneurs, who own multiple firms sequentially (Ucbasaran et al., 2008), each of which may differ from those of novice entrepreneurs. Both experienced portfolio and serial entrepreneurs are likely to benefit from the enhancement to information processing routines resulting from PBOE, which can enable the transfer of learning from an initial firm to a subsequent new firm, as noted above.

Portfolio entrepreneurs associated with an entrepreneurship anchor (Katz, 1994) may seek additional wealth creation opportunities by investing in innovative work practices and/or innovative products/services. Further, portfolio entrepreneurs with broader resource pools may find it easier to circumvent barriers to innovation. Portfolio entrepreneurs, on average, may be more entrepreneurial than novice entrepreneurs. They are more likely to start firms because they want to be challenged by the opportunities and problems involved; more likely to enjoy just thinking about and looking for new business opportunities; to have a special alertness towards spotting opportunities; to be more likely to find new markets; and to consider that identifying good opportunities usually requires immersion in a particular market (Westhead et al., 2005b). Portfolio entrepreneurs may recognize the need to foster innovation across the board, and due to the accumulation of several assets of PBOE they may more able to circumvent resource barriers to all types of innovation activity pursued. Conversely, novice entrepreneurs with no PBOE to mobilize may fail to recognize the benefits of introducing several types of innovation, and they do not have the broad pool of experience and social capital to mobilize against the attitudinal and resource barriers associated with each type of innovation activity.

Innovation involves risk. Portfolio entrepreneurs may be willing to engage in a more innovative activity, because if the innovation activity in one of their firms is not successful, they have other firms in their portfolio to fall back on. Westhead et al. (2005b) found that portfolio entrepreneurs were more innovative than novice entrepreneurs. They were more likely than novice entrepreneurs to have reported that they were innovative with regard to the introduction of 'a new product or a new quality of an existing product'; 'a new method of production or modified an existing method'; and/or 'a new culture especially through the induction of innovative people at the lower levels'. Further, Westhead et al. (2005b) detected that serial entrepreneurs may be more likely than novice entrepreneurs to engage in innovation activity. Serial entrepreneurs reported they were more likely than novice entrepreneurs to have introduced a new product/service and/ or to have developed a new distribution approach. Guided by PBOE, some serial entrepreneurs may more easily address attitudinal barriers to innovation relative to novice entrepreneurs. On the downside, the accumulation of liabilities associated with PBOE by some serial entrepreneurs may lead to resource deficiencies that retard their ability to exploit pursued innovative activity. This discussion suggested the following hypotheses:

Hypothesis 6.9: *Portfolio entrepreneurs are more likely than novice entrepreneurs to innovate.*

Hypothesis 6.10: *Serial entrepreneurs are more likely than novice entrepreneurs to innovate.*

6.5.3 Methodology

6.5.3.1 Data

The data collection process has been discussed in Section 4.2.3.1 relating to Robson et al. (2013). Issues relating to innovation were explored with regard to a hand-collected survey dataset involving 496 entrepreneurs who owned private, independent firms engaged in a broad spectrum of industrial

108   *Opportunity Discovery*

activities. The effective response rate to the survey was 68%. In total, 198 respondents were habitual entrepreneurs (40%), among whom 61 (12%) were serial entrepreneurs and a further 137 respondents (28%) were port-folio entrepreneurs. These proportions are comparable to those reported in developed country studies (Ucbasaran et al., 2008).

6.5.3.2 *Dependent Variables*

The following information was provided to the entrepreneurs (Cosh and Hughes, 1998): "Innovation is concerned with the application of new ideas. Often, these ideas take the form of new products and services or new pro-duction processes. Also, innovation may refer to new work practices and workforce organisation, to new sources of supply or materials (or new ways of working with key suppliers), to the exploitation of new markets or means of reaching those markets (including innovations in marketing, selling and distribution) and to new administration and office systems. In the following section we would like you to tell us about innovation introduced into your business. Unless otherwise specified, the term innovation should be taken to encompass any of the categories described above. However, innovations should involve substantive changes."

Entrepreneurs were asked, "In the last three years, has your firm under-taken any form of innovation with regard to seven statements relating to the following"—product or services, production processes (including storage), work practices or workforce organization, supply and supplier relations, markets and marketing, administration and office systems, and product or service distribution were presented. The authors operationalized innovation activity with reference to each statement by asking, respondents to select one of the four following responses: innovation not tried (scored 1), inno-vation tried and failed (scored 2), innovation new to firm but not new to the industry (scored 3) and innovation new to industry (scored 4). With reference to these statements, the following four dependent variables were operationalized.

The first dependent related to a simple distinction between non-innovative and innovative respondents with reference to at least one type of innovation. Entrepreneurs that reported innovation not tried with regard to all seven types of innovations (i.e., product or services (ProductI), production pro-cesses (including storage) (ProcessI), work practices or workforce orga-nization (WorkI), supply and supplier relations (SupplyI), markets and marketing (MarketsI), administration and office systems (AdministrationI) and product or service distribution (DistributionI)) were termed '*innovation not tried*' respondents (scored 0), whilst entrepreneurs that reported inno-vation tried with regard to at least one of the seven innovation types were termed '*innovation tried*' respondents (scored 1).

Finer-level analysis of innovation type activity was also considered. With reference to each of the seven types of innovations, a distinction was made between '*innovation not tried*' (scored 0), '*innovation tried and failed*' (scored 1) and '*innovation tried and introduced*' (scored 2) respondents. The second dependent variable related to '*innovation tried and failed*' respondents relative to the reference category of '*innovation not tried*' respondents. '*Innovation tried and failed*' related to entrepreneurs that undertook activities to generate and introduce an innovation, but they were unable for internal and/or external reasons to introduce the pursued innovation. The third dependent variable related to '*innovation tried and introduced*' respondents relative to the reference category of '*innovation not tried*' respondents. '*Innovation tried and introduced*' related to entrepreneurs that were able to introduce the innovation that was either new to the firm but not to the industry, or an innovation that was new to the firm and the industry.

Sensitivity analysis relating to the operationalization of the first dependent variable was conducted with regard to a composite ordinal innovation outcome dependent variable. With reference to each of the seven types of innovations, a distinction was made between respondents that '*always not tried*' with regard to all seven types of innovation (scored 0), '*tried and always failed*' with regard to all seven types of innovations, '*mixture of failed and introduced*' (scored 2) and '*always introduced*' the seven types of innovations (scored 3).

6.5.3.3 Independent Variables

Entrepreneurs were asked to report the number of years they had owned and run a business (*Experience*). Further, entrepreneurs were asked to indicate the total number of businesses they had established and/or purchased in which they had minority or majority ownership stakes. Because a high proportion of entrepreneurial activity is team-based, the definitions used include both minority and majority ownership stakes. A distinction was made between habitual (i.e., serial and portfolio) (i.e., individuals who at the time of the survey had prior minority or majority ownership experience in two or more prior independent businesses) and novice entrepreneurs (i.e., individuals who at the time of the survey had a minority or majority ownership stake in a single business that was new or purchased). Moreover, a distinction was made between serial (i.e., individuals who had sold/closed a business which they had a minority or majority ownership stake in, and who at the time of the survey had a minority or majority ownership stake in a single independent business that was new or purchased) and portfolio entrepreneurs (i.e., individuals who at the time of the survey had minority or majority ownership stakes in two or more independent businesses that were new and/or purchased). Four binary variables were operationalized: habitual entrepreneurs (*Habitual*), serial entrepreneurs (*Serial*), portfolio entrepreneurs (*Portfolio*) and novice entrepreneurs (*Novice*). The Serial and Portfolio variables were included in the regression models, and the reference category was Novice entrepreneurs.

110   *Opportunity Discovery*

6.5.3.4 Techniques

Logistic regression estimation was used to identify the combination of variables associated with the propensity of entrepreneurs to report '*innovation tried*' across all the seven specified innovation outcomes. A base model of the control variables relating to the firm and the domestic external environment was presented. Alternative measures of business ownership experience were then added to the base model. Entrepreneur demographic characteristics and other dimensions of human capital were also introduced. With regard to each of the seven individual innovation outcomes, multinomial logistic regression models were estimated. The authors reported '*innovation tried and failed*' and '*innovation tried and introduced*' outcomes against the reference category, which is '*innovation not tried*'. With regard to the composite innovation outcome across all seven innovation outcomes, multinomial logistic models were estimated for the '*tried and always failed*' outcome, the '*mixture of failed and introduced*' outcome and the '*always introduced*' outcome. The reference category was '*always not tried*'.

6.5.4 Findings

In total, 23% (n = 112) of the respondents had 'always not tried' to innovate, 7% (n = 36) had 'tried and always failed' to innovation, 53% (n = 265) cited a 'mixture of failed and introduced' and 17% (n = 83) had 'always introduced' an innovation.

With regard to the '*innovation tried*' dependent variable, logistic regression analysis models were computed (i.e., binary dependent variable relating to '*innovation tried*' (scored 1) and '*innovation not tried*' respondents (scored 0)). Entrepreneurs reporting longer durations of experience were significantly more likely to have reported '*innovation tried*'. Hypothesis 6.7 was supported. Habitual entrepreneurs were more likely at the 0.1 level to have reported '*innovation tried*'. Hypothesis 6.8 was weakly supported. Portfolio entrepreneurs were significantly more likely to have reported '*innovation tried*'. Hypothesis 6.9 was supported. Serial entrepreneurs were not significantly more likely to have reported '*innovation tried*'. Hypothesis 6.10 was not supported.

In relation to the '*innovation tried and failed*' dependent variable, multinomial logistic estimation was used because the dependent variable was nominal and related to two or more categories (Aldrich and Nelson, 1984). In several models, the dependent variable '*innovation tried and failed*' was scored 1, whilst the reference category '*innovation not tried*' was scored 0. In several other models, the dependent variable '*innovation tried and introduced*' was scored 2 and was compared against the reference category '*innovation not tried*'.

Control and independent variables relating to the propensity to report the '*innovation tried and failed*' outcome were included in multinomial logistic models relating to product or services innovation (ProductI), production

Opportunity Discovery 111

processes (including storage) (ProcessI), markets and marketing (MarketsI), administration and office systems (AdministrationI) and product or service distribution (DistributionI) innovation type outcomes. Across all five innovation type outcomes, serial entrepreneurs were not significantly more likely than novice entrepreneurs to have reported *'innovation tried and failed'*. Portfolio entrepreneurs were significantly less likely than novice entrepreneurs to have report *'innovation tried and failed'* relative to the *'innovation not tried'* reference category.

With regard to the *'innovation tried and introduced'* dependent variable, multinomial logistic estimation models were computed. Control and independent variables relating to the propensity to report the *'innovation tried and introduced'* outcome were included in the multinomial logistic models relating to ProductI, ProcessI, MarketsI, AdministrationI and DistributionI innovation type outcomes. With reference to each of the five innovation type outcomes, portfolio entrepreneurs were more likely than novice entrepreneurs to have reported *'innovation tried and introduced'* relative to the *'innovation not tried'* reference category. Hypothesis 6.9 was supported. Serial entrepreneurs were more likely than novice entrepreneurs to have reported *'innovation tried and introduced'* with regard to ProcessI, and weakly in relation to ProductI. Hhypothesis 6.10 was not conclusively supported.

In relation to the *'composite innovation outcomes'* dependent variable, multinomial logistic estimation models were computed. The composite innovation dependent measure considered responses to all seven innovation type outcomes with reference to a single index, which had the following four categories: *'always not tried'* (scored 0), *'tried and always failed'* (scored 1), *'a mixture of failed and introduced'* (scored 2) and *'always introduced'* (scored 3). Multinomial logistic analysis explored the likelihood of a dependent variable relative to the *'always not tried'* reference category. Portfolio entrepreneurs were significantly more likely than novice entrepreneurs to have reported *'always introduced'*. This sensitivity analysis relating to the composite measure of innovation suggested that portfolio entrepreneurs, but not serial entrepreneurs, were more likely than novice entrepreneurs to have exploited all pursued innovative activity. Hypothesis 6.9 was supported, but again, there was no conclusive support for hypothesis 6.10.

6.5.5 Conclusions and Implications

The authors found support for several hypotheses relating to the broad *'innovation tried'* dependent variable across the seven types of innovations. As hypothesized, entrepreneurs reporting longer durations of PBOE, and habitual entrepreneurs, particularly portfolio entrepreneurs, were more likely to have engaged in innovative activity. Serial entrepreneurs were not more likely than novice entrepreneurs to have engaged in innovative activity. Presented findings suggested that PBOE is a key resource associated with

112   *Opportunity Discovery*

the ability to introduce innovations into the market. However, habitual entrepreneurs should not be viewed as a homogeneous entity.

The contrasting ability of portfolio and serial entrepreneurs to address attitudinal and resource barriers to specific types of innovation was confirmed with reference to the finer-level analysis, which focused on the *'innovation tried and failed'* and the *'innovation tried and introduced'* dependent variables. The benefits of PBOE appeared to be more readily mobilized by portfolio rather than serial entrepreneurs. It was inferred that portfolio entrepreneurs in general potentially acquire more resources and learn more from their PBOE relative to serial entrepreneurs. Despite accumulating liabilities associated with PBOE, there is weak and inconclusive evidence to suggest that serial entrepreneurs were more likely than novice entrepreneurs to have circumvented attitudinal and resource barriers to more resource demanding innovation relating to ProcessI and ProductI exploitation. The analysis failed to conclusively support the view that serial entrepreneurs were more likely than novice entrepreneurs to have exploited different types of innovation activity.

To detect whether the results were sensitive to the innovation variable operationalized, a composite innovation dependent measure was computed that considered responses to all seven innovation type outcomes with reference to the composite innovation index. This sensitivity analysis confirmed that habitual entrepreneurs should not be viewed as a homogeneous entity, and the assets of PBOE were more readily used by portfolio rather than serial entrepreneurs to address attitudinal and resource barriers to innovation. Portfolio entrepreneurs appeared to more readily recognize the potential competitive advantage benefits associated with innovation relating to both product and work practices innovation, and they had accumulated the resources required to circumvent barriers to all types of innovation.

6.6 Summary

This chapter has reviewed three themes relating to opportunity identification and creation in developed and developing economy contexts from the perspective of the entrepreneur as the unit of analysis. The first theme explored differences between types of entrepreneurs with regard to their business opportunity identification activities. Portfolio entrepreneurs generally reported more opportunistic business opportunity behaviour than novice or serial entrepreneurs. Further, a larger proportion of portfolio entrepreneurs, rather serial or novice entrepreneurs, had identified two or more opportunities.

The second theme explored the relationship between the nature and extent of entrepreneurs' PBOE and the number of business opportunities identified, as well as the innovativeness of the latest business opportunities exploited. PBOE was considered in relation to the total number of businesses owned by entrepreneurs (TOTAL), and the total number of failed businesses they had owned (FAILURE). Curvilinear relationships with the dependent variables were considered. A quadratic term of the total number of businesses owned by entrepreneurs (TOTAL^2) was operationalized, and a quadratic term of the total number of failed businesses they had owned (FAILURE^2) was operationalized. A non-linear relationship between the extent of PBOE and the number of business opportunities was detected. An inverse U-shaped relationship between entrepreneur PBOE and the number of business opportunities identified was found. Up to 4.5 business ownership experience, PBOE was positively associated with the number of business opportunities identified. However, above 4.5 business ownership experience, PBOE was negatively associated with the number of business opportunities identified. This suggested that beyond a certain level, the benefits associated with PBOE can be outweighed by the biases that can be accumulated by habitual entrepreneurs from PBOE. Business failure experience was associated with more business opportunities identified, but when habitual entrepreneurs cited that 20% or more of their businesses had failed they identified fewer business opportunities. Some habitual entrepreneurs were, therefore, only able to 'stomach' a certain level of business failure. Habitual entrepreneur prior business failure experience, however, was not significantly associated with the innovativeness of the latest exploited opportunities.

The third theme explored the relationship between opportunity creation and focused on four measures of PBOE. It was assumed that the entrepreneur positive signal of PBOE would increase the likelihood that entrepreneurs would engage in innovation activity. Innovation could relate to new products and services or new production processes, as well as new work practices and workforce organization, to new sources of supply or materials (or new ways of working with key suppliers), to the exploitation of new markets or means of reaching those markets (including innovations in marketing, selling and distribution) and to new administration and office systems. The link between the quality signal of entrepreneur PBOE and several innovation activity dependent variables was explored in a multivariate statistical framework. Entrepreneurs with longer durations of PBOE were more likely to engage in innovation activity. Habitual entrepreneurs were weakly significantly more likely than novice entrepreneurs to engage in innovation activity. Portfolio entrepreneurs were significantly more likely than novice entrepreneurs to engage in innovation activity (i.e., innovation tried). Contrary to expectation, serial entrepreneurs were not significantly more likely than novice entrepreneurs to engage in innovation activity (i.e., innovation tried). The sensitivity of the findings was, in addition explored in relation to a *'composite innovation outcomes'* dependent variable. The latter dependent variable considered responses to all seven innovation type outcomes with reference to a single index, which had the following four categories: *'always not tried'*, *'tried and always failed'*, *'a mixture of failed and introduced'* and *'always introduced'*. The sensitivity analysis confirmed that portfolio entrepreneurs were significantly more likely than novice entrepreneurs to have reported

114   *Opportunity Discovery*

'always introduced'. However, the sensitivity analysis detected that portfolio entrepreneurs but not serial entrepreneurs were significantly more likely than novice entrepreneurs to have exploited all pursued innovative activity.

6.7 Reflection Questions

In Chapter 6, entrepreneur PBOE was assumed in the reported quantitative article to be a resource that could be mobilized to 'discover' business opportunities and/or engage in innovation activity to 'create' business opportunities. The reported quantitative articles detected several links between 'type' of entrepreneur PBOE and dimensions of opportunity discovery and/or creation. Please consider the following reflection questions:

- *What theories have been presented to explain why entrepreneurs 'discover' or 'create' business opportunities? What are the key assumptions and parameters of each theory?*
- *Why do portfolio entrepreneurs identify more business opportunities than other entrepreneurs?*
- *Is there a simple linear link between entrepreneur PBOE and the number of business opportunities identified by entrepreneurs?*
- *Is there a simple linear link between entrepreneur PBOE failure experience and the number of business opportunities identified by entrepreneurs?*
- *Is there a simple linear link between entrepreneur PBOE failure experience and the innovativeness of the latest business opportunity exploited by entrepreneurs?*
- *Why should entrepreneurs invest in innovation?*
- *What are the barriers to entrepreneurs investing in innovation?*
- *Is there an agreed definition of innovation?*
- *What types of innovation can entrepreneurs invest in?*
- *What innovation measures have been operationalized in innovation studies?*
- *Can entrepreneurs PBOE shape the likelihood to engage in innovation activity?*
- *Are serial and portfolio entrepreneurs equally likely to engage in innovation activity?*

7 Learning

7.1 Learning Objectives and Overview

Entrepreneurs may transform prior experience into knowledge that furthers their subsequent entrepreneurial behaviour in different ways (Politis, 2005). Habitual entrepreneurs may learn and accumulate human capital from PBOE 'success' firm closure and/or PBOE 'failure' firm closure (i.e., for economic and/or non-economic reasons). Entrepreneur experimental learning experience from PBOE may, in part, enhance subsequent entrepreneur opportunity creation and discovery, as well as superior firm development. In this chapter, we focus on entrepreneur rather than organization learning. The article by Ucbasaran et al. (2003) is a theory-building study that builds upon insights from human capital theory and RBV of entrepreneurship. Adopting theoretical sampling of eight habitual starter and acquirer entrepreneurs, this study explored whether the nature and extent of entrepreneurs PBOE shaped their subsequent behaviour and learning. Similarities and differences between habitual starter and acquirer entrepreneurs are highlighted. Several theoretically and empirically derived propositions are developed.

7.2 Learning

7.2.1 Gaps in the Knowledge Base and Research Questions

Ucbasaran et al. (2003) focused upon the actual behaviour of habitual starter entrepreneurs (i.e., entrepreneurs who have established more than one business) and habitual acquirer entrepreneurs (i.e., entrepreneurs who have purchased/acquired more than one business). The authors highlighted that an entrepreneur's human capital can impact on the first as well as the subsequent venture(s) owned by habitual entrepreneurs. A human capital perspective was used to explore the dynamic entrepreneurial process. This perspective appreciates that habitual entrepreneurs can acquire resources during their entrepreneurial careers. Although not formally stated in the article, the grand tour research question was as follows:

- *Does the nature and extent of entrepreneurs' PBOE shape their subsequent behaviour and learning?*

116   *Learning*

The article explored whether PBOE impacted on how habitual entrepreneurs searched for information, as well as their exploitation of business opportunities. Over time, habitual entrepreneurs acquire human specific resources, skills and capabilities (i.e., human capital) that can be utilized to start and/or acquire businesses. The nature and extent of an entrepreneur's human capital is crucial in accessing and mobilizing social, financial, physical and organizational resources. A case study approach was used to develop propositions that highlighted the similarities and differences between habitual starter and acquirer entrepreneurs. Below, material from the article focusing upon the dynamic aspects of human capital relating to entrepreneurial learning is summarized.

7.2.2 Human Capital Perspective Explaining the Emergence of Types of Habitual Entrepreneurs

A resource-based perspective of entrepreneurship suggests that business owners are an organization's key resource (Westhead, 1995). The ability to pursue opportunities is, in part, influenced by an entrepreneur's resource endowment, or 'human capital'. An entrepreneur's human capital can be mobilized to gain access to a predictable, uninterrupted supply of critical resources. Entrepreneurs are heterogeneous with respect to their resources and capabilities. In response to environmental opportunities and threats, an entrepreneur can acquire during their careers in entrepreneurship (Dyer, 1994; Katz, 1994), a profile of human-specific resources, skills, competencies and capabilities. Experienced habitual entrepreneurs are assumed to utilize their human capital to create, discover and exploit additional business opportunities. Due to human capital resource differences, contrasts in behaviour and learning are assumed to be expected between different types of habitual entrepreneurs.

7.2.3 Methodology

Low and MacMillan (1988) suggested that studies focusing upon entrepreneurial behaviour should consider contextual issues and identify the processes that explain rather than merely describe the entrepreneurial phenomenon. A case study approach was selected to provide a wider theoretical understanding of the habitual entrepreneur phenomenon. This methodological approach focused on understanding the dynamics present within a single setting (Eisenhardt, 1989; Yin, 1989). A discovery-oriented approach (Desphande, 1983) was utilized. Theoretical rather than probability sampling of entrepreneurs was conducted. The authors did not seek to generalize the findings to the population of habitual entrepreneurs. Rather, the aim of the study was to build theory and to generalize evidence from the case studies to the human capital perspective. Empirical evidence was combined with existing knowledge to develop theoretical insights that could inform further research in the area.

A longitudinal approach was utilized to focus upon the entrepreneurial learning reported by habitual entrepreneurs. Because there is no direct means of identifying habitual entrepreneurs, the respondents interviewed were indirectly identified from three sources. These sources enabled the authors to identify habitual starter and habitual acquirer entrepreneurs. Six out of the eight cases were identified in 1994 from two sources. The habitual acquirer entrepreneurs were selected from the CMBOR database, which effectively comprises the population of MBOs and MBIs in the United Kingdom. Two of the habitual starter entrepreneurs were identified as a result of discussions with venture capitalists. Face-to-face interviews were conducted. Interviews were conducted utilizing a semi-structured questionnaire derived from the existing literature. Each interview lasted between one and two hours. The habitual entrepreneurs were contacted a second time twelve months later. These telephone interviews focused upon the development of the ventures after the original interviews. Further, they allowed the cross-checking of information gathered during the initial interview.

Interviews were undertaken to gather broad information relating to habitual entrepreneurs. Eisenhardt (1989) suggests that theory building from case studies requires theoretical sampling of cases. Further, Eisenhardt suggests it is more appropriate to choose cases that highlight extreme situations or polar types in which the process of interest is transparently observable. The aim of the study was to explore differences and similarities between two polar extreme types of habitual entrepreneurs. At different points in time, some habitual entrepreneurs may both start and acquire businesses. For the purpose of the current study, habitual starter entrepreneurs were defined as those entrepreneurs who had established more than one business, whereas habitual acquirer entrepreneurs were regarded as entrepreneurs who had purchased/acquired more than one business. Responses from habitual entrepreneurs that have both started and acquired businesses were not discussed in the study.

The original interviews gathered information from four habitual acquirer entrepreneurs and a further two habitual starter entrepreneurs. An equal number of habitual starter and acquirer entrepreneurs were compared in order to allow findings to be replicated within categories (Eisenhardt, 1989). Comparable information from an additional two habitual starter entrepreneurs was gathered. Two habitual starter entrepreneurs were identified from a list of respondents who responded to a survey of privately owned businesses conducted in 1990/91 (Birley and Westhead, 1992). The authors interviewed the two habitual starter entrepreneurs in late 1998 and early 1999. For consistency, the face-to-face interviewing technique utilized to gather information from respondents drawn from the CMBOR database was again utilized. The data available from the survey conducted in 1990/91 allowed the authors to cross-check information provided by the habitual starter entrepreneurs relating to their PBOE. Informal meetings and reviews of media reports in addition allowed the authors to monitor the activities of all eight habitual starter and acquirer entrepreneurs over time. Follow-up

118   *Learning*

contacts were made with the eight selected habitual entrepreneurs between late 1998 and May 1999, mainly by telephone, but also through face-to-face discussions. Table 7.1 presents an overview of the habitual entrepreneur cases in terms of their type. This table also provides a description of the first and subsequent venture(s) owned by the habitual entrepreneurs.

7.2.4 Findings

Entrepreneurial experience can be viewed as a dynamic concept where entrepreneurs learn from their PBOE. This experience provides some habitual entrepreneurs with a framework for identifying and processing appropriate information. If previous business ownership experiences are seen as experiments, habitual entrepreneurs should evaluate carefully and objectively the feedback from these experiences (Nystrom and Starbuck, 1984). Human processing research has revealed that decision-makers often use cognitive styles associated with biases and heuristics that enables them to deal with complex and uncertain situations, such as anchoring, adjustment and availability (Tversky and Kahneman, 1974). Evidence suggests that entrepreneurs can be distinguished from other groups in terms of their cognitive mindset (i.e., the way they perceive and view the external world). Decision-making associated with 'entrepreneurial cognition' (Wright et al., 2000) is viewed as relying to a greater extent on biases and heuristics, as opposed to a systematic decision-making style. Biases and heuristics can be an effective and efficient guide to decision-making, particularly under conditions of environmental uncertainty and complexity. These mental shortcuts may also influence the way in which habitual entrepreneurs evaluate, and learn from their PBOE. Busenitz and Barney (1997) argue that cognitive biases and heuristics are difficult to change. Moreover, they may represent sustained sources of differences between individuals (i.e., advantage or disadvantage). Habitual entrepreneurs exhibit heuristic-based logic in decision-making (Busenitz and Barney, 1997). This form of decision-making enables them to quickly understand uncertain and complex situations. In addition, it can encourage forward-looking approaches that allow habitual entrepreneurs to exhibit faster learning and be associated with unorthodox interpretations.

The eight interviewees were asked to evaluate what they had learnt from owning their first venture. Habitual acquirer entrepreneurs emphasized that they had learnt what venture capitalists expect and how to negotiate with them (e.g., Jacks, Cooper and Guthrie). Some habitual entrepreneurs highlighted the importance of being aware of the problems associated with debt finance and high gearing with regard to their first venture (e.g., Harris and Guthrie). Harris claimed that outside assistance from a venture capitalist had ensured that his second venture was appropriately geared.

Some respondents suggested that PBOE enabled them to secure better deals with customers and suppliers (e.g., Guthrie and Case 'R'). Case 'R' demonstrated this with the following statements:

Table 7.1 Demographic Characteristics of the Habitual Entrepreneurs and Their Ventures

Entrepreneur	Entrepreneurial Type (no. of ventures)	Description of first venture	Description of second venture
Habitual Starters			
Curtis	Habitual starter (three)	Founded business in area of expertise in outdoor advertising in 1985; sale to achieve growth.	Start-up again (1990) plus initial acquisition (1993) in niche sector with organic growth.
Harris	Habitual starter (two)	Start-up of house builder, aborted floatation (1987) followed by trade sale and departure of entrepreneur.	Start-up again in the same sector but with different size and growth expectations. Initial limited regional diversification replaced by concentration in the London area.
Evans	Habitual starter (two)	Founded consultancy business in area of expertise in 1983 in pharmaceuticals; bought out by a client, operated as a sole trader until 1991.	Start-up in different sector in 1986 to work with wife. Initially started off with the manufacturing side of embroidery then focused on the finishing operation.
Case 'R'	Habitual starter (two)	Founded business in 1987 in area of expertise to commercialize technology developed by team member; growth achieved through merger with U.S. company in 1995.	Start-up around 1996/7 in same sector with available technology and EU grant; dissolved due to insufficient time (now MD for Europe of initial venture).

(Continued)

Table 7.1 (Continued)

Habitual Acquirers			
Cooper	Habitual acquirer (two MBIs)	Following managerial career, MBI of bearings company in 1987 needing turnaround; successful trade sale in 1991.	Larger MBI of engineering division with turnaround and organic growth potential in 1993. Business sold in 1995 having met targets.
Timpson	Habitual acquirer (two MBOs)	Buyback of family shoe business from acquirer in 1983. Exit simultaneous to MBO of second venture in same industry.	Second MBO much smaller but based on identifying new product opportunities. Major acquisition in 1995 increasing number of outlets by a half and change in strategy.
Guthrie	Habitual acquirer (five MBO/ MBIs)	MBO in 1985 of company in leisure sector where employed for considerable time; floatation followed by acquisition and departure of entrepreneur.	Started up in eating out sector in 1991, then several MBIs; several different types of strategy adopted.
Jacks	Habitual acquirer (four MBO/ MBIs)	MBO of software company in 1980. Following deferral of floatation in 1987, trade sale in 1988.	MBI/rescue of small engineering company, then same for a facilities management company. Acquired small garden furniture business; turnaround and product development.

Source: Authors.

Learning 121

> We went into [the first venture] with no contacts, with an unknown name, we didn't know an awful lot about the companies we were trying to sell to and we had a real credibility problem. . .But we did learn reasonably quickly and we realized very early on that it was going to be very important to establish that credibility and build a customer base. . .We had done a lot of research especially in terms of technology but that was about it. . .I would say I would never start a business without having some kind of ready made customer base and some kind of credibility in the area I was working.
>
> (Case 'R')

Another entrepreneur (e.g., Evans) asserted that s/he had learnt the need to acknowledge the downside of strong ties. Most notably, s/he learnt to formalize business relationships through contracts rather than informal 'handshake' agreements. Some habitual entrepreneurs also appreciated the need for planning. Timpson, for example, noted the importance of planning in terms of investigating all tax angles, while Cooper emphasized the need for planning in order to maintain the focus of the business (i.e., acquisitions carried out in the first venture were seen as a distraction). Case 'R' highlighted the importance of planning right from the outset in the form of a clear business plan that considered various contingencies.

Several habitual entrepreneurs (e.g., Case 'R' and Cooper) appreciated that some business development issues were beyond their own control, and they had benefited from 'luck'. Ignoring pertinent internal and external environmental factors may be associated with habitual entrepreneurs exhibiting overconfidence. Cooper expressed the learning aspects of previous experience as follows:

> I had a very clear idea on how I wanted the deal structured, and experience saved a lot of grief. [The venture capitalist] wanted to see if, having made money out of the first deal, did I still have the bottle for the second. The danger is overconfidence, losing sight of what [you] are really trying to achieve or getting carried away with your ego. . .What I'm saying is that when you are successful apart from being a good manager usually somewhere along the line you will find that the gods are smiling on you, so don't get too cocky with it. . .In my case learning from experiences was crucial—in terms of understanding better the structure of the deal but also largely to do with lessons relating to managing the business.
>
> (Cooper)

This liability of experience may retard their subsequent performance. While the habitual entrepreneurs in this study were all successful entrepreneurs, overconfidence to a certain extent may be observed in the case of entrepreneurs who chose to own more than one venture at the same time. For example, the closure of a previous business may encourage a habitual entrepreneur to come back and to be more successful the second time around (e.g.,

122 *Learning*

Harris). On the downside, some habitual entrepreneurs reported 'burnout' (i.e., health problems) after owning more than one venture (e.g., Guthrie).

Active external and independent non-executive directors not only provide the firm with additional resources, they can also control the behaviour of habitual entrepreneurs who are exhibiting overconfidence. Some habitual entrepreneurs seek to address business development hurdles by assembling dynamic and broadly based management teams that can proactively ensure business development. One of the respondents (e.g., Cooper) argued that business decisions had to be made on the basis of detailed evaluations of the venture's current managerial capabilities and limitations. Several habitual entrepreneurs indicated that they had learned from their PBOE. Most notably, they knew when to close or sell a venture (e.g., Case 'R' and Cooper), or delegate managerial responsibility to more able entrepreneurial team members (e.g., Guthrie and Jacks). As Case 'R' noted in respect of both ventures:

> . . .at the beginning I could work at weekends, stay till late but towards the end it became very intrusive. The attraction of selling to [business X] was to maybe get back a bit more free time.
>
> (Case 'R', first venture)

> We dissolved the company. I reached a point where I knew I couldn't do the two things and we were going through quite a critical time here [first venture which had been sold with Case 'R' remaining in post] too—reorganization. So I chose to stay here.
>
> (Case 'R', second venture)

This discussion suggested the following propositions:

> Proposition 7.1: *As a result of their PBOE, both habitual starter and acquirer entrepreneurs are likely to cite that they have learnt about negotiating with financiers.*
>
> Proposition 7.2: *As a result of their PBOE, both habitual starter and acquirer entrepreneurs are likely to cite the need to identify appropriate levels of leverage.*
>
> Proposition 7.3: *As a result of their PBOE, both habitual starter and acquirer entrepreneurs are likely to cite the importance of planning.*
>
> Proposition 7.4: *As a result of their PBOE, both habitual starter and acquirer entrepreneurs are likely to cite the need to identify factors that are beyond their control.*

7.2.5 Conclusions and Implications

The study demonstrated additional dimensions of the heterogeneity of habitual entrepreneurs. In relation to PBOE, a distinction was made between habitual starter and acquirer entrepreneurs. Relating to a dynamic human capital perspective, case study evidence explored similarities and differences in the learning reported by the two types of habitual entrepreneurs. Particularly habitual acquirer entrepreneurs were more likely to have learnt the importance of planning the path of their subsequent ventures, including the timing of business exit. This may reflect the fact that habitual acquirer entrepreneurs typically originate from a managerial position in an existing organization with established systems for planning and control. Habitual entrepreneurs, particularly individuals who had previously used VC, were more likely to have learnt how to re-contract with financiers to obtain favourable investment terms. The case analysis of learning experiences did not reveal any distinct differences between the habitual starter and acquirer entrepreneurs. This may be because habitual entrepreneurs as a group display common learning patterns based on their distinctive 'entrepreneurial cognition'. The authors' interpretation was consistent with the view that habitual entrepreneurs may rely on heuristic-based thinking to a greater extent than novice entrepreneurs (Busenitz and Barney, 1997). Case study respondents highlighted areas where they had learned from their PBOE. However, PBOE can be associated with several liabilities. Habitual entrepreneurs need to be aware of cognitive biases such as overconfidence and attribution problems by identifying when favourable outcomes are due to factors external to the individual entrepreneur. While PBOE may be generally useful in subsequent ventures, habitual entrepreneurs still need to learn, 'adapt' and modify their behaviour in line with changing external environmental conditions. Results from the case studies cannot be generalized to the population of habitual entrepreneurs. They can, however, be generalized analytically (Yin, 1989) to the human capital perspective of habitual entrepreneurs discussed in the article.

7.3 Reflection Questions

The experimental learning PBOE experience can be associated with several assets and liabilities. Presented case evidence suggested entrepreneurs can learn from their PBOE. Please consider the following reflection questions:

- *What similarities in learning are reported by habitual starter and habitual acquirer entrepreneurs?*
- *What differences in learning are reported by habitual starter and habitual acquirer entrepreneurs?*

8 Entrepreneur and Firm Performance

8.1 Learning Objectives and Overview

Firm performance needs to be explored with regard to a range of performance indicators (Cooper, 1993; Storey, 1994). 'Hard' economic firm financial and non-financial performance (or firm growth) outcomes have individually or collectively been monitored in firm performance studies. However, entrepreneurs have contrasting thresholds of economic performance (Gimeno et al., 1997). These thresholds can be influenced by the objectives of entrepreneurs. Entrepreneurs may have growth objectives as well as a desire to draw regular income streams from the business(es) in which they have ownership stake(s) (Westhead, 1997). Some entrepreneurs set higher economic thresholds, and the extent to which they are satisfied with the performance of the surveyed venture may impact on the decision to stay with this venture or exit from it and/or the intention to start or purchase another firm.

Firm and entrepreneur performance needs to be monitored. Entrepreneurial performance is a subjective concept, depending on the personal expectations, aspirations and skills of the individual entrepreneur. Measuring entrepreneurial performance is a challenging task (Davidsson et al., 2006). Entrepreneurial performance can be assessed relating to all firms currently owned (i.e., minority and/or majority ownership stakes) by a portfolio entrepreneur (Rosa, 1998). 'Entrepreneurial career performance' relating to serial and portfolio entrepreneurs can also be assesses with regard the number and proportion of successful new enterprise processes or the total net worth created (Davidsson and Wiklund, 2001; Parker, 2013).

Entrepreneur performance can be assessed with regard to firm performance indicators relating to sales revenues, profitability, employment, propensity and intensity of exporting activity, etc (Storey, 1994). Also, entrepreneur performance can be assessed in relation to entrepreneur goals such as to the desire to grow the surveyed firm; desire to increase the total employment size of the surveyed firm; the amount of money drawn out of the surveyed firm; household income (Rønning and Kolvereid, 2006); satisfaction with the surveyed firm; standard of living today compared to when they first established/owned

Performance 125

the surveyed firm; and willingness to start or purchase a business again in the future.

Relatively few studies have compared the performance of novice, serial and portfolio entrepreneurs with regard to firm and entrepreneur performance indicators. Even fewer studies have monitored the total performance of portfolio entrepreneurs, and the 'entrepreneurial career performance' of serial and portfolio entrepreneurs.

In this chapter, the link between entrepreneurs PBOE is explored with regard to the performance of the surveyed firm and entrepreneur performance. Two quantitative articles relating to Scotland and Ghana are summarized. The first quantitative article used non-parametric statistical tests to ascertain whether portfolio entrepreneurs reported superior performance relative to novice entrepreneurs, and whether serial entrepreneurs reported superior performance relative to novice entrepreneurs, with a particular focus on growth. Surveyed firm performance indicators as well as entrepreneur performance indicators were monitored. The second quantitative article builds upon insights from human capital theory, particularly specific human capital relating to the nature and extent of PBOE, to detect whether various measures of PBOE were significantly associated within a multivariate statistical framework with entrepreneurs reporting higher exporting intensities.

8.2 Entrepreneur and Firm Performance: Growth

8.2.1 Gaps in the Knowledge Base and Research Questions

Despite growing interest in the portfolio entrepreneur phenomenon, there is scant evidence relating to the performance of firms owned by serial and portfolio entrepreneurs. As intimated throughout this book, it is generally assumed that serial and portfolio entrepreneurs with PBOE to mobilize will generally own more successful firms than novice entrepreneurs with no PBOE to mobilize. There is, therefore, a gap in the knowledge base relating to the performance of serial and portfolio relating to both the entrepreneur and the firm as the unit of analysis. Previous studies have failed to detect any statistically significant size and performance differences between firms owned by novice, serial and portfolio entrepreneurs (Westhead and Wright, 1998).

The article by Westhead et al. (2005b) sought to explore gaps in the knowledge base surrounding the entrepreneur and firm performance reported by inexperienced novice entrepreneurs, as well as experienced serial and portfolio entrepreneurs in Scotland. The study focused on the performance of each surveyed businesses. Reflecting a common weakness of studies focusing upon portfolio entrepreneurs, the survey instrument utilized failed to gather information on the characteristics and the performance of the other business(es) in which portfolio entrepreneurs have ownership stake(s) in.

126   *Performance*

As a result, the full economic contribution of portfolio entrepreneurs in Scotland was not assessed. Although not formally stated in the article, the following two broad research questions were explored:

- *Do portfolio entrepreneurs report superior performance relative to novice entrepreneurs and serial entrepreneurs?*
- *Do serial entrepreneurs report superior performance relative to novice entrepreneurs and portfolio entrepreneurs?*

8.2.2 Hypotheses Tested

This univariate statistical study did not formally test any hypotheses.

8.2.3 Methodology

The data collection process relating to this study conducted in Scotland was reported in Section 3.3.3.1. Non-parametric Chi-square tests and Mann-Whitney U tests were conducted to detect statistically significant differences in performance between the types of entrepreneurs.

8.2.4 Findings

The authors explored the performance of portfolio entrepreneur surveyed firms against the surveyed firms owned by novice and serial entrepreneurs. A larger proportion of portfolio, rather than other entrepreneurs, reported that they received income from sources other than the surveyed businesses. Also, a larger proportion of portfolio, rather than novice entrepreneurs, had drawn out more than £75,000 during the previous twelve months. A larger proportion of portfolio rather than other entrepreneurs indicated that they intended to establish or purchase an additional business.

In 1999, the average sales revenues of businesses owned by portfolio entrepreneurs were larger than those owned by other entrepreneurs. On average, businesses owned by portfolio entrepreneurs reported larger absolute sales growth over the 1996 to 1999 period than those owned by novice entrepreneurs. Further, a larger proportion of portfolio rather than novice entrepreneurs reported that their current operating profit performance was above average relative to competitors.

Supporting the finding relating to sales, portfolio entrepreneur firms were larger than those owned by other entrepreneurs in terms of total employment size in 2001. Moreover, portfolio entrepreneur firms, on average, reported higher absolute and percentage total employment growth over the 1996 to 2001 period than firms owned by other entrepreneurs.

Additional analysis revealed that the top 4% of fastest growing firms owned by portfolio entrepreneurs generated 55% of gross new jobs created by portfolio entrepreneur firms, while the comparable sub-sample of firms owned by novice entrepreneurs generated 44% of gross new jobs. In contrast, the comparable serial entrepreneur sub-sample only generated 38% of gross new jobs. Relatively few entrepreneurs have the inclination, or the ability to be wealth creators (Storey et al., 1987), with reference to the surveyed firms alone that leading 'winning entrepreneurs' within the portfolio entrepreneur category accounted for more absolute employment growth than leading 'winning entrepreneurs' in the other entrepreneur categories.

The authors explored the performance of serial entrepreneur surveyed firms against the surveyed firms owned by novice and portfolio entrepreneurs. Less than a third of serial entrepreneurs intended to establish or purchase an additional business in the future. In 1999, the average sales revenues of businesses owned by serial entrepreneurs were larger than those owned by novice entrepreneurs. Further, a larger proportion of serial rather than novice entrepreneurs reported that their current profit performance was above average relative to competitors.

8.2.5 Conclusions and Implications

Presented evidence relating to entrepreneur performance in Scotland highlighted that entrepreneurs should not be considered a homogenous entity with regard to their economic contributions. Notably, there is some tentative evidence that suggests that portfolio entrepreneurs own superior performing firms. There may be lessons for both novice and serial entrepreneurs from the behaviour of portfolio entrepreneurs regarding the strategies they might usefully adopt in order to enhance the performance of their ventures. To maximize the returns from public policy intervention in the short term, there may be a case to identify the portfolio entrepreneurs who want to grow their ventures, and provide to them with the information and other resources required to facilitate firm growth.

8.3 Entrepreneur and Firm Performance: Exporting

8.3.1 Gaps in the Knowledge Base and Research Questions

Engagement in exporting activities can be viewed as a measure of firm performance. International entrepreneurship theorists (McDougall and Oviatt, 2000) appreciate that the human capital of lead entrepreneurs can shape the exporting process (Wright et al., 2007). However, the link between a lead entrepreneur's PBOE and the propensity to export has generally been ignored (Wheeler et al., 2008). Robson et al. (2012b) explored this research gap in the article summarized below. The lead entrepreneur who shapes resource allocation and strategy in smaller private firms was the unit of analysis. With respect to replicating previous work, the authors explored whether an entrepreneur's ability to assemble and mobilize human capital was associated with the widely explored intensity of

128　*Performance*

exporting measure (i.e., sales revenue generated by exports as a proportion of total sales revenue). Export intensity as a measure of internationalization performance has attracted some criticism (Katsikeas et al., 2000), but it is widely used and it allowed comparison with the existing body of knowledge. With respect to extending previous work, the authors explored whether the extent and nature of an entrepreneur's PBOE (i.e., specific human capital) shaped exporting intensity. The authors considered both the *extent* and *nature* of entrepreneurs' PBOE with regard to three dimensions: years of business ownership experience, habitual entrepreneurs compared with novice entrepreneurs and portfolio entrepreneurs compared with serial entrepreneurs (i.e., novice entrepreneurs as the reference category). They also extended understanding by examining the relationship between PBOE and exporting outside North America and Europe.

The following research question was explored:

- *Does an entrepreneur's human capital, particularly PBOE, increase the intensity of exporting?*

8.3.2 Hypotheses Tested

Experiential knowledge can shape opportunity exploitation. Entrepreneurial experience can add to human capital through enhanced reputation and better understanding of the requirements of financial institutions. Human capital from entrepreneurial experience may be interrelated with greater social capital associated with diverse networks (Davidsson and Honig, 2003). Ties with external actors can be utilized to accumulate and mobilize additional resources for firm development (Kim and Aldrich, 2005). Experienced entrepreneurs can mobilize their human capital and broader social capital developed through PBOE exposure to access resources that are critical for exporting. Entrepreneurs reporting long durations of PBOE may have had more opportunities to accumulate and mobilize their specific human capital. Further, experienced entrepreneurs associated with legitimacy, financial resources, production and/or marketing and distribution skills accumulated due to prior and current business ownership experience may have exporting opportunities presented to them (Ucbasaran et al., 2008). This discussion suggested the following hypothesis:

Hypothesis 8.1: *Entrepreneurs with longer durations of PBOE are more likely to report higher exporting intensities.*

The extent and nature of PBOE can shape opportunity identification and exploitation behaviour. Habitual entrepreneurs may have learnt from their PBOE successes and mistakes compared to novice entrepreneurs with no prior experience (Ucbasaran et al., 2008). Notably, habitual entrepreneurs can learn from the feedback from that experience to enhance their exporting activity compared to novice entrepreneurs. This discussion suggested the following hypothesis:

> Hypothesis 8.2: *Habitual entrepreneurs are more likely than novice entrepreneurs to report higher exporting intensities.*

The goals, resources and assets and liabilities reported by portfolio entrepreneurs can differ from those cited by serial entrepreneurs (Ucbasaran et al., 2008). Portfolio entrepreneurs with a broader resource pool (i.e., ownership of two or more ventures concurrently) may find it easier to circumvent barriers to exporting. Portfolio entrepreneurs, on average, may be more entrepreneurial than novice entrepreneurs. They are more likely to start firms because they want to be challenged by the opportunities and problems involved, more likely to enjoy just thinking about and looking for new business opportunities and to have a special alertness towards spotting opportunities (Westhead et al., 2005b). Portfolio entrepreneurs may, therefore, be more likely to engage in exporting activity than novice entrepreneurs. Serial entrepreneurs appear more likely than novice entrepreneurs to have gained experience in a variety of settings; to have introduced a new product/service and/or to have developed a new distribution approach; to make more use of information from customers and suppliers; to seek to grow their business; and to perceive unmet needs of customers (Westhead et al., 2005b). This discussion suggested the following hypotheses:

> Hypothesis 8.3: *Portfolio entrepreneurs are more likely than novice entrepreneurs to report higher exporting intensities.*
>
> Hypothesis 8.4: *Serial entrepreneurs are more likely than novice entrepreneurs to report higher exporting intensities.*

8.3.3 Methodology

8.3.3.1 Data

The data collection process has been discussed in Section 4.2.3.1 relating to Robson et al. (2013). In total, 432 respondents provided complete data for the selected variables explored, yielding a response rate of 59%. This rate is considerably higher than similar entrepreneur, SMEs and international business studies (Yang et al., 2006). Also, the authors concluded there was no evidence to suggest that the results would be affected by common method bias.

8.3.3.2 Dependent Variables

Entrepreneurs reported the sales revenue generated by exports as a proportion of total sales revenue. Two dependent variables were computed. Firms that exported 1% or more of their total sales reported export propensity

130 *Performance*

(i.e., exporters were scored 1, whilst non-exporters were scored 0 (Export propensity). This exporting intensity variable was converted into a percentage (Export intensity). Exporting intensity ranged from 0% to 85%.

8.3.3.3 Independent Variables

Entrepreneurs were asked to report the number of years they had owned and run a business (*Experience*). Because a high proportion of entrepreneurial activity is team-based, the definitions used include both minority and majority ownership stakes. Entrepreneurs were asked to indicate the total number of businesses they had established and/or purchased in which they had minority or majority ownership stakes. A distinction was made between habitual (i.e., serial and portfolio) (i.e., individuals who at the time of the survey had prior minority or majority ownership experience in two or more prior independent businesses) and novice entrepreneurs (i.e., individuals who at the time of the survey had a minority or majority ownership stake in a single business that was new or purchased). Moreover, a distinction was made between serial (i.e., individuals who had sold/closed a business which they had a minority or majority ownership stake in, and who at the time of the survey had a minority or majority ownership stake in a single independent business that was new or purchased) and portfolio entrepreneurs (i.e., individuals who at the time of the survey had minority or majority ownership stakes in two or more independent businesses that were new and/or purchased). Four binary variables were operationalized: habitual entrepreneurs (*Habitual*), serial entrepreneurs (*Serial*), portfolio entrepreneurs (*Portfolio*) and novice entrepreneurs (*Novice*). The Serial and Portfolio variables were included in the regression models, and the reference category was Novice entrepreneurs.

8.3.3.4 Techniques

A Heckman two-stage test was conducted to explore for potential sample selection bias between exporters and non-exporters (Greene, 2000). This technique ascertains whether the sub-sample of exporting firms are not random (i.e., the unobservable variables associated with the propensity to export are associated with the unobservable variables associated with export intensity). The first step of the Heckman test explored the issue of respondent selection bias relating to the profiles of exporters. With regard to the total sample of exporting and non-exporting respondents, a probit regression analysis was estimated relating to the propensity to export or not. Variables (i.e., observables) included in step 1 need to be different from those included in step 2. At least one independent variable has to be included in step 1 but not step 2, which is theoretically associated with export propensity but not export intensity. Some studies use a measure of productivity such as output per employee (Wagner, 2007). In line with previous studies, the authors used total sales revenue divided by the number of employees, and this measure was included in step 1 but not step 2. Independent variables were considered within step 1. A generalized residual variable, which is a function of the correlation between the disturbances of the probit model, was considered during step 2, which related to an OLS regression analysis focusing upon export intensity. If the generalized residual coefficient was significant within the OLS model, it suggests that the OLS model would be distorted by bias. However, if the generalized residual variable was not statistically significant, the OLS model related to a random sample of exporters. The authors did not detect any selection bias. They concluded it was appropriate to conduct OLS regression analysis relating to the exporting intensity dependent variable.

8.3.4 Findings

In total, 95 respondents (22%) suggested their firms were exporters and 337 firms (78%) were non-exporters. The average export intensity was 9.5% (when excluding non-exporters, the average level was 43%). Further, 60 firms (14% of all firms) reported international sales of 25% or more. In total, 177 respondents were habitual entrepreneurs (41%), among whom 56 (13%) were serial entrepreneurs and a further 121 respondents (28%) were portfolio entrepreneurs. These proportions are comparable to those reported in developed country studies (Ucbasaran et al., 2008).

The length of experience variable (*Experience*) was included in an OLS model. Entrepreneurs with longer durations of business ownership experience were more likely to export, and to report higher exporting intensities. However, the relationships were not statistically significant at the 0.1 level. Hypothesis 8.1 was not supported.

In another OLS model, the *Experience* variable was replaced with the *Habitual* variable. Habitual entrepreneurs were significantly more likely to be exporters and to report higher exporting intensities. Hypothesis 8.2 was supported.

In a further OLS model, the *Habitual* variable was replaced with the *Serial* and *Portfolio* variables. Portfolio entrepreneurs reported significantly higher exporting intensities. Serial entrepreneurs did not report significantly higher exporting intensities. Hypothesis 8.3 was supported, but hypothesis 8.4 was not supported.

8.3.5 Conclusions and Implications

The authors presented new insights into the under-researched area of the links between entrepreneur PBOE and exporting intensity. With reference to the private SME context, a novel contribution of this study is the exploration of the relative importance of PBOE vis-à-vis other firm, entrepreneur and domestic environmental resources that may shape variations in a widely respected exporting intensity performance outcome. Entrepreneur-specific

132 *Performance*

human capital relating to PBOE was found to be a key driver associated with superior exporting performance.

One of the most striking findings was that habitual, particularly portfolio, entrepreneurs were more likely than novice entrepreneurs to report higher exporting intensities. Habitual entrepreneurs are not a homogenous entity. Serial entrepreneurs need to further accumulate additional specific human capital and social capital to fully engage in the exporting process. Novice and serial entrepreneurs may compensate for their human capital deficiencies by investing in social capital, particularly links with private sector organizations with increased legitimacy and broader technical and financial resources.

8.4 Summary

Westhead and Wright (1998) suggested that the entrepreneur should be the unit of policy analysis throughout all stages of the entrepreneurial process. They highlighted that an entrepreneur's PBOE relating to resource accumulation and mobilization could impact on the subsequent performance of firms owned by habitual entrepreneurs. Few studies have monitored the performance of serial and portfolio entrepreneurs relative to novice entrepreneurs with regard to firm and entrepreneur performance indicators. This chapter summarized two quantitative articles relating to the Scotland and Ghana contexts where the entrepreneur was the unit of analysis. The first article used univariate non-parametric statistical tests to detect firm and entrepreneur differences in growth between serial, portfolio and novice entrepreneurs in Scotland with regard to the surveyed businesses. Tentative evidence was presented suggesting that portfolio entrepreneurs owned superior performing businesses. The second article used multivariate statistical analysis to explore whether the nature and extent of entrepreneurs' PBOE in relation to four measures of PBOE was associated with entrepreneurs in Ghana reporting higher exporting intensities. Habitual entrepreneurs relative to novice entrepreneurs were significantly more likely to be exporters and to report higher exporting intensities. However, habitual entrepreneurs with longer durations of PBOE were not significantly more likely to be exporters or to report higher exporting intensities. Finer-level analysis revealed portfolio entrepreneurs reported significantly higher exporting intensities, whilst serial entrepreneurs did not report significantly higher exporting intensities.

8.5 Reflection Questions

In Chapter 8, entrepreneur PBOE was assumed to enhance firm and entrepreneur performance. The reported quantitative articles detected several differences (and similarities) between serial, portfolio and novice entrepreneurs. Please consider the following reflection questions:

- *What 'hard' firm performance indicators should be monitored in habitual entrepreneur studies?*
- *What entrepreneur performance indicators should be monitored in habitual entrepreneur studies?*
- *Do portfolio entrepreneurs report superior firm performance relative to novice entrepreneurs?*
- *If the goal of policy is to maximize the returns from public policy intervention, is there a case to target resources to portfolio entrepreneurs?*

9 Conclusions and Implications

9.1 Future Research Directions

Additional studies are warranted exploring how PBOE can enable habitual entrepreneurs to better assemble a resource base that enables them to invest in and mobilize resources (such as innovation) to promote competitive advantage for the individual and/or group of firms they own (Westhead and Wright, 2014). The external environment can shape access to resource accumulation and mobilization. PBOE may counter issues that can impede the entrepreneurial process and venture development. Additional research is warranted surrounding how types of habitual entrepreneurs may compensate for location disadvantages by mobilizing their PBOE. The role of context is increasingly being recognized in entrepreneurship research (Zahra and Wright, 2011). Future studies need to explore how context in developed and developing economies promote or impede habitual entrepreneurship. Further, different context may influence the particular configurations of the phenomenon and they need to be examined. For example, to what extent do some contexts promote habitual entrepreneur start-ups versus habitual entrepreneur venture purchase modes? To what extent do some contexts favour portfolio forms of entrepreneurship involving family networks?

Some habitual entrepreneurs realize that they were initially too optimistic, and subsequently adjust their thinking. Consequently, they report a more realistic outlook in a subsequent venture(s). Entrepreneurs with PBOE, particularly business failure experience, may be less likely to subsequently report comparative optimism. Alternatively, experienced entrepreneurs may accumulate biases and hence can be subsequently more likely to report comparative optimism. Additional research is warranted surrounding how the extent and nature of PBOE enables types of habitual entrepreneurs to (more quickly) address barriers (i.e., success syndrome, illusion of control, blind spots, denial and overconfidence) to the entrepreneurial process.

Storey (2011) suggested that superior business performance is due to luck, and that entrepreneur resources and learning do not play significant roles in explaining variations in firm performance. The latter view has been questioned (Westhead and Wright, 2014). Because habitual entrepreneurs

Conclusions 135

can accumulate both assets and liabilities associated with their PBOE, it may be misleading to assume that all habitual entrepreneurs are successful and outperform novice entrepreneurs (Ucbasaran et al., 2006). The current stock of novice entrepreneurs is the breeding ground (i.e., pool) for future experienced habitual entrepreneurs. Some highly successful entrepreneurs are associated with PBOE 'failure(s)', which represent potentially valuable opportunities for learning, and the revision of expectations (Ucbasaran et al., 2010). Notably, some entrepreneurs respond to and learn from failure PBOE. Here, there is a need to differentiate economic (i.e., firm bankruptcy) from non-economic failure (i.e., the venture closed because its performance was too low in relation to the entrepreneur's expectations) PBOE. In addition, some entrepreneurs learn from PBOE success and/or a diverse pool of success and failure PBOE success. If failure of one business is an isolated case among a series of successes, or among a portfolio of ventures, it may weigh less heavily in the entrepreneur's cognitive processes. Policies aimed at incentivising all failed entrepreneurs to re-enter business ownership on the grounds that they will have learnt from their experience could be too simplistic. Currently, we know very little about how habitual entrepreneurs learn from their POBE, and how this learning is implemented in subsequent ventures. Detailed, longitudinal case studies, perhaps involving ethnographic research, are needed to open the present black box relating to this process. Similarly, we do not know whether all entrepreneurs that learn from PBOE failure become better entrepreneurs. Further research is, therefore, also warranted relating to the links between PBOE success and/or failure experience and learning, and the linkage between entrepreneurial learning reported by types of habitual entrepreneurs and subsequent entrepreneur attitudes, cognition, behaviour in relating to economic and non-economic firm and entrepreneur performance outcomes (Ucbasaran et al., 2010).

Previous studies have explored cross-sectional survey evidence. There is a need for longitudinal quantitative studies and studies that explore the performance of sub-types of serial and portfolio entrepreneurs with regard to pools of prior success and economic and non-economic failure experience. Studies have generally monitored the performance of a surveyed venture and not the performance of each business currently owned by portfolio entrepreneurs. Additional research is warranted relating to the total wealth contributions of portfolio entrepreneurs. Most habitual entrepreneur studies have explored survey evidence. To build theory, there is a need for more qualitative studies and longitudinal studies (Perks and Medway, 2012) to ascertain the environment, firm and external environmental stimuli and barriers to the entrepreneurial process reported by types of habitual entrepreneurs who have diverse PBOE to mobilize in relation to the entrepreneurial process and venture development. In sum, due to two decades of evolving research, as reflected in this volume, we now know a great deal more about the habitual entrepreneur phenomenon, but there still remains a vibrant and varied research agenda.

136 *Conclusions*

9.2 Summary and Reflection Questions

Notwithstanding the extensive evidence that we have presented in this book, further avenues remain for research in this area. Please consider the following research-oriented reflection questions:

- *Research question 1: What approaches can be developed to best research how portfolio and serial entrepreneurs create and develop their ventures over their entrepreneurial careers?*
- *Research question 2: There may be differences between habitual entrepreneurs in the goals they have for their ventures. How might research be designed to study the implications of these different goals for assessing the impact of habitual entrepreneurs?*
- *Research question 3: The extent and nature of habitual entrepreneurship may vary across country contexts. What factors might need to be taken into account in researching habitual entrepreneurs across these different contexts?*
- *Research question 4: Research on the habitual entrepreneur phenomenon has largely focused on individuals that create multiple ventures. How might research be developed to explore the impact of habitual entrepreneurs through other channels such as 1) multiple purchase of businesses; 2) multiple investments in ventures as a business angel; and 3) multiple engagement with entrepreneurial ventures as a member of multiple boards?*

References

Acs, Z.J., Audretsch, D.B., and Feldman, M.P. (1992). Real Effects of Academic Research. *American Economic Review*, 82(1): 363–367.

Adler, P., and Kwon, S. (2002). Social Capital: Prospects for a New Concept. *Academy of Management Review*, 27(1): 17–40.

Aldrich, J.H., and Nelson, F.D. (1984). *Linear Probability, Logit and Probit Models*. Newbury Park, CA: Sage Publications.

Alsos, G.A., and Kolvereid, L. (1998). The Business Gestation Process of Novice, Serial and Parallel Business Founders. *Entrepreneurship Theory and Practice*, 22(4): 101–114.

Alvarez, S.A., and Barney, J.B. (2007). Discovery and Creation: Alternative Theories of Entrepreneurial Action. *Strategic Entrepreneurship Journal*, 1(1–2): 11–26.

Alvarez, S.A., and Busenitz, L. (2001). The Entrepreneurship of Resource-Based Theory. *Journal of Management*, 27(6): 755–775.

Amabile, T.M. (1997). Motivating Creativity in Organizations: On Doing What You Love and Loving What You Do. *California Management Review*, 40(1): 39–58.

Amit, R., and Shoemaker, P.J.H. (1993). Strategic Assets and Organizational Rent. *Strategic Management Journal*, 14(1): 33–46.

Ardichvili, A., Cardozo, R., and Ray, S. (2003). A Theory of Entrepreneurial Opportunity Identification and Development. *Journal of Business Venturing*, 18(1): 105–123.

Babcock-Lumish, T.L. (2009). *Financing Clusters of Innovation: The Geography of Venture Capital Investment, US and UK*, Available at SSRN: http://ssrn.com/abstract=1358931

Backes-Gellner, U., and Werner, A. (2007). Entrepreneurial Signaling via Education: A Success Factor in Innovative Start-Ups. *Small Business Economics*, 29(1–2): 173–190.

Baerts, C., Meuleman, M., Debruyne, M., and Wright, M. (2016). Portfolio Entrepreneurship and Resource Orchestration. *Strategic Entrepreneurship Journal*.

Bandura, A. (1995). Perceived Self-Efficacy. In A.S.R. Manstead and M. Hawstone (Eds.) *The Blackwell Encyclopaedia of Social Psychology*. Oxford: Blackwell Publishers, pp.434–436.

Barney, J.B. (1991). Firm Resources and Sustained Competitive Advantage. *Journal of Management*, 17(1): 99–120.

Barney, J.B. (2001). Is the Resource-Based "View" a Useful Perspective for Strategic Management Research? Yes. *Academy of Management Review*, 26(1): 41–56.

Barney, J.B., Wright, M., and Ketchen, D. (2001). The Resource-Based View of the Firm. *Journal of Management*, 27(6): 625–642.

138　References

Baron, R.A. (1998). Cognitive Mechanisms in Entrepreneurship: Why and When Entrepreneurs Think Differently Than Other People. *Journal of Business Venturing*, 13(4): 275–294.

Baron, R.A. (2004). The Cognitive Perspective: A Valuable Tool for Answering Entrepreneurship's Basic "Why" Questions. *Journal of Business Venturing*, 19(2): 221–239.

Baron, R.A., and Ensley, M.D. (2006). Opportunity Recognition as the Detection of Meaningful Patterns: Evidence from Comparison and Novice and Experienced Entrepreneurs. *Management Science*, 52(9): 1331–1344.

Baron, R.A., and Henry, R.A. (2006). The Role of Expert Performance in Entrepreneurship: How Entrepreneurs Acquire the Capacity to Excel. *Paper Presented at the Babson Kauffman Entrepreneurship Research Conference*, Indiana University.

Bazerman, M.H. (1990). *Judgement in Managerial Decision Making* (2nd edition). New York, John Wiley and Sons.

Becheikh, N., Landry, R., and Amara, N. (2006). Lessons from Innovation Empirical Studies in the Manufacturing Sector: A Systematic Review of the Literature from 1993–2003. *Technovation*, 26(5–6): 644–664.

Becker, G.S. (1975). *Human Capital: A Theoretical and Empirical Analysis, with Special Reference to Education* (2nd edition). New York: National Bureau of Economic Research.

Becker, G.S. (1993). Nobel Lecture: The Economic Way of Looking at Behavior. *The Journal of Political Economy*, 101(3): 385–409.

Birley, S., and Westhead P. (1992). A Comparison of New Firms in 'Assisted' and 'Non-Assisted' Areas in Great Britain. *Entrepreneurship and Regional Development*, 4(3): 299–338.

Birley, S., and Westhead, P. (1993). A Comparison of New Businesses Established by 'Novice' and 'Habitual' Founders in Great Britain'. *International Small Business Journal*, 12(1): 38–60.

Blossfeld, H-P., Golsch, K., and Rohwer, G. (2007). *Event History Analysis with Stata*. London: Routledge Academic.

Bodas Freitas, I.M., and von Tunzelmann, N. (2008). Mapping Public Support for Innovation: A Comparison of Policy Alignment in the UK and France. *Research Policy*, 37(9): 1446–1464.

Brailey, K., Vasterling, J.J., and Franks, J.J. (2001). Memory of Psychodiagnostic Information: Biases and Effects of Expertise. *American Journal of Psychology*, 114(1): 55–92.

Brunstein, J.C., and Gollwitzer, P.M. (1996). Effects of Failure on Subsequent Performance: The Importance of Self-Defining Goals. *Journal of Personality and Social Psychology*, 70(2): 395–407.

Burt, R.S. (1982). *Toward a Structural Theory of Action*. New York: Academic Press.

Burt, R.S. (1992). *Structural Holes: The Social Structure of Competition*. Cambridge: Harvard University Press.

Busenitz, L.W., and Barney, J.B. (1997). Differences between Entrepreneurs and Managers in Large Organizations: Biases and Heuristics in Strategic Decision-Making. *Journal of Business Venturing*, 12(1): 9–30.

Callon, M., Laredo, P., and Mustar, P. (1997). *The Strategic Management of Research and Technology*. Paris: Economica Int.

Cantillon, R. (1755). *Essai sur la Nature du Commerce en General*. Translated by H. Higgs (1931). London: Macmillan.

References 139

Carter, S., and Ram, M. (2003). Reassessing Portfolio Entrepreneurship: Towards a Multidisciplinary Approach. *Small Business Economics*, 21(4): 371–380.

Casson, M. (1990). *Introduction*. In M. Casson (Ed.) *Entrepreneurship*. Aldershot: Edward Elgar, pp. xiii–xxvi.

Castanias, R.P., and Helfat, C.E. (2001). The Managerial Rents Model: Theory and Empirical Analysis. *Journal of Management*, 27(6): 661–678.

Cavalluzzo, K., Cavalluzzo, L., and Wolken, J. (2002). Competition, Small Business Financing, and Discrimination: Evidence from a New Survey. *Journal of Business*, 75(4): 641–679.

Chandler, G.N., and Hanks, S.H. (1998). An Examination of the Substitutability of Founders Human and Financial Capital in Emerging Business Ventures. *Journal of Business Venturing*, 13(5): 353–369.

Cohen, J., Cohen, P., West, S., and Aiken, L. (2003). *Applied Multiple Regression / Correlation Analysis for the Behavioral Sciences* (3rd edition). Mahwah, NJ: Lawrence Erlbaum Associates, Inc., Publishers.

Colombo, M.G., and Grilli, L. (2005). Founders' Human Capital and the Growth of New Technology-Based Firm: A Competence-Based View. *Research Policy*, 34(6): 795–816.

Connelly, B.L., Certo, S.T., Ireland, R.D., and Reutzel, C.R. (2011). Signaling Theory: A Review and Assessment. *Journal of Management*, 37(1): 39–67.

Cooper, A.C. (1993). Challenges in Predicting New Firm Performance. *Journal of Business Venturing*, 8(3): 241–253.

Cooper, A.C., Gimeno-Gascon, F.J., and Woo, C.Y. (1994). Initial Human and Financial Capital Predictors of New Venture Performance. *Journal of Business Venturing*, 9(5): 371–395.

Cooper, A.C., Woo, C., and Dunkelberg, W. (1988). Entrepreneurs' Perceived Chances of Success. *Journal of Business Venturing*, 3(2): 97–108.

Cope, J. (2011). Entrepreneurial Learning from Failure: An Interpretative Phenomenological Analysis. *Journal of Business Venturing*, 26(6): 604–623.

Cosh, A., and Hughes, A. (1998). *Enterprise Britain: Growth, Innovation and Public Policy in the Small and Medium Sized Enterprise Sector 1994–1997*. Cambridge: ESRC Centre for Business Research, Cambridge University.

Cosh, A., and Hughes, A. (Eds). (2003). *Enterprise Challenged*. Cambridge: Centre for Business Research, Cambridge University.

Cosh, A., and Wood, E. (1998). Innovation: Scale, Objectives, and Constraints. In A. Cosh and A. Hughes (Eds.) *Enterprise Britain: Growth, Innovation and Public Policy in the Small and Medium Sized Enterprise Sector 1994–1997*. Cambridge: ESRC Centre for Business Research, Cambridge University, pp. 38–48.

Covey, J.A., and Davies, A.D.M. (2004). Are People Unrealistically Optimistic? It Depends How You Ask Them. *British Journal of Health Psychology*, 9(1): 39–49.

Crook, J. (1996). Credit Constraints and US Households. *Applied Financial Economics*, 6(6): 477–485.

Davidsson, P. (2006). The Entrepreneurial Process. In S. Carter and D. Jones-Evans (Eds.) (2nd edition). *Enterprise and Small Business: Principles, Practice and Policy*. Harlow: Financial Times, Prentice Hall, pp. 129–151.

Davidsson, P., Delmar, F., and Wiklund, J. (2006). *Entrepreneurship and the Growth of Firms*. Cheltenham, UK: Edward Elgar.

Davidsson, P., and Honig, B. (2003). The Role of Social and Human Capital among Nascent Entrepreneurs. *Journal of Business Venturing*, 18(3): 301–331.

140 *References*

Davidsson, P., and Wiklund, J. (2001). Levels of Analysis in Entrepreneurship Research: Current Research Practice and Suggestions for the Future. *Entrepreneurship Theory and Practice*, 25(4): 81–100.

Delmar, F., and Shane, S.A. (2004). Legitimating First: Organizing Activities and the Survival of New Ventures. *Journal of Business Venturing*, 19(3): 385–410.

Department of Trade and Industry. (2004). *A Government Action Plan for Small Business. Making the UK the Best Place in the World to Start and Grow a Business: The Evidence Base*. London: DTI, Small Business Service.

Desphande, R. (1983). "Paradigms Lost": On Theory and Method in Research in Marketing. *Journal of Marketing*, 47(4): 101–110.

DeTienne, D.R., and Koberg, C.S. (2002). The Impact of Environmental and Organizational Factors on Discontinuous Innovation within High-Tech Industries. *IEEE Transactions on Engineering Management*, 49(4): 346–364.

Donckels, R., Dupont, B., and Michel, P. (1987). Multiple Business Starters: Who? Why? What? *Journal of Small Business and Entrepreneurship*, 5(1): 48–63.

Drakopoulou Dodd, S., and Anderson, A.R. (2007). Mumpsimus and the Mything of the Individualistic Entrepreneur. *International Small Business Journal*, 25(4): 341–360.

Dyer, W.G.Jr. (1994). Toward a Theory of Entrepreneurial Careers. *Entrepreneurship Theory and Practice*, 19(2): 7–21.

Eisenhardt, K. (1989). Building Theories from Case Study Research. *Academy of Management Review*, 14(4): 532–550.

Eisenhardt, K.M. and Martin, J.A. (2000). Dynamic Capabilities: What Are They? *Strategic Management Journal*, 21(11): 1105–1121.

Fiet, J.O. (2002). *The Systematic Search for Entrepreneurial Discoveries*. Westport, CT: Quorum Books.

Forbes, D. (2005). Are Some Entrepreneurs More Overconfident than Others? *Journal of Business Venturing*, 20(5): 623–640.

Franklin, S., Wright, M., and Lockett, A. (2001). Academic and Surrogate Entrepreneurs and University Spinout Companies. *Journal of Technology Transfer*, 26(1–2): 127–141.

Fraser, S., and Greene, F. (2006). The Effects of Experience of Entrepreneurial Optimism and Uncertainty. *Economica*, 73(290): 169–192.

Gaglio, C.M. (1997). Opportunity Identification: Review, Critique and Suggested Research Directions. In J.A. Katz (Ed.) *Advances in Entrepreneurship, Firm Emergence and Growth*. Greenwich, CA: JAI Press, pp. 139–202.

Gaglio, C.M., and Katz, J.A. (2001). The Psychological Basis of Opportunity Identification: Entrepreneurial Alertness. *Small Business Economics*, 16(2): 95–111.

Garnsey, E., and Heffernan, P. (2005). High-Technology Clustering Through Spin-Out and Attraction: The Cambridge Case. *Regional Studies*, 39(8): 1127–1144.

Gartner, W.B. (1985). A Conceptual Framework for Describing the Phenomenon of New Venture Creation. *Academy of Management Review*, 10(4): 696–706.

Gedajlovic, E., Honig, B., Moore, C., Payne, T., and Wright, M. (2013). Social Capital and Entrepreneurship: A Schema and Research Agenda. *Entrepreneurship Theory and Practice*, 37(3): 455–478.

Gimeno, J., Folta, T.B., Cooper, A.C., and Woo, C.Y. (1997). Survival of the Fittest? Entrepreneurial Human Capital and the Persistence of Underperforming Firms. *Administrative Science Quarterly*, 42(4): 750–783.

References   141

Gioia, D.A., Corley, K., and Hamilton, A. (2013). Seeking Qualitative Rigor in Inductive Research: Notes on the Gioia Methodology. *Organizational Research Methods*, 16(1): 15–31.

Greene, W.H. (2000). *Econometric Analysis* (5th edition). Upper Saddle River, NJ: Prentice Hall.

Gustafsson, V. (2006). *Entrepreneurial Decision-Making: Individuals, Tasks and Cognitions*. Northampton, MA and Cheltenham: Edward Elgar Publishing Ltd.

Hamilton, L.C. (2003). *Statistics with Stata*. Belmont, CA: Duxbury Thomson Learning.

Hannan, M.T., and Carroll, G.R. (1992). *Dynamics of Organizational Populations: Density, Legitimation and Competition*. New York: Oxford University Press.

Hausman, A. (2005). Innovativeness among Small Businesses: Theory and Propositions for Future Research. *Industrial Marketing Management*, 34(8): 773–782.

Hayward, M.L.A., Shepherd, D.A., and Griffin, D. (2006). A Hubris Theory of Entrepreneurship. *Management Science*, 52(2): 160–172.

Hébert, R., and Link, A.A. (2006). Historical Perspectives on the Entrepreneur. *Foundations and Trends® in Entrepreneurship*, 2(4): 261–408.

Helweg-Larsen, M., and Shepperd, J. (2001). Do Moderators of the Optimistic Bias Affect Personal or Target Risk Estimates? *Personality and Social Psychology Review*, 5(1): 74–95.

Hillerbrand, E. (1989). Cognitive Differences between Experts and Novices: Implications for Group Supervision. *Journal of Counselling and Development*, 67(3): 293–296.

Hills, G.E., Lumpkin, G.T., and Singh, R.P. (1997). Opportunity Recognition: Perceptions and Behaviors of Entrepreneurs. In P.D. Reynolds, W.D. Carter, P. Davidsson, W.B. Gartner and P. McDougall (Eds.) *Frontiers in Entrepreneurship Research 1997*. Wellesley, MA: Babson College, pp. 330–344.

Hmieleski, K.M., and Baron, R.A. (2009). Entrepreneurs' Optimism and New Venture Performance: A Social Cognitive Perspective. *Academy of Management Journal*, 52(3): 473–488.

Hoang, H., and Antoncic, B. (2003). Network-Based Research in Entrepreneurship: A Critical Review. *Journal of Business Venturing*, 18(2): 165–187.

Holcomb, T.R., Ireland, R.D., Holmes, R.M., and Hitt, M.A. (2009). Architecture of Entrepreneurial Learning: Exploring the Link among Heuristics, Knowledge, and Action. *Entrepreneurship Theory and Practice*, 33(1): 167–192.

Jovanovic, B. (1982). Selection and Evolution of Industry. *Econometrica*, 50(3): 649–670.

Katsikeas, C.S., Leonidou, L.C., and Morgan, N.A. (2000). Firm Level Export Performance Assessment: Review, Evaluation, and Development. *Journal of Academy of Marketing Science*, 28(4): 493–511.

Katz, J.A. (1994). Modelling Entrepreneurial Career Progressions: Concepts and Considerations. *Entrepreneurship Theory and Practice*, 19(2): 23–39.

Kim, P.H., and Aldrich, H.E. (2005). Social Capital and Entrepreneurship. *Foundations and Trends® in Entrepreneurship*, 1(2): 1–52.

Kirzner, I. (1973). *Competition and Entrepreneurship*. Chicago: Chicago University Press.

Knight, F.H. (1921). *Risk, Uncertainty and Profit*. (Ed. G. J. Stigler). Chicago: University of Chicago (1971).

Knight, F.H. (1942). Profit and Entrepreneurial Functions. *The Tasks of Economic History: Supplement to Journal of Economic History*, 2(S1): 126–132.

142 *References*

Koellinger, P., Minniti, M., and Schade, C. (2007). "I Think I Can, I Think I Can": Overconfidence and Entrepreneurial Behavior. *Journal of Economic Psychology*, 28(4): 502–527.

Kolb, D.A. (1984). *Experimental Learning: Experience as the Source of Learning and Development*. Englewood Cliffs, NJ: Prentice-Hall.

Landier, A., and Thesmar, D. (2009). Financial Contracting with Optimistic Entrepreneurs. *Review of Financial Studies*, 22(1): 117–150.

Landström, H. (2005). *Pioneers in Entrepreneurship and Small Business Research*. New York: Springer.

Larson, A., and Starr, J.A. (1993). A Network Model of Organizational Formation. *Entrepreneurship Theory and Practice*, 17(2): 5–15.

Lawton Smith, H. (2007). Universtities, Innovation, and Territorial Development: A Review of the Evidence. *Environment and Planning C*, 25(1): 98–114.

Lazaric, N., Longhi, C., and Thomas, C. (2008). Gatekeepers of Knowledge Versus Platforms of Knowledge: From Potential to Realized Absorptive Capacity. *Regional Studies*, 42(7): 837–852.

Lockett, A., and Wright, M. (2005). Resources, Capabilities, Risk Capital and the Creation of University Spin-Out Companies. *Research Policy*, 34(7): 1043–1057.

Lockett, A., Wright, M., and Franklin, S. (2003). Technology Transfer and Universities' Spin-Out Strategies. *Small Business Economics*, 20(2): 185–203.

Lord, R., and Maher, K. (1990). Alternative Information Processing Models and Their Implications for Theory, Research and Practice. *Academy of Management Review*, 15(1): 9–28.

Low, M.B., and MacMillan, I.C. (1988). Entrepreneurship: Past Research and Future Challenges. *Journal of Management*, 14(2): 139–161.

MacMillan, I.C. (1986). To Really Learn about Entrepreneurship, Lets's Study Habitual Entrepreneurs. *Journal of Business Venturing*, 1(3): 241–243.

Manimala, M.J. (1992). Entrepreneurial Heuristics: A Comparison between High PI (Pioneering-Innovative) and Low PI Ventures. *Journal of Business Venturing*, 7(4): 477–504.

Marshall, A. (1920). *Principles of Economics* (8th edition, reset 1949). London: Macmillan.

Martin, R., Berndt, C., Klagge, B., and Sunley, P. (2005). Spatial Proximity Effects and Regional Equity Gaps in the Venture Capital Market: Evidence from Germany and the United Kingdom. *Environment and Planning A*, 37(7): 1207–1231.

McDougall, P.P., and Oviatt, B.M. (2000). International Entrepreneurship: The Intersection of Two Research Paths, Special Research Forum. *Academy of Management Journal*, 43(5): 902–906.

McGrath, R.G. (1999). Falling Forward: Real Options Reasoning and Entrepreneurial Failure. *Academy of Management Review*, 24(1): 13–30.

Minniti, M., and Bygrave, W.B. (2001). A Dynamic Model of Entrepreneurial Learning. *Entrepreneurship Theory and Practice*, 25(3): 5–16.

Mitchell, R.K., Busenitz, L., Lant, T., McDougall, P., Morse, E.A., and Smith, J.B. (2002). Toward a Theory of Entrepreneurial Cognition: Rethinking the People Side of Entrepreneurship Research. *Entrepreneurship Theory and Practice*, 27(2): 93–105.

Moroz, P., and Hindle, K. (2012). Entrepreneurship as a Process: Toward Harmonizing Multiple Perspectives. *Entrepreneurship Theory and Practice*, 36(4): 781–818.

References   143

Morris, M.H., Kuratko, D.F., Schindehutte, M., and Spivack, A.J. (2012). Toward a Dynamic Learning Perspective of Entrepreneurship. *Entrepreneurship Theory and Practice*, 36(1): 11–40.

Mosey, S., and Wright, M. (2007). From Human Capital to Social Capital: A Longitudinal Study of Technology-Based Academic Entrepreneurs. *Entrepreneurship Theory and Practice*, 31(6): 909–936.

Mueller, C., Westhead, P., and Wright, M. (2012). Formal Venture Capital Acquisition: Can Experienced Entrepreneurs Compensate for the Spatial Proximity Benefits of 'Star Universities'? *Environment and Planning A*, 44(2): 281–296.

Mustar, P., Renault, M., Colombo, M., Piva, E., Fontes, M., and Wright, M. (2006). Conceptualising the Heterogeneity of Research-Based Spin-Offs: A Multi-Dimensional Taxonomy. *Research Policy*, 35(2): 289–308.

Northcraft G.B., and Neale, M.A. (1987). Experts, Amateurs and Real Estate: An Anchoring and Adjustment Perspective on Property Pricing Decisions. *Organizational Behavior and Human Decision Processes*, 39(1): 84–97.

Nystrom, P., and Starbuck, W. (1984). To Avoid Organizational Crises, Unlearn. *Organizational Dynamics*, 12(4): 53–65.

Office for National Statistics. (1999). *PA 1003 Commerce, Energy and Industry: Size Analysis of the United Kingdom Businesses*. London: Office for National Statistics.

Organisation for Economic Co-Operation and Development (OECD). (1998). *Fostering Entrepreneurship*. Paris: Organisation for Economic Co-Operation and Development.

Otani, K. (1996). A Human Capital Approach to Entrepreneurial Capacity. *Economica*, 63(250): 273–289.

Otten, W., and ven der Pligt, J. (1996). Contexts Effects in the Measurement of Comparative Optimism in Probability Judgments. *Journal of Social and Clinical Psychology*, 15(1): 80–101.

Ozgen, E., and Baron, R. (2007). Social Sources of Information in Opportunity Recognition: Effects of Mentors, Industry Networks, and Professional Forums. *Journal of Business Venturing*, 22(2): 174–192.

Parker, S.C. (2013). Do Serial Entrepreneurs Run Successively Better-Performing Businesses? *Journal of Business Venturing*, 28(5): 652–666.

Penrose, E.T. (1959). *The Theory of the Growth of the Firm*. New York: John Wiley.

Perks, H., and Medway, D. (2012). Examining the Nature of Resource-Based Processes in New Venture Development Through a Business-Duality Lens: A Farming Sector Taxonomy. *International Small Business Journal*, 30(2): 161–188.

Politis, D. (2005). The Process of Entrepreneurial Learning: A Conceptual Framework. *Entrepreneurship Theory and Practice*, 29(4): 399–424.

Porter, M.E. (1985). *Competitive Advantage: Creating and Sustaining Superior Performance*. New York: Free Press.

Rabin, M. (1998). Psychology and Economics. *Journal of Economic Literature*, 36(1): 11–46.

Rerup, C. (2005). Learning from Past Experience: Footnotes on Mindfulness and Habitual Entrepreneurship. *Scandinavian Journal of Management*, 21(4): 451–472.

Reuber, A.R., and Fischer, E. (1999). Understanding the Consequences of Founders Experience. *Journal of Small Business Management*, 37(2): 30–45.

Robson, P.J.A., Akuetteh, C.K., Stone, I., Westhead, P., and Wright, M. (2013). Credit-Rationing and Entrepreneurial Experience: Evidence from a Resource Deficit Context. *Entrepreneurship and Regional Development*, 25(5–6): 349–370.

144 *References*

Robson, P.J.A., Akuetteh, C.K., Westhead, P., and Wright M. (2012a). Innovative Opportunity Pursuit, Human Capital and Business Ownership Experience in an Emerging Region: Evidence from Ghana. *Small Business Economics*, 39(3): 603–625.

Robson, P.J.A., Akuetteh, C.K., Westhead, P., and Wright M. (2012b). Export Intensity, Human Capital and Business Ownership Experience. *International Small Business Journal*, 30(4): 367–387.

Robson, P.J.A., and Obeng, B.A. (2008). The Barriers to Growth in Ghana. *Small Business Economics*, 30(4): 385–403.

Rocha, H.O. (2004). Entrepreneurship and Development: The Role of Clusters. *Small Business Economics*, 23(5): 363–400.

Rønning, L., and Kolvereid, L. (2006). Income Diversification in Norwegian Farm Households, Reassessing Pluriactivity. *International Small Business Journal*, 24(4): 405–420.

Ronstadt, R. (1982). Does Entrepreneurial Career Path Really Matter? In K.H. Vesper (Ed.) *Frontiers of Entrepreneurship Research*. Wellesley, MA: Babson College, pp. 540–567.

Ronstadt, R. (1988). The Corridor Principal and Entrepreneurial Time. *Journal of Business Venturing*, 1(4): 295–306.

Rosa, P. (1998). Entrepreneurial Processes of Business Cluster Formation and Growth by 'Habitual' Entrepreneurs. *Entrepreneurship Theory and Practice*, 22(4): 43–61.

Rosa, P., and Scott, M. (1999). The Prevalence of Multiple Owners and Directors in the Same Sector: Implications for Our Understanding of Start-Up and Growth. *Entrepreneurship and Regional Development*, 11(1): 21–37.

Rothaermel, F.T., Agung, S.D., and Jiang, L. (2007). University Entrepreneurship: A Taxonomy of the Literature. *Industrial and Corporate Change*, 16(4): 691–791.

Rutherford, M.W., Buller, P.F., and McMullen, P.R. (2003). Human Resource Management Problems Over the Life Cycle of Small to Medium-Sized Firms. *Human Resource Management*, 42(4): 321–335.

Schein, E.H. (1978). *Career Dynamics: Matching Individual and Organizational Needs*. Reading, MA: Addison-Wesley.

Schultheiss, O., and Brunstein, J. (2000). Choice of Difficult Tasks as a Strategy of Compensating for Identity-Relevant Failure. *Journal of Research in Personality*, 34(2): 269–277.

Schumpeter, J.A. (1934). *The Theory of Economic Development*. Cambridge: Harvard University.

Scott, M., and Rosa, P. (1996). Has Firm Level Analysis Reached Its Limits? *International Small Business Journal*, 14(4): 81–89.

Shane, S. (2000). Prior Knowledge and the Discovery of Entrepreneurial Opportunities. *Organization Science*, 11(4): 448–469.

Shane, S. (2003). *A General Theory of Entrepreneurship*. Northampton, MA: Edward Elgar Publishing.

Shane, S., and Khurana, R. (2003). Bringing Individuals Back In: The Effects of Career Experience on New Firm Founding. *Industrial and Corporate Change*, 12(3): 519–544.

Shane, S., and Stuart, T. (2002). Organizational Endowments and the Performance of University Start-Ups. *Management Science*, 48(1): 154–170.

References 145

Shane, S., and Venkataraman, S. (2000). The Promise of Entrepreneurship as a Field of Research. *Academy of Management Review*, 25(1): 217–226.

Shepherd, D.A. (2003). Learning from Business Failure: Propositions of Grief Recovery for the Self-Employed. *Academy of Management Review*, 28(2): 318–329.

Shepherd, D.A., and DeTienne, D.R. (2005). Prior Knowledge, Potential Financial Reward, and Opportunity Identification. *Entrepreneurship, Theory and Practice*, 29(1): 91–112.

Shrader, R., and Siegel, D.S. (2007). Assessing the Relationship between Human Capital and Firm Performance: Evidence from Technology-Based New Ventures. *Entrepreneurship Theory and Practice*, 31(6): 893–908.

Simon, M., Houghton, S.M., and Aquino, K. (2000). Cognitive Biases, Risk Perception, and Venture Formation: How Individuals Decide to Start Companies. *Journal of Business Venturing*, 15(2): 113–134.

Sirmon, D.G., and Hitt, M.A. (2003). Managing Resources: Linking Uniques Resources, Management, and Wealth Creation in Family Firms. *Entrepreneurship, Theory and Practice*, 27(4): 339–358.

Sirmon, D.G., Hitt, M.A., and Ireland, D. (2007). Managing Firm Resources in Dynamic Environments to Create Value: Looking Inside the Black Box. *Academy of Management Review*, 32(1): 273–292.

Sitkin, S.B. (1992). Learning Through Failure: The Strategy of Small Losses. In B.M. Staw and L.L. Cummings (Eds.) *Research in Organizational Behavior*, 14. Greenwich, CT: JAI Press, pp. 231–266.

Spanos, Y.E., and Lioukas, S. (2001). An Examination into the Causal Logic of Rent Generation: Contrasting Porter's Competitive Strategy Framework and the Resource-Based Perspective. *Strategic Management Journal*, 22(10): 907–934.

Spence, M. (2002). Signaling in Retrospect and the Informational Structure of Markets. *American Economic Review*, 92(3): 434–459.

Starr, J., and Bygrave, W. (1991). The Assets and Liabilities of Prior Start-Up Experience: An Exploratory Study of Multiple Venture Entrepreneurs. In N.C. Churchill, W.D. Bygrave, J.G. Covin, D.L. Sexton, D.P. Slevin, K.H. Vesper and W.E. Wetzel (Eds.) *Frontiers of Entrepreneurship Research 1991*. Wellesley, MA: Babson College, pp. 213–227.

Stinchcombe, A.L. (1965). Social Structure and Organizations. In J.G. March (Ed.) *Handbook of Organizations*. Chicago: Rand McNally, pp. 142–193.

Storey, D.J. (2011). Optimism and Chance: The Elephants in the Entrepreneurship Room. *International Small Business Journal*, 29(4): 303–321.

Storey, D.J. (1994). *Understanding the Small Business Sector*. London: Thomson Learning.

Storey, D.J., Keasey, K., Watson, R., and Wynarczyk, P. (1987). *The Performance of Small Firms: Profits, Jobs and Failures*. London: Croom Helm.

Tagoe, N., Nyarko, E., and Anuwa-Amarh, E. (2005). Financial Challenges Facing Urban SMEs Under Financial Sector Liberalization in Ghana. *Journal of Small Business Management*, 43(3): 331–343.

Teece, D.J., Pisano, G., and Shuen, A. (1997). Dynamic Capabilities and Strategic Management. *Strategic Management Journal*, 18(7): 509–533.

Thorgen, S., and Wincent, J. (2015). Passion and Habitual Entrepreneurship. *International Small Business Journal*, 33(2): 216–227.

Tötterman, H., and Sten, J. (2005). Business Incubation and Social Capital. *International Small Business Journal*, 23(5): 487–511.

146 References

Tversky, A., and Kahneman, D. (1974). Judgement Under Uncertainty: Heuristics and Biases. *Science*, 185(4157): 1124–1131.

Ucbasaran, D., Alsos, G.A., Westhead, P., and Wright, M. (2008). Habitual Entrepreneurs. *Foundations and Trends® in Entrepreneurship*, 4(4): 309–449.

Ucbasaran, D., Westhead, P., and Wright, M. (2001). The Focus of Entrepreneurial Research: Contextual and Process Issues. *Entrepreneurship Theory and Practice*, 25(4): 57–80.

Ucbasaran, D., Westhead, P., and Wright, M. (2006). *Habitual Entrepreneurs*. Aldershot, UK: Edward Elgar.

Ucbasaran, D., Westhead, P., and Wright, M. (2009). The Extent and Nature of Opportunity Identification by Experienced Entrepreneurs. *Journal of Business Venturing*, 24(2): 99–115.

Ucbasaran, D., Westhead, P., Wright, M., and Flores, M. (2010). The Nature of Entrepreneurial Experience, Business Failure and Comparative Optimism. *Journal of Business Venturing*, 25(6): 541–555.

Ucbasaran, D., Wright, M., and Westhead, P. (2003). A Longitudinal Study of Habitual Entrepreneurs: Starters and Acquirers. *Entrepreneurship and Regional Development*, 15(3): 207–228.

Unger, J.M., Rauch, A., Frese, M., and Rosenbusch, N. (2011). Human Capital and Entrepreneurial Success: A Meta-Analytical Review. *Journal of Business Venturing*, 26(3): 341–358.

Vanacker, T.R., and Manigart, S. (2010). Pecking Order and Debt Capacity Considerations for High Growth Companies Seeking Finance. *Small Business Economics*, 35(1): 53–69.

Van de Velde, F., Hooykaas, C., and van der Pligt, J. (1992). Risk Perception and Behavior: Pessimism, Realism and Optimism about AIDS-Related Health Behavior. *Psychology and Health*, 6(1–2): 23–38.

Venkataraman, S. (1997). The Distinctive Domain of Entrepreneurship Research: An Editor's Perspective. In J.A. Katz (Ed.) *Advances in Entrepreneurship, Firm Emergence and Growth*, 3. Greenwich, CA: JAI Press, pp. 119–138.

Vohora, A., Wright, M., and Lockett, A. (2004). Critical Junctures in the Development of University High-Tech Spinout Companies. *Research Policy*, 33(1): 147–174.

Wagner, J. (2007). Exports and Productivity: A Survey of the Evidence from Firm-Level Data. *The World Economy*, 30(1): 60–82.

Wales, W.J., Patel, P.C., Parida, V., and Kreiser, P.M. (2013). Nonlinear Effects of Entrepreneurial Orientation on Small Firm Performance: The Moderating Role of Resource Orchestration Capabilities. *Strategic Entrepreneurship Journal*, 7(2), 93–121.

Wang, C.L., and Chugh, H. (2014). Entrepreneurial Learning: Past Research and Future Challenges. *International Journal of Management Reviews*, 16(1), 24–61.

Ward, T. (2004). Cognition, Creativity and Entrepreneurship. *Journal of Business Venturing*, 19(2): 173–188.

Weinstein, N.D. (1980). Unrealistic Optimism About Future Life Events. *Journal of Personality and Social Psychology*, 39(5): 806–820.

Westhead, P. (1995). Survival and Employment Growth Contrasts between Types of Owner-Managed High-Technology Firms. *Entrepreneurship Theory and Practice*, 20(1): 5–27.

References   147

Westhead, P. (1997). Ambitions, 'External' Environment and Strategic Factor Differences between Family and Non-Family Unquoted Companies. *Entrepreneurship and Regional Development*, 9(2): 127–157.

Westhead, P., Ucbasaran, D., and Wright, M. (2003). Differences between Private Firms Owned by Novice, Serial and Portfolio Entrepreneurs: Implications for Policy-Makers and Practitioners. *Regional Studies*, 37(2): 187–200.

Westhead, P., Ucbasaran, D., and Wright, M. (2005a). Decisions, Actions and Performance: Do Novice, Serial and Portfolio Entrepreneurs Differ? *Journal of Small Business Management*, 43(4): 393–417.

Westhead P., Ucbasaran, D., Wright, M., and Binks, M. (2005b). Novice, Serial and Portfolio Entrepreneur Behaviour and Contributions. *Small Business Economics*, 25(2): 109–132.

Westhead, P., Ucbasaran, D., and Wright, M. (2005c). Experience and Cognition: Do Novice, Serial and Portfolio Entrepreneurs Differ? *International Small Business Journal*, 23(1): 72–98.

Westhead, P., and Wright, M. (1998). Novice, Portfolio and Serial Founders: Are They Different? *Journal of Business Venturing*, 13(3): 173–204.

Westhead, P., and Wright, M. (2013). *Entrepreneurship: A Very Short Introduction*. Oxford: Oxford University Press.

Westhead, P., and Wright, M. (2014). The Habitual Entrepreneur Phenomenon. *International Small Business Journal*, 29: virtual special issue.

Westhead, P., Wright, M., and McElwee, G. (2011). *Entrepreneurship: Perspectives and Cases*. Harlow: Pearson Education Limited.

Wheeler, C., Ibeh, K., and Dimitratos, P. (2008). UK Export Performance Research. *International Small Business Journal*, 26(2): 207–239.

Wiklund, J., and Shepherd, D. (2008). Portfolio Entrepreneurship, Habitual and Novice Founders, New Entry and Mode of Organizing. *Entrepreneurship Theory and Practice*, 32(4): 701–725.

Witt, U. (1998). Imagination and Leadership—The Neglected Dimension of an Evolutionary Theory of the Firm. *Journal of Economic Behavior and Organization*, 35(2): 161–177.

Wood, R., and Bandura, A. (1989). Social Cognitive Theory of Organizational Management. *Academy of Management Review*, 14(3): 361–384.

Wright, M., Birley, S., and Mosey, S. (2004). Entrepreneurship and University Technology Transfer. *Journal of Technology Transfer*, 29(3–4): 235–246.

Wright, M., Clarysse, B., Lockett, A., and Binks, M. (2006). University Spin-Out Companies and Venture Capital. *Research Policy*, 35(4): 481–501.

Wright, M., Hmieleski, K.M., Siegel, D.S., and Ensley, M.D. (2007). The Role of Human Capital in Technological Entrepreneurship. *Entrepreneurship Theory and Practice*, 31(6): 791–806.

Wright, M., Hoskisson, R., Busenitz, L., and Dial, J. (2000). Entrepreneurial Growth Through Privatization: The Upside of Management Buyouts. *Academy of Management Review*, 25(3): 591–601.

Wright, M., Robbie, K., and Ennew, C. (1997). Venture Capitalists and Serial Entrepreneurs. *Journal of Business Venturing*, 12(3): 227–249.

Wright, M., Westhead, P., and Ucbasaran, D. (2007). The Internationalization of Small and Medium-Sized Enterprises (SMEs) and International Entrepreneurship: A Critique and Policy Implications. *Regional Studies*, 41(7): 1013–1029.

148 *References*

Yang, Z., Wang, X., and Su, C. (2006). A Review of Research Methodologies in International Business. *International Business Review*, 15(6): 601–617.

Yin, J. (1993). *Case Study Research*. London: Sage.

Yin, R. (1989). *Case Study Research, Design and Methods*. Beverly Hills, CA: Sage.

Yip, P.S.L., and Tsang, E.W.K (2007). Interpreting Dummy Variables and Their Interaction Effects in Strategy Research. *Strategic Organization*, 5(1): 13–30.

Zahra, S.A. (1993). Environment, Corporate Entrepreneurship, and Financial Performance: A Taxonomic Approach. *Journal of Business Venturing*, 8(4): 319–340.

Zahra, S.A., and George, G. (2002). Absorptive Capacity: A Review, Reconceptualization, and Extension. *Academy of Management Review*, 27(2): 185–203.

Zahra, S.A., and Wright, M. (2011). Entrepreneurship's Next Act. *Academy of Management Perspectives*, 25(4): 67–83.

Zhang, J. (2009). The Performance of University Spin-Offs: An Exploratory Analysis Using Venture Capital Data. *Journal of Technology Transfer*, 34(3): 255–285.

Index

Note: Page numbers in italics indicate tables and figures

Alvarez, S. A. 18
Antoncic, B. 71
assets and liabilities reported, resource profile 29–35; findings 32–4; hypotheses tested 29–31; knowledge base, gaps in 29; methodology 31–2; research questions 29; study conclusions/implications 34–5

Baerts, C. 80–1
Barney, J. B. 118
Baron, R. A. 15
Becker, G. S. 13
biases 16–17
Birley, S. 3, 6, 22, 23
British Venture Capital Association 64
Busenitz, L. 18, 118
business failure: definitions of 96; experience 44–5, 96–7
business ownership 4
buyouts 4–5

Cantillon, R. 1
capabilities 19
Centre for Management Buyout Research (CMBOR) 64
cognition 14–17; biases and 16–17; entrepreneurial, defined 14; experience-based knowledge and 14–15; expert information processing theory and 16; heuristics and 16–17; prototype theory and 15–16; schema theory and 15
cognitive profiles 29–35; findings 32–4; hypotheses tested 29–31; knowledge base, gaps in 29; methodology 31–2; research questions 29; study implications 34–5

Cohen, J. 100
comparative optimism, resource profile 35–45; findings 43–4; hypotheses tested 37–9; knowledge base, gaps in 35–7; methodology 39–42; research questions 37; study conclusions/implications 44–5
Cooper, A. C. 36, 40
Cosh, A. 53

debt finance 48–56; findings 54–5, 55; hypotheses tested 49–52; knowledge base, gaps in 48–9; methodology 52–4; research questions 49; study conclusions/implications 55–6
decision-making roles 4
demographic characteristics, general human capital and 13–14
dominant logic 30
Donckels, R. 3

Eisenhardt, K. 19, 117
entrepreneur, types of 9
entrepreneur diversity 2–3
entrepreneurial cognition 14–17
entrepreneurial endeavours, outcomes of 10
entrepreneur resources 12–21; capabilities and 19; cognition and heuristics 14–17; human capital theory 12–14; learning 20; overview of 12; resource-based view of firm 17–19; signalling theory 19–20
entrepreneurs; see also habitual entrepreneurs: business failure experience 44–5; cognitive profiles 29–35; comparative optimism 35–45; diversity and 2–3; portfolio

150 *Index*

4, 5; resources (*see* entrepreneur resources); roles of 1, 2; serial 4, 5; stock of experience 6–7; studies of 2–3; theoretical insight to (*see* entrepreneur resources)

entrepreneurship 1; dimensions of 4; elements of 4; external environment for 8–9; habitual, categorization of 4–5, 5; learning and 20; opportunity-based 4, 90 (*see also* opportunity discovery theory); process of 9; team-based 4; types of 1–2

entrepreneur theoretical resources 12–21; capabilities 19; cognitive psychology 14–17; heuristic-based information 16–17; human capital theory 12–14; learning process 20; overview of 12; resource-based views 17–19; signalling theory 19–20

experience: stock of 6–7; stream of 7, 7

experimental learning theory (ELT) 20

expert information processing theory 16

exporting, firm performance and 127–32; findings 131; hypotheses tested 128–9; knowledge base, gaps in 127–8; methodology 129–31; research questions 128; study conclusions/implications 131–2

external environments, finance and 47

filter of knowledge 18

finance 47–68; debt 48–56; external environments and 47; overview of 47–8; serial entrepreneurs and VC reinvestment 61–7; venture capital 56–61

financing business comparisons: portfolio to novice and serial entrepreneurs 27; serial to novice and portfolio entrepreneurs 27–8

firm: as knowledge community 18; resource-based view of 17–19

first formal venture capital investment (FFVCI) 48

Fischer, E. 6–7, 12, 30, 87, 90, 91, 105

Fraser, S. 36

Gaglio, C.M. 15, 16

Gartner, W.B. 8

general human capital 12–14; cognitive approaches to 13; inputs *vs.* outputs of 12–13; measures of 13–14

Gimeno, J. 37

Gioia, D.A. 81

Greene, F. 36

growth, firm performance and 125–7; findings 126–7; hypotheses tested 126; knowledge base, gaps in 125–6; methodology 126; research questions 126; study conclusions/implications 127

habitual entrepreneur phenomenon: definitions of 3–5; entrepreneurship process 9; entrepreneur types 9; external environment 8–9; organization types 9–10; outcomes of endeavours 10; scale of 5–6; theories of 8, 9, 12–21

habitual entrepreneurs; *see also* portfolio entrepreneurs; serial entrepreneurs: categorization of 4–5, 5; comparative optimism 35–45; defined 4, 10, 73; human capital accumulation of 13–14; networking and 75–6; *vs.* novice entrepreneurs 4; profile of 2; research relating to 6–8; specific human capital and 14; study of 1–2

heuristic-based information 16–17

Hoang, H. 71

hubris 30

Hughes, A. 53

human capital comparisons: portfolio to novice and serial entrepreneurs 25–6; serial to novice and portfolio entrepreneurs 26

human capital theory 12–14; general human capital 12–14; inputs *vs.* outputs and 12–13; specific human capital 14

innovation, definition of 104

Katz, J.A. 15, 16, 91

Kirzner, I. 15, 89

Knight, F.H. 1

knowledge community, firm as 18

knowledge gaps, research themes and 6–7

Landier, A. 36

learning 20, 115–23; findings 118–22; habitual entrepreneur case types *119–20*; human capital aspects of 116; knowledge base, gaps in

115–16; methodology 116–18; overview of 115; research questions 115; study conclusions/implications 122–3

learning process 20

Lioukas, S. 18

Low, M. B. 116

MacMillan, I. C. 116

management buy in (MBI) 4

management buyout (MBO) 5

Manimala, M. J. 99

Marshall, A. 90

Martin, J. A. 19

McGrath, R. G. 96–7

Mosey, S. 70

Mueller, C. 56

nascent entrepreneurs: defined 73; networking and 74

networking 69–80; findings 73–9; habitual entrepreneurs and 75–6; knowledge base, gaps in 70–2; methodology 72–3; nascent entrepreneurs and 74; novice entrepreneurs and 74–5; overview of 69; propositions, development of 76–9; research questions 70, 71, 72; social capital development patterns 73–4, 77; study conclusions/implications 79–80

new firm formation (NFF) 4

novice entrepreneurs: cognitive profiles 29–35; comparative optimism 35–45; defined 4, 24, 73; financing business comparisons 27–8; vs. habitual entrepreneurs 4; human capital accumulation of 13–14; human capital resource profiles of 25–6; networking and 74–5; opportunity identification/sources comparisons 26–7; organizational capabilities comparisons 28

opportunity-based entrepreneurship 4

opportunity creation theory 87–90, 102–14; findings 110–11; hypotheses tested 105–7; innovation and 89–90; key elements of 88, 88–9; knowledge base, gaps in 102–5; methodology 107–10; overview of 87–8; research questions 104; study conclusions/implications 111–12

opportunity discovery theory 87–102; see also opportunity creation theory; extent and nature of experience 93–102; key elements of 88, 88–9; nature of experience 90–3; overview of 87–8

opportunity discovery theory, extent and nature of experience 93–102; findings 101; hypotheses tested 94–8; knowledge base, gaps in 93–4; methodology 98–100; research questions 94; study conclusions/implications 101–2

opportunity discovery theory, nature of experience 90–3; findings 92; hypotheses tested 91–2; knowledge base, gaps in 90–1; research questions 91; study conclusions/implications 92–3

opportunity identification/sources, comparisons of: portfolio to novice and serial entrepreneurs 26; serial to novice and portfolio entrepreneurs 26–7

optimistic bias 35

organizational capabilities comparisons: portfolio to novice and serial entrepreneurs 28; serial to novice and portfolio entrepreneurs 28

organizations, types of 9–10

outputs 12–13

overconfidence 35

over-optimism 35

PBOE see prior business ownership experience (PBOE)

pecking order hypothesis 47–8

Penrose, E. T. 17–18

performance 124–33; exporting 127–32; growth 125–7; overview of 124–5

portfolio entrepreneurs; see also habitual entrepreneurs: categorization of 4, 5; cognitive profiles 29–35; comparative optimism 35–45; definition of 24; financing business comparisons 27–8; human capital resource profiles of 25–6; opportunity identification/sources comparisons 26–7; organizational capabilities comparisons 28

prior business ownership experience (PBOE) 1; assets and liabilities of

152 *Index*

29–34, 48–56; cognition and 14–15; comparative optimism and 36–45; exporting and 127–9, 131–2; extent and nature of 93–6; future research directions 134–5; human capital and 13; learning and 20, 115–18, *119–20*, 122–3; length of debt finance gap 55; liabilities of 16–17; networking and 69–78; opportunity creation and 102–7; opportunity discovery and 87–8, 90–1, 111–12; performance and 125–6; resource profiles and 23–8; specific human capital and 14; stream of experience and 7; variations in 3; venture capital reinvestment and 61

propositions, development of 76–9; network content 76–8, 77; network government 77, 78–9; network structure 76, 77; venture development 79

prototype theory 15–16

resource accumulation; *see also individual headings*: finance 47–68; networking 69–80; resource orchestration 80–6

resource-based view (RBV) of firm 17–19; capabilities and 19

resource configurations, harmonizing 83–4

resource orchestration 80–6; findings 82–4; knowledge base, gaps in 80; methodology 81; overview of 69; research questions 80; resource/ capability harmonizing configuration process 83–4; resource/capability sharing 82–3; study conclusions/ implications 85; theoretical background 80–1

resource profile dimensions 23–9; business ownership 24–5; descriptive analysis 24; financing business 27–8; findings 24–9; human capital comparisons 25–6; knowledge base, gaps in 23; methodology 24; opportunity identification/sources 26–7; organizational capabilities 28; research questions 23; study conclusions/implications 28–9

resource profiles 22–46; *see also individual headings*; assets and

liabilities reported 29–35; cognitive profiles 29–35; comparative optimism 35–45; dimensions of 23–9; overview of 22–3

Reuber, A.R. 6–7, 12, 30, 87, 90, 91, 105

Robson, P.J.A. 48, 102, 107, 127, 129

Rosa, P. 3, 91

sameness 30

Schein, E.H. 87, 91

schemas 15

Schumpeter, J.A. 89–90

Scott, M. 3

serial entrepreneurs; *see also* habitual entrepreneurs: categorization of 4, 5; cognitive profiles 29–35; comparative optimism 35–45; definition of 24; financing business comparisons 27–8; human capital resource profiles of 25–6; opportunity identification/sources comparisons 26–7; organizational capabilities comparisons 28; venture capital reinvestment in 61–7

Shane, S. 90

Shepherd, D.A. 96

signalling theory 19–20

Sirmon, D.G. 82, 83

Sitkin, S.B. 96

social capital development patterns 73–4, 77

Spanos, Y.E. 18

specific human capital 14

stock of experience 6–7

Storey, D.J. 134

stream of experience 7, 7

team-based entrepreneurship 4

Thesmar, D. 36

Thorgen, S. 3–4

Tsang, E.W. K 60

Ucbasaran, D. 35–6, 93, 115

university spin-outs (USO) 48; *see also* venture capital (VC)

unrealistic optimism 35

VC *see* venture capital (VC)

Venkataraman, S. 90

venture capital (VC) 56–61; defined 56–7; findings 60; hypotheses tested 58; knowledge base, gaps in 56–7; methodology 58–60; reinvestment in serial entrepreneurs 61–7, 66; research questions 57; study conclusions/implications 60–1

venture capital reinvestment 61–7; findings 65, 66; hypotheses tested 62–3; knowledge base, gaps in 61–2; methodology 63–4; study conclusions/implications 67

Vohora, A. 73

Westhead, P. 3, 6, 7, 22, 23, 29, 90–1, 107, 125, 132

Wincent, J. 3–4

Wright, M. 23, 62, 132

Yip, P. S. L. 60